A Seat at the Table

A SEAT AT THE TABLE

AN INSIDER'S GUIDE FOR AMERICA'S NEW WOMEN LEADERS

PATRICIA HARRISON

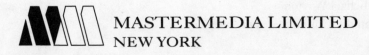

MASTERMEDIA LIMITED
NEW YORK

MASTERMEDIA and colophon are registered trademarks
of MasterMedia Limited.

Library of Congress Cataloging-in-Publication Data
Harrison, Patricia, 1943-
    A seat at the table: an insider's guide for America's new women
leaders / Patricia Harrison.
        p.   cm.
    ISBN 1-57101-013-0 : $19.95
    1. Women executives—United States. 2. Women
government executives—United States. 3. Women in business—
United States. 4. Women in the professions—United States.
5. Women in politics—United States. 6. Success in business—
United States. I. Title.
    HD6054.4.U6H373   1995
    658.4'0082—dc20   94-44759
                                               CIP

Production services by Martin Cook Associates, Ltd.
Designed by Michael Woyton
Manufactured in the United States of America

❖ ❖ ❖

Special thanks to my in-house editor and counsel, Elise Garfinkel; Christopher, Claudia and Courtney, the A Team that makes it all worthwhile; Marguerite De Stacy, my mother, who continues to inspire all of us and Bruce Harrison who helps me do it all and still keep my day job.

❖ ❖ ❖

Contents

INTRODUCTION

When I was asked to write this introduction, I considered a variety of approaches to the subject. For example, I am very proud of my company, NYNEX, for being a positive example, and I would point to the statistical evidence of the progress that NYNEX has made in providing seats for women at its table: two female directors on each of our three principal boards; four female officers; and more than 2,000 women in the upper-and-middle management ranks. So we are moving in the right direction, but we know we still have much further to go.

And that is more than just idealism. Diversity adds excitement and innovation to the workplace. When you are searching for potential employees, it always makes good business sense to draw on the largest possible talent pool, without regard to gender or race or religion.

This book recognizes that women have a vast diversity of their own: a diversity of goals, choices, lifestyles and ambitions. And if I were to give advice to the reader, I would begin by emphasizing that fact: Look inside yourself, and maximize whatever is special in you, rather than searching a single, all-purpose pattern to guide to you to success.

The key to this kind of growth is to keep on learning, throughout your career, thoughout your life, and make your strengths even stronger.

In *The Fifth Discipline*, business analyst Peter M. Senge, describes what he calls a "learning organization," an organization that is constantly re-creating itself in order to compete successfully in a constantly-changing world. On an individual level, that same kind of success is achievable in the same way. As Senge says, "Through learning we re-create ourselves."

Set the highest possible standards for yourself, and seek out role models and coaches who can help you along the way. And that means doing lots of networking.

Be a risk-taker. You can't learn if you never make a mistake. Don't be rash, but be bold.

Think of your career as a series of steps, and as you move up, keep pushing the top rung higher and higher until you reach the place you want to be.

Have faith in yourself, and even if you have doubts, show the world your confident side. As Eleanor Roosevelt once said, "No one can make you feel inferior without your consent."

Don't ever give anyone that kind of permission. And you can remind people how terrific you are by the superior work you perform.

That is the kind of spirit, the kind of attitude, that will earn you a seat at the table.

Ivan G. Seidenberg
CEO, NYNEX

FOREWORD

When I first began my career in the telecommunications industry, more than twenty years ago, I could have used a book like *A Seat at the Table*. Unfortunately, there weren't many books on the market geared toward helping women get ahead in the business world. Nonetheless, women like myself turned to these books for wisdom and advice. We listened to what they had to say, including how to dress, how to speak, how to behave (for the most part, like men!). It took a while for us to realize that the best advice on how to succeed comes from within. Each of us is an accumulation of life experiences unique unto ourselves. We all have individual ways of handling things. It is this varied set of strengths and weaknesses that makes us who we are, and constitutes what we have to offer to the world. *A Seat at the Table* will guide you through a process of self-discovery that will enable you to find your own voice, your own style, your own dreams, and the path to take you there.

Despite the fact that I had few role models to follow, I did make my way up the corporate ladder. I now fill seats at a number of decision-making tables both at work and in my community. And if I were asked to choose one factor that got me where I am today it would be this: my willingness to stand up to fear, as Susan Jeffers says, and do it anyway.

I was fortunate to work for a company like NYNEX that viewed the world both progressively and pragmatically, realizing the tremendous contribution women and minorities can make to their corporation's success and have! At a critical point in my career, when I was struggling through one of the most difficult battles of my life — a bout with breast cancer — NYNEX promoted me into the officer position I hold today, in spite of my physical disability. Perhaps, they felt that if I could overcome breast cancer, I could overcome anything.

I also attribute my success to the network of women I was privileged to work with through the years. Women who have supported, encouraged and mentioned me along the way. There's no substitute for women helping women. That's why I believe so strongly in the importance of mentoring groups and organizations like the NYNEX Association of Management Women. By working together, we enable each other to bloom where we are planted, by providing a rich soil in which to grow and a stong stable trellis to cling to on our way up.

"Throwing little torches out to the next step to lead people through the dark," as Whoopi Goldberg puts it, is what mentoring and networking is all about. Unfortunately, not every woman has a mentor readily available to help her, or an organization or support group nearby that she can easily join. *A Seat at the Table* fills that void. I encourage you to take advantage of the resource guide in the back of this book. The people listed are genuinely interested in helping you to reach your goals.

I also urge you to read *A Seat at the Table* with a notebook and pen in hand. Answer the questions. Jot down the lists. In the process, you'll be formulating a strategic plan of action, a way to reach your own individual idea of success. And that will be different for all of us. I believe Anna Quindlen put it best when she defined feminism as "ordinary women who want the best for themselves, the best for their daughters, the best for their sons. Women who want to decide what the best is and don't want anybody saying, 'You can't stay home because that's not cool,' or 'You can't be vice president because you'll just leave and have babies,' or 'You can't grow up and collect trash, because women don't know how to collect trash.' You can do and be anything you want to be."

A Seat at the Table will show you how.

Judy Haberkorn
Vice President, Consumer Markets
NYNEX

PREFACE

"When it comes to power, there is no substitute for a seat at the table."
LINDA ELLERBEE

For the past 10 years, from my vantage as an entrepreneur and the founder of an organization which identifies qualified women for corporate boards, I have worked with men and women leaders in all kinds of business, industry, government and volunteer organizations. A Seat at the Table reflects my experience with and observations of outstanding women in the corporation, in government, in politics, in the volunteer community, in the arts, in the media, and in the work force at all levels. "Outstanding women" is a redundancy. What I have observed is the incredible ability and talent demonstrated by women who do not really acknowledge their own ability, by women who just do the job and do it so well, that in the process they redefine the job or position.

This ability is not restricted to women in the corporation or women business owners or women in government. It is equally evident in communities, in schools, and in volunteer organizations where women are seeking to have a voice in order to make a difference. Women know how to work hard. Women have a great deal to contribute. Why not make this contribution where our voice is heard, with other decision-makers around the leadership table? Women have learned that work without strategy just leads to more work and someone else making the decisions. With planning and thinking, focus and commitment, women can take their place at the table of their choice.

There have always been power tables from medieval times and the Knights of the Round Table to today's equivalents in the corporate board room or in the White House. The difference is, depending upon the moustache or beard fashion of the time, the faces around those tables have remained pretty much the same — all male, until recently. Now, more than ever before, women, building on a base of talent, expertise and experience, are setting their sights on higher and higher levels of responsibility in business, in politics, in the corporation, in the media, in the workplace and in the community arena.

Women are doing this for the best reason possible: The opportunities are there. Women today have all the options and examples they need. There is a potential leadership table wherever you are.

As a parent, it may be in your home. In many American homes, the table is becoming a ceremonial relic, a reminder of a place and time when families actually sat down to eat together at least once a day. Around this kitchen or dining room table, families had a chance to catch up with one another, to learn about what had happened during the day. A lot of counseling, complaining, cajoling and commending also went on around that table.

Today, the pressures of time and money make it a challenge for many of us to gather around the table as a family ritual. It may be time for new rituals. The table for single-parent homes can also be the place where self-respect and learning are explored. One parent and one child can be a power table. Put yourself at the table with one or more family members and consider that the knowledge, which begins with the exchange of information, is power. Is your home table a power table? Is information being shared? Is it being shared in a way that is conducive to mutual respect? Do things happen as a result of this shared information, counseling, admonishing, suggesting? Do the people who sit at the table in your life, believe they have a voice. Do you?

In the process of identifying what you want (what fits your talents or your interests or your passions), you will be embarking on an exciting trip, one in which you will have an opportunity to not only find a seat at the table, but to create a model for the table you want.

A Seat at the Table does not ask you to succeed by being more feminine or less feminist. It will not ask you to view men or the universe as your natural enemy. It is not about villains or victims. It is about an opportunity to realize your own goals at higher and higher, but reachable levels. Only you can claim these opportunities. And only you can decide when you will. Obtaining a seat at the table requires a true strategy with clear goals, planning and specific action items.

What is your goal? If you can't identify it, chances are you won't get it. Goals are the first step. The good news is that they can be expressed without immediately knowing exactly how you will reach them. A goal is simply your vision, such as: One day I would like a seat at the school board table. Or, I would like to be CEO of my own business. I want to create an organization that can really make a difference.

So, right now, identify your goal. Go ahead write it down.

My goal is to:

_____

_____

Don't worry about how or if you will reach it. This book will show you ways of moving toward a goal. We will listen to women with different experiences who have moved toward the leadership table in their lives and who have really enjoyed the trip. Cosmetics giant Estee Lauder said, "First, comes the shy wish, then you must have the heart to have the dream. Then, you work and work."

THE SHY WISH

In 1983, I founded the National Women's Economic Alliance for the purpose of helping women increase their opportunities for economic and career advancement. Even 10 years ago, it didn't make much sense to the leadership of the Alliance to tell women to strive for a seat at the table by totally lobotomizing the very qualities that they would need to be effective. Our goal: to identify our strengths and talents and to move forward from that base.

If you talk to former Secretary of Commerce Barbara Franklin; former Secretaries of Labor Elizabeth Dole and Lynn Martin; current Secretary of Energy Hazel O'Leary or Secretary of the Department of Health and Human Services Donna Shalala, you'll find great similarities among these women, although they represent different political parties. All of them had a strong sense of self, which gave them the strength to move forward table-by-table from volunteer to paid positions. In the process, they built reputations for leadership, for always following through, for working well with teams or committees. They brought a leader's commitment to every job.

They also had a vision for their own lives. In 1977, a young Donna Shalala was interviewed by Jane Trahey for a book, *On Women and Power*. Shalala at that time was an assistant secretary in the now-defunct U.S. Department of Housing and Urban Development (HUD). She was also an economics professor with tenure at Columbia. Shalala told Trahey, "Yes, there is one job that I'd like. I'd like to be where I could influence public policy and the perfect spot for this is a cabinet office."

That specific goal took Shalala 15 years to achieve.

The women I've met, who have a seat at many different tables, did not have a map or guide book to show them which road to take. But they listened and learned until the lightbulb flashed: "I can do that." and "I want to do that." As Barbara Walters says, "Follow your passions."

When she was the highest paid woman anchor on network television, Walters had a seat at the table, but it was in danger of being pulled out from under her. The ratings were down, the chemistry was wrong with her co-anchor. The publicity about her salary had created a go-ahead-we-dare-you-to-succeed attitude on the part of the public and her fellow journalists. Walters believes if she had not failed in this format, she would not have gone on to create her own successful style of interviewing and reporting.

After failure, she built her own table and has been seated at the head ever since.

Follow your interests. In order to do that, you have to keep your passions alive. You have to feed the flame and work very hard to protect it from the harsh judgment of naysayers, critics, discouragers, underminers, and most important, your own self-doubt.

When I wrote *America's New Women Entrepreneurs* in 1986, I talked to hundreds of women, who worked hard and worked smart and succeeded, but none of them were aiming for the Cabinet or government service. Their motives were different. Some just wanted a way to earn a living so that they could stay at home with their children because they couldn't afford child care. Others had an idea and wanted to risk time and resources to see it take life.

Still others, frustrated by the corporate-climb stagnation, decided to take their expertise and apply it to the marketplace on behalf of a service or a product. These women triumphed over obstacles of prejudice, lack of support, limited resources, and, in some cases, minimal education. They ignored the chorus of naysayers warning them that they would fail, and in fact, did not deserve to win. They left unread all those magazine articles suggesting that success was a lonely trip and, if it were the road chosen, women would pay a high price for achievement.

It was curious that none of these articles ever talked about the joy of succeeding, about the increase in personal power that comes when one overcomes personal fears and doubts to finally reach a goal. There was no mention of the opportunity to learn and to grow as you consistently moved up your ladder, which included contribution, ideas, constant challenge and stimulating people.

Women, who have achieved and surpassed their goals, have done it against a backdrop of negative factors. Whether it was a glass ceiling, tight credit, scarce resources, no mentor, or no help, they continued to move onward and upward. They were not born automatically knowing what to do and when to do it. And they were definitely not superwomen.

The journey to the table is about personal growth, leadership, power, and money. It is about success; and part of the joy of this success is deciding what form and style your success will take. One size does not fit all. The table I'm aiming for may hold no interest for you. Choosing one table does not commit you for a lifetime. As you get to know the women in this book, you'll see how they effectively table-hopped from one area of interest to another while learning along the way, building self-esteem and confidence, and making a measurable contribution at each table level.

WHERE DO YOU WANT TO GO AND WHAT DO YOU NEED TO GET YOU THERE?

"The question of the future will no longer be how much shall women be permitted to do, for all artificial barriers will have been withdrawn; but rather, first, how far will her own strength of body and mind be likely to carry her in the open competition with men on their own ground, and more importantly still, among the many diverse tasks and objects proposed to mankind in the great and laborious future, which shall seem most worthy of the woman's choice and pursuit? She may do what she chooses, but what will she choose to do?" So asked Florence Ravenal in 1918!

The choice will start you toward a destination where the trip is just as important as the arrival point. Along the way, you will experience triumphs and setbacks. You'll meet many interesting people, some of whom, will help you on your journey. Your time is of value. Your goal is important. It should be something that comes from your heart and sustains you through challenging times.

What seems worthy of your choice and pursuit? What seat at what table do you want to occupy and why? Where can you make your unique contribution and be rewarded financially, professionally or emotionally?

There is no better time than now to find out.

A Seat at the Table is a guide to help you perfect your work in progress. There are action items and lists in every chapter. Women, in their historic caretaker roles, have been great at making lists for others — forever. These are for you. "The discipline you impose upon yourself by writing things down is the first step toward getting them done," said Lee Iacocca.

As you move toward a seat at the table in your area of interest or passion, you'll find out what you are good at doing. You'll spend a lot of time getting better at it. You'll try to do whatever it takes to be the best. You'll establish a standard of performance that is high yet achievable and you will compete only with yourself. In the process, you'll discover the power of being yourself and then you can help others along the same route.

A Seat at the Table is about you and how you can start from wherever you are to begin your journey, or to consider a few alternate routes, if you've already begun. You'll hear from other women and men, who want to talk to you not just about their own success, but also the value they have learned along the way.

The stories are only guidelines; you are the leader on this trip.

1

THERE IS A TABLE FOR YOU

"Would you tell me, please, which way I ought to go from here?" she asked. "That depends a good deal on where you want to get to," said the cat.
LEWIS CARROLL, *ALICE'S ADVENTURES IN WONDERLAND*

"We're definitely headed for the White House and to the Congress and the state house, the mayor's office, the board room and every other seat of wordly power. But when we get there, we must arrive as women, not men in drag."
MARIANNE WILLIAMSON, *A WOMAN'S WORTH*

Within the last 10 years alone, there have been many books and articles written about women and power, women and money, women and love, women and management, and women as losers and victims. We've been advised how to dress, how to talk, how to swim with the sharks, how to practice the teachings of Attila the Hun; and, at the same time, cautioned not to lose our kinder and gentler instincts.

It seems like only yesterday, that women worked hard to eradicate any signs that they might actually be women, in order to move up the corporate ladder, achieve success and be accepted in the worlds of business, industry and government. The now infamous little blue suit and floppy little bow tie were just one sign that we were willing to do almost anything to gain respect.

The smart money told us then, "Don't put photos of your children on your desk. It will indicate you are not really committed." In fact, as late as 1988, Albert Heur in *Moving Up the Corporate Ladder* said, "Please, no photographs of cats, dogs or small children," as one of his eight rules to follow for corporate success.

We were told not to be "too emotional." In some firms, that could mean not saying "God bless you" after a sneeze. We learned "never let them see you sweat,"

1

"never let them see you cry," "don't get mad, get even." We knew acting "too feminine" was inappropriate, but short of showing up at work wearing a hoop skirt and flourishing a fan at meetings, what exactly did that mean? We didn't want to be "too masculine" either; that was just as bad. That could mean anything from wearing low-heeled shoes to asking for a key to the men's room.

Most of us spent a lot of time trying to discern the difference between aggression (bad) and assertion (sort of good). In the meantime, we took on everything from the car pool to the board room, with very little time to think about what we really wanted. We went from "I am woman, hear me roar!" to "I am working so hard, I haven't time to whimper." All of this against a backdrop of countless news articles warning of the unhappiness of success and the loneliness of achievement. In the meantime, someone else, usually one of the guys, moved ahead.

If the unexamined life was not worth living, we had more reasons to live than anyone. We examined exhaustively. We went along because we wanted to be the best. We knew we were invading territory that had been occupied for a very long time. As the new kids on the block, we had to learn the customs and the language before we could even play the game. Forget about win!

Former Secretary of Labor Lynn Martin recalled her swearing in as a member of Congress in 1977. "I look back at that photo and see me in that gray-flannel, pin-striped suit with the striped blouse and little bow tie. I guess I was thinking that if I looked enough like the guys, maybe I could pass. You know, they never made that mistake. They knew I was a woman."

Luckily, just as we were on the cusp of irrevocably turning ourselves inside out in an attempt to please and succeed, something changed and the changes were in our favor. "We see," says Lynn Martin, "that business, industry and government cannot effectively be run by just the 'heads' or the 'hearts.' We need both."

"Business has changed," according to Robert Lear, executive in residence at Columbia University School of Business and president and COO of Indian Head, Inc., "but a lot of people haven't learned how to change with it."

In the mid-1980s, the corporate giants began to wobble. In a fiercely competitive worldwide marketplace, American business and industry began to lose. CEO's were toppled from formerly secure perches and with them went the my-way-or-the-highway and ready-fire-aim approach to management. Rosabeth Kantor, author of *The Change Masters*, and Tom Peters, who coined "management by walking around," were key cheerleaders advocating an end to corporate bureaucracy, affirming the need for intrapreneurship, and empowering talent whatever it looked like. "The United States' relatively greater emphasis on women in management could well be a strong competitiveness advantage in the emerging global economy," said Peters.

"Segmentalism (the old bureaucracy) inhibits the entrepreneurial spirit and makes the organization a slave of its past, a victim, not a master of change," adds Kantor.

The enormous numbers of women in the work force and the numbers of women in middle and senior management represented a talent base too large to ignore.

An article in *Time* by Barbara Rudolph predicted, "Work force demographics suggest that the emerging female style of management will become more prevalent, not only because more women will achieve positions of power but also because a flexible, mediating approach will be vital in dealing with America's ever more heterogeneous workers."

Megatrends 2000 authors John Naisbitt and Patricia Aburdene called the 1990s the Decade of Women in Leadership, and underscored that the influx of women in the work force will continue to change the dynamics of the workplace. A new emphasis, on teams, personal responsibility, self-management and an entrepreneurial approach to industry and business challenges, begins to be valued over the old autocratic, omniscient style of CEO's of the '60s and '70s and '80s.

Corporations with an eye on surviving the present and thriving in the future encourage intrapreneurial talent no matter what the gender. At the same time, the increased numbers of women achieving as entrepreneurs raises their business profile and value in the marketplace.

Service industries, jobs in which women have always excelled, take the lead over manufacturing jobs. By the year 2000, 80 percent of all jobs will be in services.

"Even in the male-dominated manufacturing world, women have made great strides," explains Naisbitt. "Between 1983 and 1988 the number of women executives, administrators, and managers in manufacturing swelled from 403,000 to 647,000 thereby increasing women's share of the top manufacturing jobs from 20 to 26.3 percent."

The rise in women's earning power is also linked to women's decision-making power, which impacts corporate marketing. Companies wake up to the fact that women in senior-level management positions may be able to market more effectively to the growing group of women consumers.

On October 18, 1992, a story in *The New York Times* (Women's Progress Stalled? Just Not So), argued that women were big winners in the 1980s and "the gains should keep coming." The headline and the story were based on research published in the following books: *Understanding the Gender Gap: An Economic History of American Women* by Claudia Goldin, a Harvard economist; *The Economics of*

Women, Men and Work by Francine Blau, vice president of the American Economics Association; and June O'Neill, an economist at Baruch College.

The winning signposts for women:

1963 Women's expectations raised. Betty Friedan writes *The Feminine Mystique*. Federal act requires equal pay for equal work.

1964 Title 7 of the Civil Rights Act outlaws discrimination against women.

1975 Court decisions back up civil rights laws.

1980s Women's unemployment rates lower than men's.

1981 For first time, more than 50 percent of women are in the paid labor force.

1984 Proportion of women in labor force with college degrees equals that of men for the first time since the 1940s. Women increasingly choose same majors as men.

1989 Women hold 40 percent of entry-level and middle-management jobs, double that of 1972.

1991 Proportion of women who work full-time year-round reaches an all-time high.

These benchmarks show that unlike their mothers, young women have not been falling further behind in salaries as they grow older. Because women are getting a larger share of new professional degrees, it seems logical that their share of jobs will increase toward the year 2000.

In the nonprofit arena more women are stepping up to the leadership table and getting high marks. "We see an increase in the pool of talented, qualified women that we can present to our clients, especially in the arena of the major nonprofits," according to Jacques Nordeman, chairman of Nordeman Grimm, a leading executive search firm.

"And," says Peter Grimm, vice-chairman of Nordeman Grimm, "we make an effort in every search to identify and include women as part of any slate of candidates to the top 1,000 corporations. In almost every search, our clients want us to do that. Five years ago they may have said, 'let's look at some women but we really want a man.' "

Human Resources, once viewed as a female ghetto, moves up in importance in the corporation. Chief executive officers are called on more and more to not only communicate, but connect! Women are perceived as having an inside edge on this skill.

In the 1990s, feminine skills are deemed of value. Now, it is very important to leave your office, talk to your employees and learn about their personal lives.

It is a good sign to have a photo of your family on your desk. Intuition is now a valued commodity.

Corporations seeking the right formula for long-term survival in today's constantly changing economic environment find there is no long-term certainty. Even within the hallowed halls of business schools, the approach to management training has changed. The Wharton School retools its program, with emphasis on leadership, innovation, people skills, and real-world experience while in school.

Equally important, as the changes occurring within corporate America, are the astounding number of women succeeding as entrepreneurs. According to the Small Business Administration, women are forming their own companies at four times the rate of men and it is predicted that by the year 2000, 50 percent of all small business will be owned by women.

Women and business is no longer an oxymoron.

Women entrepreneurs refuse to read from the old rule book. They don't have any answers, so they ask a lot of questions, ignore the naysayers, and make a substantial contribution to the economy.

More women have made the decision to run for political office, with surveys showing women have advantages as candidates. According to a poll commissioned by RENEW (Republican Network to Elect Women) and conducted by Public Opinion Strategies, voters may believe that women's strengths lie being "negotiators or pragmatists, interested in getting things done."

And, in that rarest of rarefied atmospheres — the corporate board — the search began for more qualified people — women — to serve as directors.

So if you are looking for signs that say this is the right time to move forward now, you have them. With great change comes great opportunity.

To Thine Own Self Be True

As we look at the women who are succeeding in many different areas, we can jump to some positive conclusions about how they got where they are. The most important finding is that they succeed by being themselves.

Judith B. Rosener, professor at the University of Colorado, looked at executive and entrepreneurial women in a 1990 study for the International Women's Forum. The study affirmed that increasing numbers of women in or out of the corporation were achieving because of their "feminine" traits, not in spite of them. But the interesting thing about this finding is that women, who do achieve, believe that they do not need to subjugate who they are in order to succeed, and the higher their aspiration levels, the higher their rewards.

This study is just one of many that supports the concept that by knowing who you are and what you want, and by focusing your talents and abilities toward a goal, you can choose a table, focus on a decision-making seat around that table, and in the process raise not only your aspirations but your chances of moving forward.

What table are you aiming for? CEO of your own company? Director on a corporate board? Running for a local or national office? Is your eye on a seat around the school board table? Would you like to really make a difference on an issue about which you care deeply? Have you considered creating your own table of influence?

Hannah M. Hawkins, director of the Children of Mine Center, an organization in Washington that provides children from three to 14 with food, shelter and mentors, positive activities and nurturing, began by feeding hungry street children in her neighborhood. In order to keep the center going she had to take her story to the media, to key politicians. She had to sit around the decision-making table and make her case for the kids. In the process, she met CEO's of major corporations and expanded her outreach and sphere of influence all to benefit the children who use the center.

Bonnie Erbe is a writer with many years experience in radio, print and television, who knew there was a need for a television program reflecting the varying opinions of women in business, government, and politics. So she created To The Contrary. Her vision took four years to come true. Erbe's all-female commentary show is now in its third season, airs in more than 240 markets, and has won many awards, including a grant from the Ford Foundation to take the show in seminar form on the road.

Erbe created the concept and sat around the table with potential funders and sponsors convincing them this was a different show with great possibilities. To The Contrary features panelists such as Linda Chavez of the Manhattan Institute; syndicated columnists Julianne Malveaux and Ellen Goodman; Harriett Woods, president of the National Women's Political Caucus; Kate O'Beirne, of the Heritage Institute; commentator Irene Natividad; Elaine Shannon of *Time* magazine; Helen Ferre, of *Diario Las Americas* in Miami and Lynn Martin, former Secretary of Labor. Erbe now enjoys several seats as an opinion leader, a journalist and an entrepreneur.

At a recent conference I attended, the keynote speaker had a resume of accomplishments so long that a woman seated next to me said, "What is the point of even trying? I will never accomplish that much in my whole life." I asked, "Do you want to?" She said, "Not really, but it makes me feel guilty knowing someone has been able to manage her time so effectively." We both laughed, but as we continued to talk, I found out that she was a small business owner, whose business was growing. She was married with three children and also was politically involved in her county. So much so that the local political leaders had tapped her as a potential candidate. She was already occupying a seat at several key tables, including that of the family, but as she said, "Those are not real boards or presidential appointments. They're just community things. And my business, is well, just my business. It's not as if I were doing something really important like inventing penicillin."

How Important Does It Have to Be Before You Can Give Yourself Credit?

This reminds me of the "Oh, this old thing" syndrome. The cliche was, because it was used so often, that if you complimented a woman on her dress or suit, she would say, "Oh, this old thing" instead of a simple "thank you." Today we are still laboring with this problem of false modesty. It is important, of course, to try not to become a raving ego maniac, but life has a way of dealing with those folks. On the other hand, give yourself credit when you get on a community board, or start a business, or work with the Girl Scouts. If you diminish your contribution you are really discouraging others from participating at a leadership level, and we need more, not fewer, women of good will doing volunteer work.

Comparisons are often self-defeating. We can count ourselves losers by what others achieve or take an objective view and identify what we can learn from their journey. Always bearing in mind, it will never be our trip. Not all of us want to invest the time and energy and single focus required to achieve CEO or senator status, but that doesn't mean we do not want to participate as a peer around some other decision-making table.

What Will You Choose?

Your trip to the table begins with the following statements:

What's your opinion?

Is this the best of times or the worst of times?

_____ BEST   WORST _____

Is the glass ceiling impassable or it is just one more challenge to overcome?

_____ PASSABLE   IMPASSABLE_____

Is this a good or bad time to start a business?

_____ GOOD   BAD _____

There will never be a female president.

_____ THAT'S RIGHT.   THAT'S WRONG. _____

Women will never hold significant seats around any table.

_____ YOU GOT THAT RIGHT.   YOU GOT THAT WRONG. _____

Women won't help other women.

_____ YOU GOT THAT RIGHT.   DEPENDS ON THE WOMAN. _____

Successful women are power hungry, unhappy people.

_____ YOU GOT THAT RIGHT.   DEPENDS ON THE WOMAN. _____

Power is bad for women.

_____ YOU GOT THAT RIGHT.   DEPENDS ON THE WOMAN. _____

I want a seat at the _____ table. I have a contribution to make.

I see myself there and I recognize myself.

_____ YOU GOT THAT RIGHT   YOU GOT THAT RIGHT. _____

There is no answer sheet with a ranking form for you to determine how right or wrong you are. That's the point. Shakespeare said, "To thine own self be true and then it will follow like the night the day, thou canst not be false to any man."

So, first find your own self. This as we all know is a lifelong endeavor. A trip not made any easier by so-called gurus of the right and left who are constantly defining what real femininity or womanhood entails. The cacaphony grows louder every day with advice about what is worthy of our pursuit.

Your answers will tell you what you already know. The interesting thing about your opinion is that studies show that a positive outlook is a critical component of any success story. Ralph Waldo Emerson said, "Nothing great was ever accomplished without enthusiasm." This doesn't mean you must be a Pollyanna refusing to acknowledge challenges and roadblocks. It does mean, that without a positive outlook in general and growing faith in your dreams, you will not have the stamina or energy or persistence to find the road behind all the roadblocks.

Examine where you are now. Have you been looking at the same scenery for a while? If so, it may take some special effort to really see what there is to see: possibilities.

Martha Stewart built an empire by noticing the ordinary and celebrating the possibilities. Her power seat is at the kitchen table where she creates the ideas for beautiful gardens, a wonderful wedding, a holiday feast, a child's birthday, a new way of preparing vegetables, or a calendar complete with a schedule for all those seasonal jobs that most of us hate doing. Stewart looked at all the same things we all see but she viewed them in a different light and a business was born.

THE FEAR LIST

In order to realize our own goals, we have to stop and take a look at where we are and what the environment looks like. We have to ask ourselves if it is possible for us to thrive where we are. And if the answer is no, we need to make plans to move on to other possibilities.

What often tips the equation to a negative result is fear. There are more excuses, more fears, than we can list. They are all valid. How each of us deals with our list makes the difference between a person who moves forward at a crossroads, and one who stays where she is.

I have listened to so many women, successful women from all walks of life express one or more of the these fears just as they were ready to consider a new venture, a new move toward a bigger goal. In fact, every woman I profiled in *America's New Women Entrepreneurs* talked openly about her fears that she wouldn't, couldn't achieve what really was in her heart to do. So how did they move forward? They put their fear on hold and went ahead anyway.

Do these fear-of-trying excuses sound like any you've thought about lately?

I am afraid to try.

No one in my family has ever done this.

I have no money.

I have no education.

I have no time to spend on myself or my dreams.

No one will help.

Only people with power and money succeed.

I am a woman.

I am the wrong race.

I am too old.

I am too young.

I am too tired.

I have tried before and it didn't work.

The economy is not booming.

I am not smart enough.

It's too hard.

I am not sure if my family and friends will be supportive.

People will resent me if I succeed and I want to keep my friends.

What if I fail?

What if I lose?

What if I succeed?

I am not an insider.

I have no connections.

I can't make a difference.

I have no time.

Someone stole my idea.

I'll think about it tomorrow.

When Nancy Kerrigan, Olympic Silver medalist in figure skating, was asked how a sports psychologist had helped her achieve her medal, she explained that although she had always tried her best, something had kept her from going to that next level. It was the fear that if she really tried and failed, it would be worse than not having tried at all. She learned that trying for the medal with everything she had strengthened her and it can strengthen you, whether you win or lose, and it provides you with personal satisfaction and real power.

Kerrigan had a choice when she received that brutal blow to her leg. She could choose one from the fear column: "I can't go to the Olympics now. I have a good excuse for not trying." Or she could choose one from the *Seat at the Table* menu: "I will overcome this and give it my best shot." That decision to go for it, made Nancy Kerrigan a winner, and financially secure. And she didn't even have to win the gold.

You've never heard of her, but one day you will when Alice Talbot becomes a judge on the Supreme Court. That's her seat at the table goal. A divorced mother of three, she married early and never completed college. Her idea of a seat at the table was to become a lawyer, but before she could even consider law school she needed a degree from a college or university. Instead, she picked several selections from the "fear" list: I can't afford to go back to school. I am too old. What if I can't keep up with the rest of the (much younger) students? What difference is it going to make at this point in my life? My family will laugh at me. My ex-husband will think I am ridiculous. What if I'm not accepted at any college? It will take too much time.

The list worked so well that it kept Talbot from applying to colleges for several years. Then she realized that the time she could have utilized to reach her goal was passing away, anyway. Four years had passed and she had not moved one step closer to her goal. "It hit me that I could have had something to show for those four years. I could have at least begun some course work," she said.

So, she threw away her first list, her fear list, and made another.

Her goal: I want to get my B.A. from a college or university in four years from this date. Today, I will: Call and write to colleges in the area to get admissions forms and catalogues. Determine how I can go part-time. Find out about loan programs. Make a list of everyone I know who may be able to help me. Make an appointment with admissions, when I narrow my college list to three.

And she kept making lists, simple lists, headed with the title, "Tasks Required Daily." Each list kept Alice Talbot going and going and going. In June, 1995, she will graduate from law school.

Two things we know: Everybody experiences fear and action starves fear. Fear thrives the more you think about how afraid you are. Fear diminishes the minute you begin to move toward a goal. The problem with most of us is that we think we must move toward the goal in big, impressive steps, instead of small, forthright ones. The goal: I want to serve on the Supreme Court. The action: I am going to register for classes so I can get my degree. Actions/objectives are specific, achievable and measurable.

Most of the time, the "announcing" portion of our plan is to effectively postpone any real activity. We all know that the minute we float an idea or announce a new move, there will be a chorus (usually relatives) responding with something from the fear list. "This is a bad time/bad idea/where are you going to get the time/money/smarts?"

There is a lot to be said for quiet reflection, but just reflect long enough to put you in charge of whatever decisions you want to make. Identify your table and quietly observe who is currently occupying all of the seats? What do they bring to the party? What do you bring? When you've satisfied yourself that your commitment is true, you can begin to selectively share your plans with those who can really help.

So, as we begin our brief journey together, let's agree that we are all afraid and quaking in our shoes 90 percent of the time. And so is everyone else.

ACTION STEP: Evaluation

I have higher personal goals than I am currently realizing.

YES _____ NO _____

I have higher financial goals than I am currently realizing.

YES _____ NO _____

I have higher career goals than I am currently realizing.

YES _____ NO _____

I have higher emotional/spiritual goals than I am now realizing.

YES _____ NO _____

When I was a child, I thought it would be great to be _____ when I grew up.

I have identified the seat at the table I want for now but there are several roadblocks:

_____

_____

_____

Review your answers. Do they describe a person who is making the decisions you want to make? If you have identified the roadblocks to your achievement can you identify how you are going to get under, over or around this roadblock? Is there real opportunity for you in your current situation?

Ask yourself:

Yes, I enjoy what I am doing and would like to be doing even more. I feel energized.

No, I wonder why I continue to show up for work every day. I feel depleted.

Burnout does not mean you are working too many hours, it means you are working too many hours at something that is not nourishing you emotionally or professionally.

If you are currently working, list three things you like about your job:

1. _____
2. _____
3. _____

If you can't come up with three, you owe it to yourself to start looking for something else now. Describe the job or position that would have what you are looking for:

If you are not currently working, list three things you enjoy doing:

1. _____
2. _____
3. _____

List three things about your current situation you would like to change:

1. _____
2. _____
3. _____

Identify two or three ways in which this change could occur:

1. _____
2. _____
3. _____

If you have no idea how change can occur. Keep reading. Without knowing anything about your situation, I can tell you the only way you can make change occur is to take a few action steps. When they asked Willie Sutton, why he robbed banks, he answered, "Because that's where the money is." You can't climb Everest if you are not at the base of Everest. I know if we could have a conversation, you would tell me exactly what three steps would put you on the positive road to change. That's the easy part. So just list them. Writing them down will help you figure out the execution.

List the first three things you would do if you won the lottery:

1. _____
2. _____
3. _____

Now that you have spent all the money you want to spend, taken all the vacations and provided for your family, what would you choose to do with your life? What seat at what table would you aim for?

In conversations with women in the work force and women currently at home, the goals identified were very different. They included:

Get a seat on the pre-school membership board.

Join one professional organization.

Move toward a seat on the senior leadership team in my company or move to another job.

Establish a family night board meeting to go over the events of the week and give everyone a chance to weigh in.

Eliminate three activities from my life that are not viable any more.

Identify one cause and concentrate on a leadership position in the organization.

Run for political office.

Establish a foundation to fund a program for grade school children on development of entrepreneurial values.

Establish an international program for women in the work force with a worldwide data base of resource and support information.

Start a new business. Research the need for a product marketed to older population in health areas.

Increase sales and move into management in my corporation.

Become president of a nonprofit organization this year.

Organize a working mothers car pool and babysitting emergency group.

Turn my volunteer experience into a paying vocation.

Become a columnist for my local shopper/newspaper.

Get into the export market for my company.

Develop an international sister city partnership with a woman business owner in the same field.

Serve on one corporate board.

Serve on board of a nonprofit organization.

Create after-school program for latchkey kids.

Write a book on political campaigning.

Form an organization for women who have never joined a political party.

This list is only of interest to you because, just like your list, there is nothing here that you can't do, if you really have the passion to follow-through. The truth is you don't need to win the lottery to begin living your dream now.

List three steps that you see as leading you toward this goal:

1. _____

2. _____

3. _____

Can you begin to take these steps now?

YES _____ NO _____

If your answer is "no," review your goals. If you can't take three steps right now, can you take one?

1. _____

How much time each day are you prepared to work toward this goal?

HOURS _____ MINUTES _____

List people, men and women, whom you admire. (You do not need to know them personally.)

_____

_____

_____

_____

What is the common link among the people you listed? Is this a value you would like to demonstrate? Can you start now right when you are building a reputation based on these values? Do you feel you would find these values demonstrated in one area over another? _____

_____

_____

_____

_____

Write your mission statement. _____

_____

I will consider myself fulfilled professionally when... _____

_____

I will consider myself fulfilled personally when... _____

_____

If I could have a seat at one table, it would be... _____

_____

What is in your way right now, blocking you from your seat at the table?

_____

_____

_____

Can you think of three things you can do to start dismantling the roadblocks?

1. _____

2. _____

3. _____

(For Talbot, the biggest roadblock preventing her from graduating from law school was the fact that she had never received a college diploma. In order to achieve her long-term goal, she had to back up and pick an immediate roadblock to dismantle: Get a college degree.)

Can you identify the one thing you will do? _____

_____

How long will it take you to do it? _____

_____

I've answered all these questions. Now what?

What is your reward for going through this exercise? To give you a chance to look at what has now become familiar surroundings. To be honest with yourself enough to know that it is time to move on or to move up. If you were not able to answer all of the questions, it is because you don't have the answers just yet. If you are currently in a situation where you wonder why you continue to show up every day, you are adding a heavy stress load to your life. Time spent now on getting out or away from this situation will enable you think more clearly about what you do want.

If you cannot answer any "future" question, or have no idea what it would take to fulfill you either personally or professionally, you have not allowed yourself to dream. Without a dream or vision for your life, you will be in a reactive mode where there is no fun or exhilaration or passion. Review your answers. Write down your thoughts and put your notepad away. Return to it at the end of the day, when you have some time for yourself. Dare to dream a little.

You may want to invest in a three-ring looseleaf notebook. Organize your book with alphabet tabs and keep notes on yourself. Use these questions as starters. You may want to ask yourself many more that are not in this book. Only you know what they are. The questions you left unanswered today, try to come back to them. They are the ones that are the most important.

2

VERY LOW AND TINY CHAIRS

"How many cares one loses when one decides not to be something but to be someone."
COCO CHANEL

The operative word here is choose and to understand enough about yourself and your passions and aptitudes to say, "I really see myself in a seat at this table." Freud asked, "What do women want?" I believe Willa Cather gave him the answer when she said, "That is happiness: to be dissolved into something complete and great."

The "something" is up to you and this can change as you change.

To be engaged in something in which you become "dissolved," requires knowing what your mind and soul requires above all else and then, having the will to go for it. Mary Cassatt knew from her first breath that she would be dissolved in and by art. Emma Goldman lived and breathed political activism, but most of us are not that clear about which road leads to happiness, professional and personal achievement and fulfillment.

The great women artists, writers, musicians, faced great challenges, but their goal was always clear: to reach the place, the point of something complete and great. Far too often, our dissolving moments are too brief and can be surrounded by hours of things we must do, have to do, and frequently don't wish to do. Our personal voice is lost in the activity of the day, the week and the years. The result is a grinding down of our hopes, dreams and desires.

In order to achieve the seat at the table of our choice, we have to listen to that small voice that may be drowning in a sea of superfluous noise. The voice that asks, "Why aren't you doing something you really love?" "How much longer are you going to take the seat in the back of the bus?" "When is it your turn?"

17

"One day, you will take the trip, lead the company, paint the picture, start the business, go for the seat at the table."

How can you start now, to keep your goal in sight? To protect it from being overwhelmed with the demands or discouragements of others? How do you know if your goal is realistic? What would you consider complete and great? How does anyone start?

On a winter's day in 1994, I broke every bone in my left ankle after an unsuccessful climb up an icy hill. Following surgery, nine pins and two plates later, I had an unusual opportunity to think about the questions I have just posed for you.

Although at this point in my life, I sit at various seats at several tables including that of chairman of the board for a corporation, my primary source of affirmation, contribution and sense of well-being comes from family and friends. My friends are an integral part of my professional life. My family is my most important table. And in a way, this commitment to family led circuitously to other seats around many tables in other arenas.

TABLE 1: VERY LOW AND TINY CHAIRS

When I was a young mother, with three small children, I wanted a seat at the table where the decisions were made at my childrens' pre-school. In this way, I could be part of the leadership of the school determining the direction this small school would take to provide the best environment for the children. I didn't sit down and write my strategy. But I did make inquiries and learned that as a parent new to the school, my chances were very slim regarding a board seat.

Those who were then on the board had served on a variety of committees including, the school improvement committee, which was responsible for raising money to provide playground equipment, books and toys. A key talent, required for this board, was the ability to repair or replace school materials and playground equipment.

My repairing talents were nonexistent, but I could help members of the improvement committee raise money for books and toys. In terms of baking talents, my cookies were more like inedible sculptures, but I was great at organizing bake sales, garage sales, and used book sales to get the funds for the classrooms. At the time, I, like so many women, did not place high value on what we did. We just did it.

After helping members of the improvement committee raise money through bake sales, rummage sales, garage sales, I was eventually invited to serve as a member of this group. Two years later I had worked myself up to board level. In the process, I learned a great deal about working with committees and about how to move toward a goal without beding torpedoed on the way.

Our board consisted of women at home and women who worked. In one sense we ran the school like a small business with the children as the customers. In order to provide the equipment, books, teachers, field trips for our customers, we had to learn about the budget process, salaries, and administrative costs. We had to look into health care and benefit packages for teachers. We developed programs and policies to help families who could not afford to pay the school tuition. In fact, within the micro-world of the nursery school we dealt with all the macro issues facing Americans today.

For the next 10 years, all of my power seats had to do with people and programs that could affect my children. As a single head of household, a great euphemism for a scared, lonely, overworked and financially challenged mother of three, I lived in a community that was distinguished by its two-parent, traditional families. I did not want my childrens' teachers assuming that my kids did not have a strong parent/ally.

Eventually, my table list increased. I served as a den mother, on the soccer committee, the teachers' helper committee. In all of these and many more activities I learned a lot about people; the ones who volunteer and never come through; the ones who do everything they promise. I witnessed the organization and turf battles. If you think the corporate board room is challenging, you have never been on a pre-school committee board.

I witnessed the antipathy between the women at home and the women at work develop when the working mothers expected those at home to shoulder all of the activities. Time paid for was considered more valuable, more precious than time volunteered. The problem could have been solved easily by more interaction between the groups and mutual respect. I learned that humor can deflect a lot of tense situations if it is not caustic or sarcastic. I learned how to express myself in a meeting, how to bring a new idea to the table without killing someone else's, how to get on the bandwagon, when my idea was rejected and work to help make happen what the group had voted for.

All of these lessons were free. If I hadn't been a parent, I would not have targeted any of these tables. So, far from my family standing in the way of my expression, they really provided the catalyst propelling me into the community.

TABLE 2: ENTREPRENEUR/FREELANCE WRITER

At the same time, I began to look for ways to supplement my income and I started writing. Like many women who must suddenly face the challenge of providing for the family and at the same time, being with the family, I wanted a home-based job.

For those of you who are working at home, you know this is not as easy as it sounds. In theory, you announce to your children that you are in your working mode and are to be left alone. My recourse, after these announcements were ignored, was to take my work in the one room that had a lock on the door — the bathroom — and try to write for a full 10 minutes before the inevitable pounding on the door began accompanied by yells, "Mom, why are you in there so long?"

If you live in an apartment or house big enough, you may be lucky to have a designated office. If you don't, there goes the bedroom or the dining room or the bathroom. It is very difficult to work at home, but fortunately today, there is the Home-Based Business Association and they can get you started on the right foot.

Eventually, I was able to come out of the bathroom with a packet of articles which I promptly sent off to a variety of magazines and waited for my checks to come in. Unfortunately, what came back were rejection slips. I had failed the first step of moving to a seat at the table. Research before you leap. Understand the market and the need to be filled.

My attempt to shortcut the process was sloppy and I didn't want to make that mistake again. I needed to know the rules and the right trade publications to read. I wanted to be around other writers who could critique my work. Through an ad in a writer's magazine, I found out about a writer's group that met weekly in the evening, across the bridge, in Washington, D.C., to read members' articles and stories.

The group was run by Pat Hass, a published author and editor who would determine if my work was good enough to join the group. I wanted a seat at this table, but I did not have the extensive portfolio of published articles, which was the required entry ticket. What I did have was a large porfolio of unpublished articles and an even greater portfolio of rejection slips. As Hass read my material, including several letters from editors praising the work but declining to publish my articles, she said, "I am going to take a chance and let you join the group. But you must make the meetings a priority and you have to commit the time between the meetings to writing, writing and rewriting."

TABLE 3: PUBLISHED WRITER

I was in this group for five years seated around a table with published writers and a few who were in my category. I never missed a meeting. During those five years, the members of the group could count among the published works: four books, many, many articles, short stories and a syndicated column. Years later when I met Mary Higgins Clark, this country's most successful mystery writer, she told me that she is still in a writers' group because it gives her a chance to be with her peers, discuss each others' works in progress, help one another and share in the good news when someone's book sells. She would not miss a meeting for anything.

As you move through your goals you may want to consider creating a resource group, if one does not already exist. A group can be invaluable helping you to understand the challenges you are currently facing and those you can expect in the future. A resource group provides an oasis within which you can be encouraged to keep trying and to improve along the way.

The writer's group increased my success rate, and taught me three lessons:

1. I learned that talent or no talent, if you want to be really good, it takes steady, hard work. One rarely hit the bull's-eye with the first draft, or the second, or the third. If you didn't really have the commitment for the task, you would give up before the final rewrite ever occurred.

2. Criticism never works. Feedback does. There is a big difference. Feedback is offered with the idea that together you are going to be part of the process improving the service, the product, the presentation, the article. This help is not overpowering, but is meant to empower someone else to find the way to use their own skills, talent and intelligence to reach a desired goal.

Gail Blanke, a senior vice president of corporate affairs and communications at Avon Products, says, "There are times when I'll say to the people who work for me prior to a major presentation, no matter what happens know that this work is good. That you are good. Feel proud starting now because nothing can take away from the excellence of work."

3. Talking is talking. Writing is writing. Doing is doing. I began to see that the only thing that really works is really working, not talking about it. So many wonderful ideas for books were discussed, but they never were written. The talk had siphoned all the energy from the idea. Overtalking can undermine your commitment and undermine the commitment of others for your project or goal. Know when it's time to be in a research mode, listening, absorbing but not "announcing."

TABLE 4: PRESIDENT, PROFESSIONAL ORGANIZATION

After a year, with a syndicated column on working women under my belt, I joined Capital Press Women (CPW), the Washington, D.C., chapter of the National Federation of Press Women. This was my first professional association and I felt I had truly arrived at a new and exciting table. Two years later, I was elected President of CPW and in that position was required to chair meetings, give speeches, raise money and increase membership.

I was very lucky because the former president, Jeanne Viner Bell, an entrepreneur and owner of a successful public relations firm took me under her wing and became a lifelong mentor. Bell wore beautiful clothes and jewelry at a time when women were told that unless they were willing to wear the "dress for success" straitjacket, no one would take them seriously. She was a great example of a successful businesswoman, a caring mother and wife, a community contributor, and a mentor to hundreds of women. Bell was the first to let me know that while it was possible to be all these things, it was impossible to be all of them at the same time.

This meant making a choice between priorities on a daily basis, but with a clear idea of what my long-term priorities would always be.

You have to choose where you will place your greatest efforts.

As your circumstances change, so will your time commitments. So, if you are unable to juggle everything perfectly in your life just now, be aware that you will one day have the time. It is important to do the groundwork now, so you will be prepared to meet opportunity when it comes.

Watch and listen. Identify someone you admire and learn from this person. Today, when I refer to Jeanne Viner Bell as my mentor, she replies, "Pat, darling. If you are going to tell people I am your mentor, at least let me 'ment' once in a while."

The writing table was very rewarding for me, personally and professionally. I kept the kids posted every step of the way. They were thrilled when the *Chicago Sun Times* published Tut, Tut, Tutsie Good-Bye, an article about the King Tut exhibit that was responsible for herding Americans to museums like never before. When I received my check in the grand amount of $65, we blew it all on dinner, but the message was clear: It would take more than my articles to pay for future college tuition.

I began to be a regular contributor to the Point of View column for the Evening Star, a newspaper in Washington, D.C., which no longer exists. Eventually I wrote a syndicated column, Women At Work. I wrote about women at home, women at work, getting my car towed, the empty nest, makeovers — all generated by my experiences as a working mother. Even the play I wrote, "Cabbage Soup," which was based on the story of Rapunzel and produced by Children's Radio Theater and finally at the Kennedy Center's Terrace Theater, was the result of telling the Rapunzel story so many times in the preschool circle group.

My "success" at this point was grounded in the world I knew: my three children, my point of view and the stories that other women were beginning to tell me about their goals and struggles and hopes for the future.

TABLE 5: ENTREPRENEUR AND CEO

I knew it was time to move on to another table. There were economic considerations, three children, who I hoped would eventually go to college, as well as professional ones. My work background prior to marriage and motherhood, had been as an account executive for an advertising firm in New York City and the experience had been a positive one. My experience as a freelance writer gave me the confidence I needed to begin thinking of myself as a business owner, although it was a very small business. I wanted a seat at the entrepreneurial table and I was willing to mortgage my house and load up my credit cards to get it.

This time the writing would be position papers, speeches, op eds, articles for clients. This was a very small table with only two seats, one for me and one for my new husband. We borrowed, mortgaged, borrowed again until the company grew.

This table demanded everything we had to give and more and more and more. Long days and weekends, conversations around the dinner table, when there was dinner, focused on work. The kids hated my obsession with every detail of the company. I longed for summer when I could send them to camp and work around the clock without guilt. I loved the work and time flew. After years of working at home, I was finally in a place where the stamps could always be found and the stapler was never broken.

What a scam, I thought. All these guys coming home saying, "Honey, what a hard day I had today!" What was hard about this? Hard was entertaining two toddlers for 14 hours. Hard was negotiating car pooling, playground duty with pre-school mother-of-the-month detail. Hard was reading *Green Eggs and Ham* for the 1,000th time. Hard was realizing that these children would probably not continue to take naps through puberty.

Today, our firm is among the top 10 owner-managed public affairs companies in the U.S with offices in New York, Dallas, San Francisco, Washington, D.C., and Brussels.

The balancing act between home and family continued for the next 10 years. No matter how organized I was, a child emergency threw every plan out the window. Despite my work addiction, my family knew they were my top priority. Without their help, I never would have been able to move forward achieving not only career goals, but economic ones as well.

Christopher, Claudia and Courtney were my not-so-silent partners as we discussed together how we could manage time and problems given the demands on all of us. My husband's children, Susan, Emmett and Joe were also part of the team, who allowed us to work on weekends, even though it cut into their time. Like most working mothers, although my children came first, I made sure the company recouped whatever time was lost. It became clear that at least for these "wonder years," my plans would have to be long range. In the meantime, though, I could get ready for the next phase:

Rip and Read: Because there never was going to be enough time to read everything I wanted to, I began to keep a subject file and zoom through the newspapers and magazines, collecting articles of interest, to be read now and filed or to be read later. *The Financial Times*, the *Journal of Commerce* in addition to *The Washington Post, The Wall Street Journal* and *The New York Times* gave me the perspective on a range of management, business, government, women in the work force, consumer and environmental issues.

Formulate an Opinion: I began to track trends and to develop a point of view on many issues having impact on our lives, not just the ones designated for women-only.

Get the Credentials: I enrolled in an M.B.A. program on International Trans-actions and took every opportunity to meet with the study group on trade and commerce issues.

Join Professional Organizations: I joined the Public Relations Society of America (PRSA) and the Counselors Academy of PRSA. I became a member of the board of the Medical College of Pennsylvania. This was made possible by a member of Capital Press Women. I joined the International Women's Forum, Washington, D.C., chapter. Susan Davis, the founder of The Susan Davis Companies, nominated me. I knew Davis through her work with the National Association of Women Business Owners which she had helped to found. One person led to another and my circle began to widen. The key to remember: Your circle will widen if you come through with the work required and the commitments promised when you become part of the organization.

Get Visible: I volunteered to speak gratis for local professional groups, including conferences sponsored by CPW. One speech led to another and the last one led to a speech coach. I needed the critique. I needed to be better.

TABLE 6: FOUNDER/NONPROFIT ORGANIZATION

As I traveled through the country, talking about women in the work force, I met many interesting men and women and discovered that although there were many women's organizations dedicated to helping women get ahead, there wasn't one with both men and women working together toward this goal. I began to talk to men and women leaders asking them if they would be interested in helping to shape a new organization dedicated to increasing career and economic opportunity for women; dedicated to helping corporations find the best talent possible for senior-level positions and corporate boards; dedicated to helping women identify their own entrepreneurial qualities so that they would be better positioned to not only access opportunity but also to create it.

That was 1983 and the first meeting of the Board of Governors of the National Women's Economic Alliance was held. Margaret Heckler, who was then a member of Congress and soon-to-be Secretary of Health and Human Services, offered her help, her contacts and her expertise to get the Alliance going.

Without her, I would never have been able to reach the opinion-makers, the men and women leaders from business, industry and government with track records of achievement in their various fields, that I needed to serve on the board. Ten years earlier when I was seated at the pre-school board of directors table, I didn't know any of these people. Looking back, I could see that so much had happened while I thought I had been in a "hold" pattern waiting for the balancing act between home and work to end.

Table 7: Political

Other than voting in national elections, I had never been involved politically prior to 1980. Although I lived in Washington, D.C., I was not part of the political echelon on either the Democratic or Republican side. My political expertise and insider knowledge was totally dependent upon what I read in *The Washington Post*.

All this changed for me when Betty Heitman, who was then co-chairman of the Republican party, organized a coalition of women business leaders. Heitman did not care what your political party happened to be, she invited Democrats and Independents to join the group as well. The focus of this coalition was on issues affecting women in the work force and women business owners. That was certainly something I could relate to.

Although I had never met Betty Heitman, she had attended several Alliance meetings where she heard me speak on the need for more access to capital for women business owners and a reduction of the capital gains tax. At this time I was writing a column on women and workplace issues and had some visibility in the media.

From the inside out, the political environment is stimulating, intriguing and addictive. I began to meet people, who managed to find time in their very busy lives for some level of political involvement, including fundraising, speech making, article writing, volunteering time on a campaign, writing checks, joining issue coalitions. For those who were political appointees and members of the Administration, I learned their day had no end.

For the most part, contrary to what you continually read, the people who come to serve in Washington, either in Congress or as political appointees are dedicated and committed. They are interesting to be around because they have a point of view, and a position on the critical issues that face our nation. Politics is really an equal opportunity employer. If you are willing to commit the time, there will be a place for you. The political table offers you a wide opportunity to participate either as a candidate, a supporter of a candidate, or an active member in the party of your choice

Irene Natividad, founder of a successful consulting company, political commentor, and former president of the National Women's Political Caucus, has built a reputation and a livelihood on her vast political knowledge regarding women candidates and women in politics. She is a panelist on To The Contrary and is sought after not only by those interested in her insights regarding the political arena, but also for her business acumen as well. The seat she enjoys at the political table is based on a lifelong commitment to helping women achieve leadership in politics.

Mary Matalin started her political career as the end of an elephant in a political parade. She was willing to work at any job they threw at her in local and national campaigns until her political savvy was recognized and rewarded. From her stint as campaign director of Bush-Quayle '92, she is now moderator of her own television show and a regular guest on the "Today" show.

Whatever route you choose, you will learn more than you ever thought possible about issues you never thought you'd care about. In order to be effective, you have to articulate what you believe and why. Depending on the level of your involvement, it is possible to become involved and keep your day job. Politics can be rewarding whether you win or lose. Winning is great, but, win or lose, the friendships you establish remain through the good and bad political times.

If you are thinking about eventually having a significant seat at this political table, I would advise you to start with fundraising. The fundraising committee comprises men and women, usually business owners, who are putting their own money where their beliefs are. You will meet some of the most successful and interesting men and women in the country. In the process, they will learn about you.

Although I was a late starter and did not have major money to contribute, my involvement has been very rewarding. My work with energy issues enabled me to be appointed by the Secretary of Energy to the National Coal

Council. I continued to work in politics, while keeping my day job, and after several years involvement with trade and small business issues, I was appointed as Chairman, International Committee, Advisory Board, Small Business Administration. One of the most interesting tables I had the honor of sitting around was the President's Export Council (PEC). Our work on the PEC led by Chairman Heinz Prechter was substantive and affirmed the old maxim, if you want to get something done, get busy people to do it. The purpose of the council is to work with the Secretary of Commerce advising the President regarding export policy and programs to help American business. The board was filled with leading chief executive officers dedicated to helping American business increase exports.

Following my term on the PEC, I was appointed by the U.S. Trade Representative to the Services Policy Advisory Council (SPAC). The goal of the SPAC was to ensure that the U.S. services industries' goals were represented in GATT and Uruguay Round discussions.

In addition to these appointments, I was invited to serve as a member of the delegation to the United Nations' Commission on the Status of Women. The work completed by the delegation under the direction of Ambassador Judy McLennan was recognized by the Department of State with the Superior Honor award. I list all of this for you to underscore that participating in the political process can provide you with an opportunity to serve around many tables.

Politics will provide you with a very big table. Do your homework and as you become involved, you will be better positioned to consider several options, which include becoming a candidate or being appointed to serve in the president's cabinet, or working at higher and higher levels and making a difference on defining issues. If more women understood the unlimited benefits connected with becoming involved at almost any level in politics, we would ultimately see more women in the House and the Senate and yes, the White House.

TABLE 8: CORPORATE BOARD TABLE

My visibility in senior-level political appointments and my reputation as a businessperson led to my appointment to the board of Guest Services Inc., a corporation established in 1917, whose excess earnings are distributed annually to charitable organizations. Today, I serve as Chaiman of the Board and among other duties, help the President, S.J. DiMeglio identify other qualified people, who happen to be women, for corporate board service. It is possible to move from "very low table and tiny chairs" to a table at the top. In my case, my interests led me up the path, one step at a time. I did not have a grand game plan.

I had simple goals, which I achieved, and which then led to other possibilities. The key for me, that continues to this day, is building relationships and building them in more than one arena. The plus with this approach is even if you don't gain the seat at the table of your choice, you have made lasting friendships along the way. It makes for a very interesting trip.

3

MOVING TOWARD YOUR TABLE

"An important question, as always, was why were we here? Answers came readily: to visit Asia, climb a mountain, test our limits, know ourselves. All these were true, yet they were not enough. Why would any woman risk her life to stand on the top of a mountain? The geese circled the summit once before resuming their flight south. Were they wheeling among the high peaks for the view? For the glory? I smiled and thought, 'I bet they're doing it for the fun of it.' "
ARLENE BLUM, *ANNAPURNA, A WOMAN'S PLACE*

What table have you targeted for the fun of it?

If you cannot tolerate the idea of having a boss, you probably are not going to be happy in a structured corporate environment with a traditional culture. But even in the hallowed halls of the top 1,000 corporations, change has occurred. Recently, KPMG, Peat Marwick's London office, conducted a visioning workshop to help people, who had lost their jobs through downsizing, find new jobs. Job change or job loss provides an opportunity to step back and ask, "What do I really want to do with the rest of my life?"

This is a question for women, who have had a solid coporate background, to ask when considering either job change or business ownership. It is the key question you should ask yourself if you are considering public office. It is a question that may take some time to answer.

According to Richard Donker, author of *Zen and the Art of finding a True Vocation*, the Peak Marwick sessions are geared to help people discover unresolved career longings. We have all met people, who have what appears to be a great job, and yet they are not happy because they want to be doing something else. A friend of mine, who is a successful executive in a leading advertising agency, has it all: money, title, office with a huge window, prerequisites and benefits. When I asked her what would she choose to do if money were not a consideration, she smiled and said without hesitation, "be a ski instructor."

Sometimes getting a seat at the table means giving up something else. Only you can determine how much personal satisfaction you will get as a result of achieving your goal. If you move toward your goal in baby steps, you can evaluate as you get nearer to the destination.

CAN YOUR FANTASY TURN INTO THE REAL THING?

I don't know anyone who hasn't at one time or another fantasized about winning millions in the lottery. But I don't know anyone who has given up her job on the strength of purchasing a ticket. Many of us have dreams about owning a business, but if the idea of entrepreneurial risk starts your stomach heaving, perhaps the role of business owner is not for you. Do you care deeply about a cause, an issue, a candidate? Do you have a vision for your community or your world? What would you choose to do if money were not a factor?

I know many women in Congress today, who would have answered these questions as follows several years ago. Do you like giving speeches? I could never stand up in front of a crowd. Do you see yourself in Congress? I can't stand politicians and I could never ask anyone to give me money. What happened to make them change their minds? They got involved in campaigns. They realized they cared very deeply about issues and believed they could make a difference. They did their homework and learned all they could about the political process in their environment. They began to believe, "I can do that." And they did.

The same goes for some of the successful women business owners I know. For example, Ellen Terry, president of Ellen Terry Realtors in Dallas, Texas, never visualized the entrepreneurial table as a goal. She was wrenched from her suburban housewife life when her husband ran off, leaving her with two children and over half a million dollars in debt. Necessity was the motivator that helped her get going. She has never stopped.

In her case, fear was a catalyst for action, fear of never seeing her children again moved her quickly forward. It enabled her to convince a real estate firm that they would more than get their investment of a draw against salary back if they gave her a chance. "I believe," says Terry, "that success can only come to each of us by stepping out and taking risks and grasping hold of that opportunity that is floating by. True success in life is not what we are, but what we are, compared to what we could have done."

Success can be anything, according to Courtney Spain, of J. Walter Thompson, "It can just be being alive. There are so many successful women who have totally different goals and objectives than I do. The important thing is to identify the goal you wish to achieve and be comfortable with it. That's success."

Many of us have arrived at a place through a process known as ready-fire-aim. If we had the opportunity to reconsider, we might first start with understanding a little more about where we can realistically contribute. Where does what we have to offer fit what the marketplace wants? Do you know enough about yourself right now to see yourself at one of the following tables or a combination of one or more?

Table: Public Service

Elaine Chao, president and CEO of the United Way and former director of the Peace Corps; Betsy Myers director of the Office of Women's Business Ownership of the Small Business Administration and former entrepreneur; Elizabeth Dole, president of The American Red Cross and former Secretary of Labor and Secretary of Transporation, are just a few examples of public service leaders. Women who "manage with a mission," according to Francis Hesselbein, former president of the Girl Scouts USA.

Does this sound like you? You want to make the world a better place. This is your number one priority. You believe you have something to contribute. You have a point of view about what can work and what doesn't. You want to make a difference. You may not be quite sure where you want to invest your time and talent but you know you must work for or with an organization or an administration that is cause-related. You are motivated by the chance to effect change. To be able to look back and say, "Because of me, this happened."

The public service table includes volunteer involvement as well as full-time paid commitment. There are different qualifications required to take the helm of a nonprofit organization as compared to a for-profit entity. "The skills requirement can crisscross," says Jacques Nordeman, chairman of Nordeman Grimm, "but we are seeing a demand that the CEO of a nonprofit be able to provide a complex list of abilities including fundraising, managerial, communication skills, knowledge of the cause or issue, political skills and leadership experience."

If volunteer service at a leadership level is your goal, you can, by developing a strategy, stay on your current career path and achieve a significant position around this table. Sharon Rockefeller spent many years as a volunteer for the Public Broadcasting System before she became president and CEO of WETA, the Washington, D.C., local PBS affiliate, in a paid and leadership position. "There is extraordinary talent represented by women who run major nonprofit organizations," says Jacques Nordeman. "We know this because the leadership role provides critical exposure for these women and makes it a viable step for them to go on to other positions."

TABLE: CORPORATION CEO OR SENIOR EXECUTIVE

A seat at the corporate table requires a track record of experience and achievement combined with the ability to rise above internal politics. You will be judged on measurable results and how your performance impacts the bottom line. There is risk-taking but the difference between the risks you take in the corporate world and those required from entrepreneurs can be very different.

If you make a mistake in the corporation it is unlikely the company will close its doors, however, your successes and failures will be noted in your personnel file.

In the corporation, the ability to move ahead can depend on those who are ahead of you, their recognition of your skills and talents. You are constantly being assessed in terms of performance, bottom-line contribution, team work, leadership qualities, communication skills, interpersonal skills. You will be judged on your ability to work through tough times and sometimes tough people. It requires hard work and unlike the entrepeneurial table, does not promise control. And it takes a great deal of self-confidence and a strong sense of self.

As a senior member of a corporate entity, your benefits can consist of substantial financial rewards, the opportunity to do work in a stimulating environment, the opportunity to deal with challenges on a global level and to have the resources you need to make things happen. William "Mo" Marumoto, founder of the Interface Group, an affiliate of Boyden, says, "It is important to understand the corporate culture. If you are making a transition from a slow-moving industry to a highly intrapreneurial company, you may have a problem fitting in."

TABLE: ENTREPRENEUR AND CEO

You thrive on doing it your way. Despite the vagaries of business ownership, you do not shrink from risk-taking. Whatever your product or service is, you enjoy most being able to make the decisions. You have confidence and a lot of drive and energy. You have a vision for your company and will work around the clock if you have to in order to achieve your goals. You may give out but you never give up. Your challenge is to manage your goals and expectations for your business against limited resources, financial and personnel. You are comfortable making decisions but you may have to learn how to delegate if your goal is to grow your company.

TABLE: CORPORATE BOARD

You have a record of achievement either in business, academe, industry or politics. You know your industry and the challenges and opportunities that must be addressed by the CEO. You may have expertise in a specific area and your appointment to the board will complement the contributions made by the other directors. You know how to be an independent thinker and a team member. You are ethical, you have integrity, vision and a sense of purpose. You have confidence and are not intimidated by other men and women of accomplishment.

TABLE: POLITICAL

CANDIDATE

You have a point of view and believe you can make a difference. You have a record of achievement as a community leader or entrepreneur or parent, who is concerned about schools, crime, health issues. You are willing to commit the time, resources and your money and the funds of others because you are on a mission. You want your voice and those you will represent to be heard. You want to run for office.

APPOINTEE

You believe in the goals identified by the president. You want to be part of a team having an impact on the key national and international issues of our day. You are at a point in your life where you can afford to take a political appointment at a senior level. You want to give back something to your country. You want to be appointed to a political position.

VOLUNTEER

You have no desire, yet, to run for office but you would like to be a "player" in a local or national campaign. You are prepared to commit the time to do what it takes to rise up the political volunteer ranks. This can include using your talents to raise money, to host events, to make calls and to stuff envelopes. You have your eye on getting a spot on the finance or communications committee depending on your talents and the needs of the campaign. You will become known to either the leaders of the Democratic National Committee or the Republican National Committee or any number of political coalitions or groups, including: Women's Campaign Fund, WISH List, Emily's List, RENEW, Women Who Win, National Women's Political Caucus.

TABLE: CREATE YOUR OWN

You have been energized to create an entity that will deal with a specific issue or problem. You are willing to raise money, establish a nonprofit organization, pull together committee members in order to make a difference. The issue can be child abuse, battered women, drunk driving, equity for women and minorities. Your commitment will give you the energy to make sure this table is viable.

It doesn't matter what your background is or what your resume looks like. If you are motivated enough, you will find a way and learn what you have to in order to succeed.

You may be motivated to create your own "table" if persistent pursuing does not allow you to move forward in your current environment.

Where are you now? Is your environment conducive to your goals and dreams? Political activist Mary Ellison says, "One of the things, I always tell young women is if you are not well-perceived in your environment or corporate culture, get out of it. No matter how good you are, and it may not be your fault if you are not perceived in the way you wish, then leave." Ellison rose up the ranks in a banking corporation in a relatively short time, but she realistically assessed that she would never rise higher than the rank of vice president.

The table she was seeking was not available at this company, so she left for a better chance to achieve her goal. Ellison believes it is important to be very simple in your goals; clearly define them so others can understand exactly what you want.

What would you consider complete and great? Do you have those moments in your life now? Do you experience them in the workplace? Ever?

TABLE HOPPING

In your life you can expect to enjoy a seat at many tables as your interests and influence increases. One table alone can not possibly fulfill all you want to accomplish.

Create your own Seat at the Table List: Write down everything you think you would like to achieve, including all the components that would fit your definition of a fulfilling life, professionally and personally. Your tables may multiply. One table truly leads to another and another.

Volunteer: You begin by contributing your time and in the process, build a reputation for commitment. As a result, you have an opportunity to become visible to a new group of opinion shapers. (Everyone is an opinion shaper if they have an opinion of you.) Your work in volunteerism becomes a passion for a cause or a specific issue. You have learned a lot about galvanizing resources, raising money, getting the job done with a non-paid group of people. You begin to speak about your cause or issue to groups. This increases your visibility. At this point you may consider forming your own organization.

This is what Ilene Leventhal did when she started the Hand to Hand Foundation, providing food for the homeless. Many organizations such as Race For The Cure, Mothers Against Drunk Driving were created in order to effect change. The women who started these and many more nonprofit entities had resumes rich with volunteer activities.

The volunteer table can also lead to business ownership. As an entrepreneur, it is important to have visibility in the community in certain kinds of businesses. Debbie Fields provided those cookies for hundreds of school events before she began to think "cookie empire."

Working as a volunteer with others enables you to "interview" future partners for a potential business. You learn quickly who you can or might even want to work with.

Entrepeneur: If you do move toward the entrepreneur table, you will find the same qualities — reputation, commitment, trust — are critical for your success as a business owner. In addition, as you work hard and increase your market and build your business, your network will increase. You will begin to interact with many people who will now be in a position to have an opinion about you.

Politics: You will involve these people as a resource group when you consider running for office. Why would an entrepreneur want to run for office? For one thing, as a small business owner you will have a hot-seat appreciation for legislation, past and pending, that will affect your ability to do business and to stay in business. Entrepreneurs become fast experts on a variety of topics including health care, tax issues in addition to a growing list of workplace issues.

Corporation: The corporate table requires a different career path, which can include volunteerism and business ownership, but usually results from a steady climb within the organization. However, the success of that climb may depend on how many seats you enjoy outside of the organization.

Board seat: All these roads can lead to the corporate board table. In fact, according to the National Women's Economic Alliance Foundation/Directors' Resource Council survey, more than 90 percent of all women, who currently serve as outside directors, count their volunteer participation at the leadership level an instrumental factor in their appointment.

One table does lead to another.

Can you identify the table in your environment?

Who is currently occupying those seats?

What would you have to do to join them?

How can you get those credentials?

Where will you begin to obtain the required experience?

Think about it and start now in a small way.

Try answering these questions using a tape recorder. Later, you can write down the goals you hope to achieve. The writing process is very important. The act of writing down your ideas is a critical imprint for your subconscious. Next best, is saying them aloud. The point is not to jump over these exercises because you don't have the time to write your responses. If taping is not a comfortable alternative, take the book to work and utilize your computer system in a private file.

MOVING TOWARD YOUR TABLE: NETWORKING

The most important thing you need to know about that overused word networking is that the net only works when you do. This means you must interact with one or more people on a regular basis in order to provide information and to receive information. How effectively you will be able to utilize the information will depend on a long list of variables, including: experience, creativity, individual or market need, commitment, drive, reputation, and likablity factor.

"Ignore the word," says Susan Bari, executive director of the American Women's Economic Development Corporation (AWED). "It is an artificial term which tends to discourage or frighten women who do not know what it is, but who have been told that it is important to their success. Bari believes that even though women have been networking since the dawn of time by exchanging information over the back fence, the difference is, it is a lot easier now. "Men and women alike are serving as mentors and are generally helpful in sharing information and providing opportunities."

How would you answer this question?

1. I find that in general people are willing to help me?

YES _____ NO _____

2. I find that in general I am willing to help people.

YES _____ NO _____

If the answer is usually no for both questions, you need to spend some time taking a hard look at how you've been networking up to this point. Or as Bonnie

Guiton Hill, dean of the McIntire School of Commerce at the University of Virginia and a member of several boards, says, "You can't network with people who don't like you to begin with."

Your answer to #1. will impact how you feel about #2.

Too simple you say? All right, let me ask you how you react to the term networking? Check one:

- ❏ **A.** Musical chairs with business cards.
- ❏ **B.** What the trapeze artist asks right before he swings.
- ❏ **C.** A good way to kill an enjoyable dinner, party, meeting.

Those of you who have checked C. probably have vivid memories of those early days of networking excess when we put on our dress-for-success suits, registered for the nearest seminar, "How to Succeed in Twenty Minutes" and armed with a year's supply of newly minted cards proceeded to hand them to anyone upright and breathing. After the meeting most of us left with as many cards as we brought. One week later we were hard pressed to remember which face matched which card and what was supposed to happen next.

Did this really work for anyone? I know it didn't work for me. I hated every minute of it. But I had read all the books that said, go and meet with people, get out of your office. Network, network, network. So, after meeting someone at a conference, I would call and invite them to lunch. If I had been lucky enough to get the person to show up, I spent most of the time during lunch not listening to what was being said, but trying to figure a way to ask for what I needed. This was such a stressful process, I just stopped. I decided this networking stuff was just not for me.

Instead, I decided to follow my interests and join organizations where I could listen and learn how others were achieving their goals. Once I changed my mind about my purpose and goals, things began to happen.

Now, it was easy. I could relax and listen. Real conversation: where you react to what you have just heard leads to more shared information. When Susan Bari was asked to attend a party for a friend of a friend she went with no other agenda other than to show support for someone who was leaving town and embarking on a new career.

At the party she learned that another woman was leaving her job at the White House. Bari asked the woman, "Would it be appropriate for me to apply?" She was encouraged to not only apply, but also to use the woman's name as a reference. This chance conversation led to Bari's job at the White House as Deputy Director of White House Personnel.

Bari would be able to answer the two questions posed earlier with a definite yes. Yes, people seem to want to help me and yes, I actively try to help as many people as possible achieve their career goals.

I took myself off the hook in regard to a timeline where something had to happen either in a meeting or lunch for me to feel successful. When I look back, I can see that my networking was responsible for everything I enjoy today, but at the time it was not clear what would lead to what or whom. And not every contact led to a relationship or business.

If you are driving yourself relentlessly to meet as many people who can help you as possible, take the time now to stop and review if you are being effective or just exhausting yourself and your contacts. Think about the people you are trying to get close to? Why? For what purpose? What's in it for them?

GIVE BEFORE YOU RECEIVE

Why not take your target contact off the hook? Reverse the equation. Instead of trying to receive something, identify how you can be of benefit to this person? What are their professional needs? One of their needs may be for you to back off, stop calling and review not what you need from him or her, but what you can provide. Is your contact person involved or highly visible with a charity or fundraising drive? Can you offer to provide your time gratis to help her meet her financial goals for the organization? Can you volunteer for an event she is involved with?

Before you call, identify what you can bring to someone else's table. The only way to do this is to understand the need, before you meet the decision-maker. "Building relationships goes beyond knowing whom to call," explains Diane Steed, president of the Coalition for Vehicle Choice. "Relationship-building requires nurturing, follow-through in commitments, staying in touch, being willing to help and advise others."

We know that in order to move toward a seat at our designated table it is important that we be known. In order to be known, we have to be visible. And here is where networking comes in. Or as Cathie Shattuck, a partner of Epstein, Becker & Green, says, "Networking is really a matter of knowing and being known to a large number of persons who may have interests or talents that may be called upon to assist oneself or others."

Whatever your definition, one thing is certain, networking involves others, it is not a game of solitaire. "Get out there! Go to lots of events. Meet lots of people," advises Paula Lambert, president of The Mozzarella Company. "Listen to what they have to say and start to sort it out as you go."

Before you even begin the process it is important to understand a lot about you first. Do you interact better in crowds or professional organizations or do you prefer to meet and talk to people in small groups or one-on-one? Are you willing to take the time to learn as much as possible about someone else's professional goals and needs before you ask for favors that will help you reach your goals?

Networking is not something outside of yourself. It is what you do when you have an encounter with anyone new. first there is an exchange of information. This is the time to listen, to try and identify if you and the person you are talking with have anything at all in common. If you can't find even a sliver of a common denominator, it will be difficult to continue the contact. If you are always being interviewed, whether you know it or not, you are always networking for friends, for information, for reassurance, for help, for an opportunity to contribute.

ESTABLISH A RELATIONSHIP AND FORGET THE NETWORKING

You are going to be in the workplace for a very long time. Take your time and be selective about the professional relationships you would like to have.

Although business may be the common denominator, your contacts, if they are to grow into mutually beneficial relationships, must be based on shared interests, friendship, something other than an immediate return on the relationship.

FORGET SCORING

The networking excesses of the past were really caused by confusion on the part of women who wanted to be as effective as possible. The ability to understand the need or find the comfort level is an essential quality of those with whom you have successful relationships. Find the base, however narrow, upon which to build a long-term mutually beneficial relationship: favors dispensed and favors received.

"I think women focus too much on women," notes Carol Cox Wait, president of the International Women's Forum, "Some of my best friends are men, and there are more men than women in positions to help us." Wait does not believe there is just one right way to network. "Networking is one strategy for finding and identifying those with whom you hope to build lasting relationships."

Networking style, as we move toward the twenty-first century, is subtle and very effective. Call it the Zen of networking. If you can see it happening, nothing's happening. "Networking," says Joan Whalen, president of The Whalen Company, "is trust, respect, but above all, friendship. You may or may not get something from the relationship immediately. I don't think of my success at networking as a 'coup' or a 'score.' When I pick up the phone, I think of the call as a natural part of my life and work. As soon as you start calculating, you're dead."

Elynor Williams, vice president of public responsibility at the Sara Lee Corporation, agrees. "I see a definite change from those early manic days. As we continue to achieve and perceive that we are not all fighting for one brass ring, we are eager to help one another. We are no longer frightened by competition as we once were. In fact, networking today is a lot more sophisticated and more fun."

Williams makes an interesting point. The higher up the rung you climb, the less likely you are to use the term networking. At this point in your career, you have built a reputation, you are visible, you have many professional relationships. You understand where people fit and what they can do. They understand the same thing about you. Because you now have worked hard and smart, you can pick up the phone and ask directly: I need you to make a call for me. I need you to weigh in on this proposal. Who do you know you can help us get this account? Will you be a speaker at our next meeting? The voice on the other end will say "yes" because you have already established a working relationship. Your goal is to reach this level.

Whether you are building relationships vertically, lower to higher career level, or horizontally among peers, whether you are just beginning or have arrived at your seat at the table, the golden rule still applies: Do unto others as you would have them do unto you. Pursue, pursue, pursue may be to networking what location, location, location is to real estate, but if you pursue without focus or consideration of the pursuee, you are working without a net and on your way to a major fall.

"Women beginning their careers always think they have to go for the top person all the time," says Elynor Williams. "You can get help from people who are not on your career level. Secretaries and receptionists can open the gate to the people you need to see. In exchange, you can provide access to them as they move up the career ladder."

Williams likens the person who is only interested in talking to the top banana, to the man who, while talking to you, is constantly looking over your shoulder, watching for a more interesting or better-looking contact. "You notice things like that and you are annoyingly aware that the person is not really interested in you but in trying to score with the big WHO, the person who can do the most for them."

As women continue to achieve, they receive recognition and while most recognition is good, sometimes it creates a very big problem for those recognized. They become targets for overzealous networkers.

I have talked to many women in the corporation, women business owners, women leaders from government and industry and they are in agreement with a woman corporate officer who said, "I truly want to help and I have helped. But I find immediately after giving a speech, I get calls from women who want employment in my company. I am happy to provide counsel regarding what is required and the steps to take to position oneself if an opening occurs. For example, I do believe there is merit in getting one's foot in the door and trying to work up within the corporation. That's what I did. However, there is little I can do if there are no openings and if the candidate is not willing to consider alternative positions with a goal to moving up. As much as I would like to help everyone, I simply can not meet with everyone who calls. Frequently, these callers do not take 'no' for an answer and believe that if they are persistent they will reach their goal. In the abstract, that may be good advice but it ignores the basic tenets of good manners and instead of building an ally for a job search or a promotion it makes me want to close the door quickly and firmly."

Bonnie Guiton Hill agrees. "The least positive aspect of achieving a seat at the table is having people come at you from all different places for nothing that has anything to do with you as a person, but what you can do for them."

How to avoid sabotaging your welcome:

Request an appointment by note. Identify a specific objective, follow up with a call. Talk to a key staff person, secretary or assistant and refer to your letter. Ask her opinion regarding a good time to schedule a short meeting. Let the assistant know exactly why you are requesting the meeting. If you have a reference, a common friend or contact, recognition point, mention this in your letter and again in your call. Of course, you will prepare for the meeting, keep it short and on target. There is no point in getting a meeting where your presentation or purpose has not been defined ahead of time.

What happens if you are unable to get a meeting? There have been many times when I am just not able to meet with someone to discuss a general career move or to offer a job. This does not mean I am not interested in eventually meeting the person. It is a clue that the approach should be changed. If your potential target does not want to meet with you, try communicating by mail, send notes on a regular basis, continue the process and eventually, perhaps several months later, ask for a meeting again.

If you do get a meeting, it is very important to follow up carefully. Always send a thank-you note and keep in touch. If the advice or counsel you received helped in any way, be sure to let your advisor know. President Bush was famous for his personal notes of thanks, or just saying "good job." It is a highly effective and meaningful way of keeping in touch. Especially, in the age of faxes, photocopies, phones and computers, personal notecards stand out and shout, "I care."

Networking is not a one-way street, with those in power dispensing favors to those seeking access. It is more like the domino effect. One domino touches the next one and eventually hundreds of dominoes are affected. If you are the head domino, your benefit in helping others can be immeasurable as you gain outreach to people and information you might not readily have access to.

Judy Ernest, a former columnist for the *Cleveland Plain Dealer*, remembers when she agreed to have lunch with a woman who had just lost her job. "She wanted information about how to write a column," said Ernest. "Since I had been a columnist for several years, I agreed to spend some time going over the basics. At the end of the lunch she happened to mention a mutual acquaintance and the interesting work he was doing. That off-hand comment triggered me to do some research which paid off in my own job."

Carole Crockett, an assistant vice president of public affairs at the American Graduate School of International Management and former director of the Office of Women's Business Ownership at Small Business Administration, says, "Winners network differently. They enjoy people first and think about networking second, if at all. Their indirect message, which is powerful says, 'I like you. I like myself. I'd not only like to work with you, I'd like to know you better.'"

Jinger Heath, chairman of the board of Beauticontrol Cosmetics, says, "Networking doesn't always have to be about contacts who can help each other only in business. It can also be about support groups that encourage each other to move forward on personal and professional issues. Networking and just making contacts are useless without long-term relationships."

Carolee Friedlander, president of Carolee Design, also serves as president of the Committee for 200 and an officer of the International Women's Forum, adds, "I find sharing experiences and contact invaluable for broadening my thinking and for insight into the place of women on today's national scene. If you are starting out in your career, join an organization of women professionals and become active in their work."

As you continue to grow professionally, you will create your own networks representing your various interests. It really gets to be fun when you are able to act as a catalyst at a senior level introducing people who you think would benefit from knowing one another.

If you feel awkward about the networking process, you are probably trying too hard. Relax and begin to build a circle of friends based on what you can contribute. As more women continue to achieve a seat at the table, a strong net woven with real friends, shared experiences, may be in and of itself the most important achievement of a successful networker.

INCREASING YOUR NETWORKS OR
BUILDING FRIENDS IN ALL PLACES

The importance of effective networking and relationship building begins to be clear as you move toward your seat at the table. Whether your objective is a corporate board or political appointment, a top-level job within your corporation or another, a speaking engagement or an opportunity to head a nonprofit organization, you will need endorsers, not only from your sphere of interest, but across the board. If throughout your career, you have been involved in a variety of activities and have enjoyed even moderate visibility, your potential network of endorsers will be plenty.

This is important because gaining a seat at a power table is easier the more senior-level people you know in diverse occupations, who are able to stand up and say, "I know and respect this person."

As your networks grow so does your ability to learn about other routes that may lead to your goal to be included at the leader's table. In the process, you will change your mind or revise your target goal. This is all part of a winning process leading to a more self-assured and satisfied you.

We can see so many examples of women in business, women leaders in the community who became involved in politics at an entry level, made contacts and friends and eventually decided to run for office. Networks are important to everyone but essential to candidates. Achieving a seat at one table enables you to build the network you need to move toward a seat at another table.

Bonnie Guiton Hill's career stands as an example to all of us. She grew up poor and on welfare, but eventually acquired three degrees: an undergraduate degree in psychology, a master's in educational psychology and a doctorate in higher education, administration and policy analysis. Not only did Guiton Hill not have a built-in network, or a powerful family, or a long list of endorsers, she began her college education at the age of 30. What she did have was the drive and determination to ensure that neither she nor her family would ever be on welfare again.

After obtaining her degrees, Guiton Hill became head of a nonprofit organization whose function was to provide funds for educational purposes. Her outreach for the nonprofit led to corporate contacts. One of these contacts, impressed with her performance, offered her a job at Kaiser Aluminum.

This was only one of five corporate positions offered to Guiton Hill. Her credentials were excellent, but so were many others who wanted these jobs. High on the list of what the companies were looking for was a person who could say: (1) In general people want to help me, and (2) I try to help others. Guiton Hill had built a positive reputation among a large group of potential endorsers and this ranged from entry to senior level.

One of the things people tend to forget in the networking process is that not all of your efforts should be directed up the ladder. Your ability to eventually obtain a seat at the table will depend in great part on how you treat the people you work with and the people who work for you, in addition to the people who work for others. Guiton Hill did not reserve special treatment for those high up and lesser treatment for those below senior level. She reserved special treatment for everyone.

"You can do anything you want when you outrank people. But I really believe it is better to try and provide a comfort level for everyone who has to work with you," says Guiton Hill. "They have the same political structure, the informal and the formal leaders. The only adjustment I had to make was whether you had to go through the extensive bureaucratic process to get something done or whether you had the power and the authority to make things happen without the bureaucracy being an impediment."

Networking to Guiton Hill just means being sensitive to people, using common sense and listening well. "Just look at it this way," she says, "almost everything you do in a business environment, where you are going to people and asking for advice, exchanging cards and information is networking. We really do not need to label it. On the other hand," she continues, "I don't spend time with people that I don't like well enough to at least be a friend, even if it's a distant friend, for the rest of my life."

Guiton Hill, who considers herself a generalist, has held positions ranging from junior level to the top appointments in the federal government. She credits her success in a great part to her involvement in many organizations such as the YWCA, the Northern California Legal Defense Fund, and the National Urban Coalition.

"At one point," says Guiton Hill, "a seat at the table to me was breaking $13,000 a year in salary, then it was $23,000 and then I remember when I said I really need to break through to six figures, make $100,000 a year. Today, I consider success right now. I have my seat at the table and it is being healthy and having enough income to pay my bills. All the rest is gravy."

In terms of building relationships or networking your way to a seat at the table, Guiton Hill says, "Just do it the way you would to make any kind of new friend. It's really just that simple."

To network, according to Meg Armstrong, president of The Leadership Group:

❖ Look around your environment for those things which really interest you, whether professionally, as a volunteer, or a hobby.

❖ Find out what organization exists, what activities are available for you to become involved.

❖ After you learn the ropes, understand the goals, know who the players are, take a leadership role. How?

❖ Raise your hand and say, "I'll do that."

4

BEING GOOD TO YOURSELF: TAKING YOUR MENTAL VITAMINS

"I used to need approbation, awards and praise, outward recognition, a lot more than I do now. It is always pleasant to be recognized by others, but more important, to 'know thyself.' "

DR. ARIEL HOLLINSHEAD, PROFESSOR EMERITA, DEPARTMENT OF MEDICINE, GEORGE WASHINGTON UNIVERSITY; PRESIDENT, HT VIRUS AND CANCER RESEARCH

The race is to the swift.

ANON

The race is not to the swift but to those who keep running.

ANON

Many of us, at the end of the week, question "why am I in a race and what am I running for?" The idea that there is a worthwhile payoff to "joyless striving" is one that women are finally rejecting. On Monday we may be quite happy as we move toward our goal of a seat around the power or decision-making table within our chosen arena. On Friday, we may be longing for a cabin by a stream with nothing more high-tech to communicate with than a pad of paper and a box of crayons. These are not necessarily contradictory desires.

If you have a desire to achieve, a desire to express yourself at higher and higher levels of responsibility, you may also have a desire to have a few friends along the way, an opportunity to spend time with your family, a chance to sit by a stream and think about something other than goals for success. One way to begin to have those varied experiences in your life, is to reframe the choice question.

Refuse to choose between power and friends. Refuse to choose between power and femininity, money or selflessness. These are choices that fit neatly within a sitcom concept but have little to do with real life. Women and men are not one-dimensional stick figures. Women leaders, women who have achieved at many levels, women who are very ambitious can be the same women who value family and friends. Susan Douglas, author of *Where the Girls Are: Growing Up Female With the Mass Media*, noted, "The stereotype that women in power are selfish, superficial and heartless is a stereotype that deserves to have as many stakes driven through its heart as possible."

These false choices can rob you of the peace of mind you need to pursue what you want to have. Which button do you push? A: Great job, economic independence, recognition but no one one will ever like you, much less love you. Or B: No job, no independent or personal goals, but you will have a family and a husband. For years we bought into the idea that these were the only choices.

How can you stay on course to follow your vision? What do others do to stay on course? Is the trip a hollow experience only rewarded by the "seat" at the end of the destination? If that is true, we will hardly be nurtured along the way. The point is for the trip to be as important as wherever we arrive. If it isn't, it is unlikely that we will have the drive, energy or the passion required to persist.

What can we do to sustain our dream and sustain us, mentally and physically on our journey? Whether we target a seat at the table or just decide to kick back and do nothing, we are choosing. But to have a dream without action is to have an unrealized dream.

Along the road to our seat or seats at various tables we will be asking ourselves, Is this path enriching? Do I still want this particular seat? Do I feel energized by the course of action I've chosen? When I think about my goal, do I feel intuitively it is the right thing? Do I feel more alive? What am I learning along the way? Where does this goal or these actions take me?

Your trip should not be anxiety-driven, although you may be fearful and anxious from time to time. Your desire for a seat at the table should be based on what you need to express, to contribute. If it is a journey toward power for power's sake, you may arrive to find that the table and the seat was not worth the trip or any of the sacrifices along the way.

By taking the time to develop a time-out plan, a self-revival plan, you will be giving yourself constant breathers which will allow you to make the corrections you feel you need to make to continue your journey for the right reasons.

IF YOU DON'T HAVE TIME TO SMELL THE FLOWERS, HAVE THEM DELIVERED

Know yourself, and pay attention to your needs. If you don't have time to stop and smell the flowers, do what I do, have them delivered. You're worth it! I love flowers and I know when I have a huge bunch of lilacs or gladiolus or roses in a vase in my office or at home, they provide me with a boost throughout the day. What is that worth to you? Do you view flowers as a luxury or a necessity? There is no right or wrong answer. The key is to understand what you need to sustain yourself. Sometimes it's flowers.

Flowers sitting on your desk or in your office communicate to everyone who enters that this is a day to celebrate; that something good is going on in your life. If you can't afford a weekly or monthly bouquet, can you afford one flower on your desk in a small bud vase? Keep the bouquets coming, even if you have to order them for yourself.

TAKE CONTROL OF YOUR IMMEDIATE ENVIRONMENT

Whether you are CEO or are a recent entry to the work force, there are things you can do now, within your space, to shape your environment. You may want to consider putting framed photos on your desk, or if you have the space, on your wall. In Washington, the power photo wall has almost become a cliche. You and famous people. However, if the photos mean something to you, go ahead and put them up. You may want to add photos of not-yet-famous people as well. Rebecca Beverley, an assistant vice president of the E. Bruce Harrison Company, has a beautiful framed photo of Cowboy on her desk. Cowboy is the newest addition to her family and is a quarter horse.

Elynor Williams, of the Sara Lee Corporation, has developed a different view of power photos. "I have a friend who is a vice president at Coca Cola and one who is a vice president at Time Warner. Every time we're together for an event we take what we call a power photo. The three of us have these photos on our desk in silver-gold frames." The photos remind Williams when she is having a particularly stressful day that she has friends whom she can call, who are a resource, who can help.

For many years, when women in the work force were trying to prove how professional we were by wearing ugly clothes, we extended this statement to our offices as well. We did not have photos of our children or family on the desk, we declined flowers as too feminine and therefore not serious enough. Usually, the color scheme of the office was a corporate gray or blue and that dictated what would be appropriate in our own offices.

But a funny thing began to happen. As more women achieved at higher levels in the work force, they began to travel and as they began to travel they let hotels know how they felt about colors, closet space, amenities. Hotels listened because women make up 50 percent of business travel and they usually are the decision-makers when it comes to luxury or vacation travel as well.

The results were open spaces and plenty of light even in the bar area, warm and inviting colors throughout, more amenities in the room, safety features, and more services. When women traveled they realized they were the customer. Perhaps the impact in the workplace has not been as dramatic because at work we don't consider ourselves the customer or the client. Perhaps we should start. It is important to really look at your work environment, a place where you will be spending a majority of time, and shape this environment according to your style and needs. Who knows, others may follow and the entire environment could improve.

Why not have an oriental scatter rug on the floor? What is wrong with a beautiful tea or coffee service? If having a silver water carafe on your desk, gives you a sense of well-being, go out and buy one. If you have a collection at home that you rarely see because you are never there, bring it into the office where you can really enjoy it. What about a sculpture or painting? A beautiful painting can provide you with a thousand time-outs.

A friend of mine loves to needlepoint and the more stress in her life, the more pillows she completes. You can always tell what kind of year it has been just by visiting her office and counting the beautiful pillows.

Take the time to look around your environment now. What can you get rid of? What is taking up space that has long since outlived its usefulness? How long has it been since you rearranged your office?

Create an environment in which your taste is reflected and your spirit restored. One of the offices I love to visit is Georgette Mosbacher's. A successful businesswoman and the author of *Feminine Force*, she has invested as much personal attention to the comfort of her business guest as she does in her home for family and friends. The result is a positive and attractive environment, one in which you truly can feel at home.

INTERNAL ENVIRONMENT: TRY TO DEVELOP A SENSE OF HUMOR

You don't have to develop a stand-up routine, but the old cliche is really true, after time, almost anything is grist for the humor mill. The trick is to find the humor, not after time, but when you need it, now. It is important that you discover the flip side of your very serious, I-mean-business personae. Tom Peters says, "If you want to win, you'll grin. If your work space doesn't ring with more than the occasional peel of bona fide belly laughter, I wouldn't waste a plug nickle on your stock."

Laughing at yourself is the best antidote to fear, loathing and that oh-boy, things are really screwed-up again feeling. A small warning: Don't go overboard on the self-deprecating humor bit. I know all the books say this is a very attractive quality, to make fun of yourself. My feeling is there are enough people out there ready to do this without your help. The kind of humor I'm talking about, is gentle, not sarcastic. It helps you through almost any situation and it can put you and those you are trying to relate to at ease. And let's face it, a lot of funny things happen on the way to a seat at the table.

KEEP A JOURNAL

Women executives have discovered journal keeping, either on their own or after taking one of psychologist Ira Progoff's Intensive Journal Method workshops in New York City or throughout the country. Keeping a daily journal provides a safe venting for wishes, goals, and situations that need resolving.

Acccording to *Working Woman* magazine, James Pennebaker, a psychologist at Southern Methodist University, found that "college students who wrote over a period of just four days had significantly better health during the course of the next several months." Journal keeping gives you a chance to be honest without worrying about consequences. (Unless, of course, you are a political appointee in Washington, D.C.) Many of Progoff's students connect their success to journal keeping.

REMEMBER THE PEARL AND THE OYSTER

"In Italy for 30 years under the Borgias they had warfare, terror, murder, bloodshed — they produced Michelangelo, Leonardo da Vinci and the Renaissance. In Switzerland they had brotherly love, 500 years of democracy and what did that produce? The cuckoo clock." Orson Welles in "The Third Man"

The historical reference is not exactly true. Switzerland had two civil wars and the derivation of the cuckoo clock is up for grabs. But the point is that very little is accomplished without conflict, internal and external.

Julie Krone, the only woman to win the Belmont Stakes or any of the Triple Crown races, crashed to the ground from her horse in a race at Saratoga, and shattered her ankle. Nine months, two operations, two metal plates, and 13 screws later she was back in the race at Belmont Park.

In an interview with Joseph Durso of *The Washington Post*, Krone asked herself, "Why am I doing this?" The answer: "a passion for riding race horses. All jockeys face danger. But that's the tradeoff you accept. And if I feel pain when

I walk 20 years from now? Even if I have to limp a little, I'll take the tradeoff to keep riding."

You can't have a pearl without the sand. You can't achieve any of your goals without the desire, the passion, the will, the commitment and yes, the stress of moving toward a goal. There is no way, no way, no way to get what you want without effort and work. Without setbacks or whatever the world calls failure. Big or little failures are just the opposite of big or little successes. They occur when you try. They can be your medal of honor that proclaims I moved toward something I cared about. I have created my own pearls.

BUILD IN TIME FOR PRAYER/MEDITATION/ QUIET TIME

This is almost as hard to do as working out on Nordic Track, but the returns are far greater. Very few of us have the time or the inclination to follow the advice in most women's magazines: "If you feel stressed, light some candles in the bathroom, fill the tub with warm water, and soak in bath salts for several hours." Busy people are basically shower people.

One woman I know, who tried the bathtub approach, brought along her reading material which she propped up on the bathtub tray. She couldn't read by candlelight and the bath oils made her feel as if she'd just landed in the middle of a bad oil spill. "This was clearly not the most relaxing thing for me to do," she said. Meditation, on the other hand, for just a few minutes in your office with the door closed, can give you a brief, quiet break from the daily frenzy. It takes practice, but after a while, it can provide you long-lasting energy and renewal.

Several years ago, Peggy Stanton, a former broadcaster with NBC, and I created a program called the Spiritual Spa. The purpose of the group was to help us build a spiritual awareness at the same time we were all so focused on external gains. The group was nondenominational and met once a month. It was a fluid group with some women attending every month and others coming for one or two meetings. Recently, one of the members of the group died after a four-year bout with cancer of the pancreas. The monthly meetings not only gave her sustenance but added value to her life and the others as she searched for and found meaning in her health challenge.

"I think it is important to develop a spirituality," says Elynor Williams. "So that you have an internal connection with a faith, with universal love. So that you can realize that universal love embraces you at all times, whatever you are doing, and if what you are doing is for the highest purpose, you will succeed."

Dr. Lillian Beard, chairman of the National Women's Economic Alliance and a practicing pediatrician in Washington, D.C., says, "It is important to try and maintain a spiritual connection. It makes no difference what your religious belief may be. It is just important that when wonderful things begin to happen to you that you can't be too full of yourself. Build in time to give thanks. Express thanks."

INDULGE IN PURPOSELESS READING

Take a mini-break of five minutes. Pick up the leather-bound volume of Emily Dickinson's poems and read one to yourself. It can only help. Or, on the way back home after a business trip, after a long day in front of your computer, after a three-hour meeting with your venture capitalist, sit back and read anything that has nothing to do with the job you just finished. In reality, nothing is purposeless. There is always something to be learned, even if you're reading a mystery or this month's copy of *Rolling Stone*. "Reading is a favorite way to unwind," says former Secretary of Commerce Barbara Franklin, especially mysteries and history "Ben Franklin's years as ambassador to France provide a good counterpoint to *Business Week* and the *Japan Economic Journal*."

TAKE A LOOK AT WHERE YOU ARE AND STAY A WHILE

Carol Brookins, chairman and CEO of World Perspectives Inc., travels to Europe and Asia on a regular basis. She tries to build in one agenda-less day in her destination country. "I always learn something new by taking this time out," she says. Brookins advises her fellow business travelers to try and take the time and stay one day later or arrive just one day earlier when possible. The mental vitamin here is a far less stressful trip and a chance to have some down time in a new culture.

Nancy Clark Reynolds, former vice chairman of Wexler, Reynolds, Harrison, Schule, Inc., serves on several boards and now lives in Santa Fe, New Mexico. When she lived in Washington, D.C., she said, "One of my favorite ways to relax is to travel and get away from it all. New Mexico and Africa are my favorite places! Planning the trips is a great way to relax." This fun and relaxation also provided her with the information she needed to choose a place to live when she left Washington.

Therese Shaheen, chief operating officer of U.S. ASIA Commercial Development Corporation, flies from Washington to Beijing and back the way most of us use the shuttle from Washington, D.C. to New York. Clearly, she is not interested in adding on a few days in China when she is scheduled to return so frequently. And in fact, most women who travel internationally, complete their business and return immediately, despite the fact they may have spent more time in travel than in the actual destination. Adding on another day is something you may want to consider doing occasionally.

Even though this extra day may appear to be down time, women on business or vacation travel, follow the trends not just by reading about them, but by observing and asking the right questions.

"No matter what country you visit," says Shaheen, "If you have an inquisitive mind and an observant eye and ask a few questions of waiters, taxicab drivers, salespersons in shops, in one day you will have a sense of where the attitudes are on economic and political issues."

Get in bed with the covers over the head.

In our survey of leading women in the workplace, some of the most successful take a Saturday or Sunday a month and have "nothing" days. "I have a king-sized bed and, when I take my day off, I gather all the magazines I've been meaning to read, all my catalogues, a box of Wheat Thins and a bottle of peach-flavored club soda and I don't budge for hours. The phone rings and I just let the answering machine record all the calls. After a day totally alone, I am really revitalized and ready to answer those calls," says Claudia Spain Grove, president of I Claudia, a Virginia interior design firm.

Buy a punching bag and take out your anger and frustrations on an inanimate object.

Barring boxing, consider golf, running, walking, fencing, swimming as long as it is something that gets your heart-rate going. Whatever you choose, it should not add to your competitive angst. No time? Put on a CD and dance by yourself at home.

"I've decided stress is something I love. Relaxation is something I don't practice well," says Susan King, president of the International Women's Media Foundation. "Exercise daily that allows me to confront the limits of my endurance adds some sweat to the usual stress experience. I try to find a 90-minute aerobics class with weights. It's ideal: long enough to be a test, hard enough to demand commitment and fun enough to forget whatever is bothering me for the moment."

Go to movies for a quick-fix.

Movies were high on the list for a quick retreat from reality. For only a two-hour investment, you can be worlds away from daily pressures and problems. I work a very long week but every Friday at 7 p.m., I have a standing date with my husband to go to the movies. It doesn't matter much what is playing. The minute we sit down with a bag of popcorn and those lights go out, I feel calm and relaxed without a thought for business for at least two hours.

Concerts and plays can provide you with restorative energy as well, usually far more than any movie. Try to schedule some art in your life, whether it is a concert, a play or a visit to a museum. Many of the senior-level women I know subscribe to music or theater programs and wind up giving the ticket away. They are simply too tired to go to something that is not directly business-related.

If this is happening to you, pay attention. You are making too many business withdrawals from your energy bank and not concentrating on deposits.

The network: Friends and family.

The stereotype of the successful businesswoman is someone who is alone and lonely. The litany usually goes something like this: Yes, she is an entrepreneur/corporate officer/committed volunteer. Perhaps her life is interesting, but is she really happy? The answer is "yes." Women leaders are by nature a gregarious group, and are eager to share their success stories and counsel with others. Women do not enjoy being loners. They seek out other women, and place high value on friendships.

Elynor Williams has a system that works for her through her network of friends. She calls them her "cheering squad" and they are the people who keep her focused when things look bleak and what she really wants to do is chuck it and ride into the sunset. She is there for them as well.

Dr. Lillian Beard says, "Long-term friendships and relationships are so important; they have to nourished all through the years. They should never be taken for granted." Beard used to rely on memory to recognize friends' birthdays or anniversaries. As her appointment schedule increased, it became more difficult to remember special occasions without a calendar notation. Now, she inserts special dates at the beginning of the year and includes a notation prior to the week so she has time to buy a gift or send a package or a card that will arrive on time.

"When we wrote *On Target,*" says Jeri Sedlar, partner of Sedlar and Miners, who co-authored the book with her husband, Rick Miners, "we found so many people who had defined themselves and their success with only material things. When the downturn in the '80s happened most of their self-esteem was tied to money. They were left with nothing, no money and no confidence."

Friends, families, networking organizations can help you be clear about why you want a seat at the table and what you will contribute when you get it.

"It all must fit together, family, friends, power and success," says Carol Cox

Wait. "And that starts by being honest. Admit that we do what we do for ourselves and once we stop pretending we are doing it for others, consciously make time for others and the things that matter to them."

"Titles don't really mean a whole lot," says Judy McLennan, ambassador to the U.N. Commission on the Status of Women. "I've seen people come and go in Washington, and titles are temporary. Unless you are a good person, you are not going to succeed in the end. However, if you have three or four really good friends count yourself successful."

Barbara Ferris, a former Peace Corps official, says, "I don't forget who was there for me when I was on the road so much on my road to success, when I was doing 100,000 and 200,000 miles a year around the world for my work. For me, the security of knowing that at 3 o'clock in the morning I could call my sister in Cleveland from Brussels and not ever have to worry that it was 3 o'clock, put my mind at rest. These are the people who have sustained me during my disappointments and that is not something I treat lightly. I am fiercely loyal to my friends as well and they know that."

Carol Brookins believes there is a great danger in losing yourself and personal relationships in trying to manage the responsibilities of leading an entrepreneurial venture. "It took a cancer experience for me to force me to 'schedule' time with friends and for recreation," she says.

THE CALENDAR

Whatever you use, day timers, Filofax, automated voice reminders, if you want to keep on course and enjoy the trip, schedule regular breaks and write them down in your appointment calendar. I found I had to write "take a walk" and schedule it for once a week after I realized I had been sitting at the computer for four straight hours. Passion and commitment to the job is great, but sometimes a walk around the block at the right time will keep the ideas coming and will help you keep a positive attitude.

TAPES

There are so many tapes available, from the great books to spy and mystery stories to advice on how to meditate. Dove, one of the most successful books-on-tape companies, was founded by Deborah Raffin and Michael Viner. The favorite listening environment seems to be the car, to and from work, though many are really hooked on listening to tapes on planes. Only the most determined seat mate will attempt conversation with a person wearing head phones. So, grab your Walkman. Now is the time to finish *Finnegan's Wake* or *War and Peace*.

LEADING ANOTHER CAUSE

The women I've talked to, entrepreneurs, women in the corporation, women on boards, are leaders because they have taken the lead in their own lives. Most of them find it stimulating to have a leadership role in something other than their daily concerns.

Jean Sisco, president of Sisco Associates also serves as chairman of the National Association of Corporate Board Directors. Georgette Mosbacher, chairman of Mosbacher Enterprises, is a board member of Child Help and has raised millions of dollars for political campaigns and programs. When you work outside your business, you exercise different muscles by taking the chance to focus on something new. It is a revitalization process that enables you to get recharged by changing your accustomed pattern.

NURTURE YOUR SELF-CONFIDENCE IN ANY WAY YOU CAN

If using the latest makeup or perfume or lipstick gives you a boost, then do it. Don't let anyone make a federal case out of it if you enjoy dressing great, wearing jewelry and wouldn't go out of doors without your eye shadow.

If you love clothes it does not mean you are a victim of anti-feminist forces or the advertising industry, it can mean you love clothes. Part of the joy of the trip to a seat at the table is a chance to make choices about what you like and don't like, what you will say and how you will say it, and, yes, what you want to wear. We are all aware now that those we meet form an opinion of us that can be long-lasting within the first three minutes of introduction. If dragon lady nails with fire engine red polish is something you can't live without, go for it. You'll know soon enough if this is something that is getting in your way, affecting the impression you are making and then you can choose for yourself, if you can't live without them.

I've always wondered why Queen Elizabeth felt it necessary to carry that pocketbook with her wherever she went. Here she is one of the world's most powerful women and in every photo, addressing the troops or giving a speech, she has that bag hanging from her wrist. If this is what makes her comfortable, who cares what fashion dictates? Of course, this attitude is easier to carry off if you're the Queen. Or if you have put enough into your self-esteem bank to realize you don't have to be the Queen in order to treat yourself like one.

As long as you are shaping your internal and external environment, you may want to consider taking a break from the constant barrage of articles that insist as women we are constantly lacking. Self-improvement is a valid objective, but constant self-flagellation, because your hips are too big or your hair is wrong, will wear you out. Working mothers are subjected to articles ad nauseum about how they are neglecting their children. If you are single and doing well in your career or running your own business, you are told that you will spend your future alone and childless in your hot tub! Yet, women at home raising families are confronted with the false information that the world is passing them by.

I travel a lot, and, invariably, I sit next to a man reading *Forbes,* or *Fortune,* or *Worth, Success, Esquire* or *Business Week.* I look across the aisle and his female counterpart is reading, "Are you too flat/full chested for success?" He is feeding his mind information, she is undermining her self-esteem.

It is important that you stay strong, feel good and give yourself credit on a daily basis. Contrary to most counsel and based on interviews with hundreds of women, I don't think it's valuable to make a list of your shortcomings. If you are a woman you will be so conscientious with this list, you are likely never to stop.

This is not to say you don't have a thorough understanding of who you are at this moment in time and what your behavior patterns have been. The shortcoming list can be a real staller. How do you know when you are through?

Focus on your strengths. Even if you feel you have only one worthwhile quality, go with that one, build and expand from that base.

Disappointment and Betrayal

There is no one right way to deal with this but the consensus seems to be, Don't Get Mad and Don't Get Even, or as Wilhelmina Holladay, founder and chairman of the board of the National Museum for Women In the Arts, advises, "Just lick your wounds and get on with it."

Not because you are such a pushover or a saint, simply because it takes too much time and energy and requires you to abandon your own goals while you focus on undermining someone else's. How many of us know women, who after years of separation, are still recounting grievances suffered with a former husband? What about a business partner that didn't work out? There will be many times when people say they will come through and they don't. How you react to disappointment and sometimes betrayal will shape the quality of your life for better or worse.

Judith Von Seldeneck, CEO of Diversified Search, says, "This is something that I do not handle well. I feel betrayed. People can trust me and I want to trust them. When I feel let down, I try to deal with it but I'm not good at it. I try to find an excuse for them but I can't truly forget it."

Carol Cox Wait admits, "I get very depressed and I might go home and throw a tantrum when I am alone or with my family. Then, I put it behind me and move on."

Ambassador McLennan agrees. "If you can change something then do it, if you can't just get on with it. If something happens and there's not a damn thing you can do about it, just keep going and put it behind you."

"I don't want to say that I enjoy being disappointed," says Barbara Ferris, "but I recognize that it is part of life and that no one escapes from it. I recognize that it is not going to last forever and it's really okay to process it for a couple of days and for me, it's necessary if I'm upset to the degree that I need to cry, or I need to swear, I need to vent. I recognize that whatever it is that I need to do to get through it, I do it and this is where my family and friends are very important. I expect them to listen."

Dr. Ariel Hollinshead adds, "I am sensitive and proud, therefore prone to sadness and sleepless nights, until one day I wake up fighting and set out to make things right. I learned to respond if appropriate and to ignore the ignorant. I don't let it rankle me for long."

Ongoing anger, disappointment, resentment all take huge withdrawals from your energy bank. These emotions can separate you from your goal, keep you from focusing on what is important. Forgive, forget or fix it, but move to move on. Elynor Williams believes that "arriving at closure on things" is a female trait. "Men don't mind having things dangling over, but I want to have closure. I want to know why 'that' happened. I am learning however that you do not have to go back to the person, who disappointed or betrayed you to find out, because many times they truly don't know. Unless there is some way to salvage the situation or the relationship, it's probably better to let it go, put it out there in the universe and let it float. Then, deal with it yourself."

"And," she emphasized, "actually nobody can really hurt or disappoint you. You allow that. But knowing it and acting on it is always a challenge."

EXERCISE THE IMPORTANT MUSCLES

The muscles I am talking about are the kind you develop when you step out and step up. When you start to move on a small wish and through a series of steps, reach a bigger vision. Courage grows in increments as you step up and do the thing you feared. One woman I know had such a negative opinion of herself, an opinion carefully built over many years and reinforced by her husband, so much so that when she decided to drive by herself from New York to California, the bet was she wouldn't make it to New Jersey.

That very real trip turned into a symbolic journey toward her seat at the table. "I realize to most people this was not a big deal, but it was to me and it provided that small amount of courage I needed to believe I could complete something; that I was worthy of greater goals," she said. That road trip led to the belief she could start and run a business and today she is CEO of a 10 million dollar environmental management firm.

A steady diet of fear constricts the heart and clouds your ability to think. Do whatever you have to to build the muscles you need, to strengthen your inner voice until you can hear it and affirm: "This is what I want and this is what I am going for."

HAVE A LIFE? HAVE YOUR OWN LIFE

Determine what having a life means to you, not to someone else. It isn't that easy as we are constantly being subjected to what society or our family or our friends think is right for us. "Why are you working so hard?" is a question successful women frequently hear. Very rarely do they answer, "Because it gives me pleasure." We are always told to "stop and smell the roses" without anyone taking the time to find out what we consider — each one us — to be "roses."

As you listen to your "voice," you will shape your life if you have the courage to pursue what you know you want. Having your own life requires courage, the courage to know yourself, what you value and accept what you know. It also means being able to change your mind and change your direction if the course is wrong. Knowing the difference between getting off the wrong course and hanging in to succeed, requires a lot of vitamins, mental, spiritual and physical.

Give yourself a break. Give yourself several breaks. As Tom Peters says, "This the wrong age to go stale."

INSTANT MENTAL SPA

Try a few of these to get you started and begin to add some of your own.
1. Read something inspirational every day.
It can be just one sentence before you go to bed or immediately when you get up in the morning. Keep a few books next to the bed and vary your readings.
2. Identify the big fear.
My biggest was the the public speaking appearance. I realized that my self-

confidence quotient could rise on fall in direct relation to how much I had prepared. So I made a deal with myself. I would prepare to the best of my ability and not beat myself up if the presentation did not win the brass ring.

Whatever your fear is, diffuse it by being pro-active, prepare a plan of action to defeat it.

3. Visualize the prize.

See yourself living the goal, arriving at the destination. What does it feel like? What are you wearing? Get comfortable with your destination and start now to look and to think like a person who has a seat at the table.

4. Make regular deposits to your mental, spiritual and physical bank.

Don't let anyone whittle away your inner core of self-esteem. Cut short a conversation that is beginning to get you angry, stressed, resentful or depressed. Walk away from negative people and negative agendas. Develop a mental flak jacket especially if office politics become sinister. Reward yourself often!

Studies show that pleasant events boost the immune system for several days. "Positive events of the day seem to have a stronger helpful impact on immune function than upsetting events do a negative one," said Dr. Arthur Stone, a psychologist at the medical school of the State University of New York at Stony Brook. "Having a good time on Monday still had a positive effect on the immune system by Wednesday. But the negative immune effect from undesirable events on Monday last just for the day." Buffer your life with "small pleasures" and you will be better able to handle the bad stuff when it happens.

5. Watch the weather.

Learn to listen and watch. Women are very good at sign reading. Get to know the behavior patterns of the people at work and in your personal life.

6. Keep learning, keep open, keep growing.

There is a correlation between self-esteem, self-confidence and what you think you deserve. "The integrated sum of self-confidence and self-respect," explains Nathaniel Branden, author of *The Psychology of Self-Esteem*, "is the conviction that one is competent to live and worthy of living."

Mental vitamins that you create for yourself will help keep you on course as you begin to build confidence, reach goals, survive through setbacks and keep on going.

7. Goals and rewards.

Get a book. Write down your goals. Look at the book every day. Cross off what doesn't make sense. Add to it. Keep it up. Don't show it to anyone. It's yours. Set wild and reasonable goals at the back of the book. Make a list of rewards, wild and reasonable. When you need a lift. Open the book, close your eyes and place your finger on that page. That is your reward for the day or the week!

Here's my reward list:

1. Exercise ankle and then go buy non-orthopedic shoes.
2. Stop by my mother's house and have coffee.
3. Call a long-distance friend and talk forever.
4. Do one pro bono speech.
5. Send myself some really great flowers from Hedgerows.
6. Pick a date to really go to the Spa at Doral.
7. Make six-month appointment for mammogram now.
8. Go to a movie or rent seven, even though I know I'll be late returning the rentals.
9. Buy or paint something for my office.
10. Call Chris, Courtney or Claudia.
11. Take Bruce to dinner and let him pay for it.
12. See and talk to no one this weekend.
13. Do not go into the office this weekend.
14. Plan to stay one extra day on next international trip.
15. Decide on charity giving for 1995 and mail check.
16. Try meditating for longer than three minutes.
17. Get the Off-the-Record Club together for a dinner and party meeting.
18. Buy six mysteries for weekend reading.
19. Buy a treadmill and really try to use it this time.

The late Ruth Gordon, who enjoyed several careers including that of actress and playwright, offered the best advice with no sermonizing: "Don't be helpless, don't give up, don't kill yourself, don't look for trouble. Stuff gets in your way, kick it under the rug. Stay well, stay with it, make it come out. Never, never, never give up."

5

Target Table:
The Entrepreneur

"The problem with the rat race is even if you win, you're still a rat."
LILY TOMLIN

Entrepreneurs consider themselves apart from the rat race. If they are in a race, it is with themselves. Are you thinking about a product or service you feel will really fill a need in the market? Does this idea dominate your thoughts? Does it keep you awake at night? Do you visualize having your own company? Can you see yourself leaving the world of 9-5 for the world of 7-WHENEVER? Can you live without weekends, job security and the benefits of your present job? Can you give up the illusion that you will have a more balanced life if you own your own company? If you answered "yes," "yes," and "yes," then be aware that the entrepreneur, a.k.a. Chief Executive Officer, Chairman of the Board, Chief Financial Officer, Maintenance Person, Human Resource Specialist, Salesperson, Marketing Whiz, Visionary, and Chief Cook and Bottle Washer, sits at the head of a very, very big table at which she may very well be required to fill every seat.

But, if you want the title and the hard work that goes along with it, unlike the corporation or the corporate board, there is immediate room at this table for you.

❖ By the year 2000, 50 percent of all small business will be owned by women, according to the Small Business Administration.

❖ Women-owned businesses are an expanding force, contributing revenue and creating jobs faster than their Fortune 500 counterparts, so reports the National Association of Women Business Owners.

❖ Women-owned businesses employed more people in 1992 than all of the Fortune 500 companies combined.

❖ 50 percent of all women-owned businesses have five or more employees; 17 percent have 25 or more; and 10 percent have payrolls above $500,000.

❖ 25 percent of women-owned businesses added employees in the past year.

❖ Women-owned companies spent an average of $27,300 on employee benefits; $23,500 on federal taxes; and $7,500 on local taxes.

❖ Women-owned businesses are no longer new or start-up businesses; more than 75 percent have been in existence more than four years; 29 percent have been in business more than 11 years.

And what about minority firms? In 1993, the largest black-owned companies in the U.S. did better than non-minority-owned firms, according to *Black Enterprise* magazine. "Revenue for the 100 largest black-owned companies rose 14 percent to break the $10 billion revenue level for the first time." The top minority firm is TLC Beatrice International headed by a woman, Loida Lewis.

Although financial success is a critical component, the real motivation is having the chance to create something that is uniquely yours, to fulfill a vision. Those who judge the entrepreneur from the outside, usually see someone who is driven and single-focused, someone who thinks, eats, and lives her business. What they can't see is the fun and excitement, the exhilaration that the entrepreneur enjoys by creating a business.

The reasons for starting a business may be varied, but one thing is universal, entrepreneurs are not looking for "easy." Ramona Arnett, president of Arnett Enterprises, says, "Being in your own business is working 80 hours a week so you can avoid working 40 hours a week for someone else."

Perhaps the key word is creation. For just a few minutes, let's put aside all those military and sports metaphors to describe business and look behind the hardware to the software. The entrepreneur creates the idea or product. She nurtures it along. She protects it until it begins to grow and can weather a few setbacks without dying. She thinks about it constantly. How can she improve the product or service? What product or service is already out there or emerging that will threaten her business? What new territories should she explore to increase the market share?

In order to grow a business, you must love it and nurture it. But that's only part of the story. In addition to these wonderful maternal instincts, you'll have to bring some hardware to your entrepreneurial table as well: a realistic appraisal of the market and the marketplace, a cold eye assessing your resources and a timeline in which to accomplish your goals.

Thousands of women are doing this on a daily basis.

Women and business is a winning partnership, but it wasn't always the case. In the past, women in the workplace could be compared to Miss Havisham in Charles Dickens' *Great Expectations*. Do you remember her? She was engaged to be married, but when the big day for the wedding arrived, the groom didn't. For the rest of her life, Miss Havisham sat in her wedding dress, surrounded by a cobweb-covered wedding feast that was never consumed.

If Miss Havisham had been an entrepreneur, after a short grieving period, she would have pulled herself together and either had a major garage sale for the wedding gifts or hung out a sign advertising wedding cake and punch. Unlike Miss Havisham, entrepreneurs are not great mopers when life or business disappoints. They may take a little time out, but generally when a promised loan falls through, or a product due is delayed indefinitely, when a client's definite "yes" turns out to be a definite "no," the entrepreneur begins to look for the new answer. She moves on to the next bank, a revised due date, a better way to meet client needs.

Therese Shaheen is a successful entrepreneur, who is succeeding in countries that are not supposed to be favorable to women in business. "Rejection? I just think of something else. I change tracks and move on. I think that agility is a universal quality women have. If what we throw our hearts into fails us, we look around and throw our hearts into something else."

In the workplace, women have been as mistakenly patient as Miss Havisham playing a losing waiting game, waiting for a promotion or a promise of moving forward, waiting until we were smarter before taking on new responsibilities, waiting until the circumstances were perfect, or we were, waiting before moving on to our hopes or dreams, waiting until someone would tell us we were ready, waiting for someone to hold out our chair at the prized table. Most entrepreneurs do not know how to play this waiting game and because of their success, women are inspired to stop waiting and start moving.

Jeri Sedlar says, "I give myself a little bit of a mourning period, but I don't every really get angry. My enthusiasm usually lets me find the silver lining in any cloud."

If Shaheen and Sedlar seem to have a Pollyanna approach to problems, many studies show that they are not alone in demonstrating this attitude. Surveys of successful men and women entrepreneurs indicate that they truly believe that if they work hard and work smart success will follow.

As Executive Director of the American Women's Economic Development Corporation, Susan Bari sees and helps hundreds of women entrepreneurs start and grow businesses. A business owner herself, and founder of Personally Yours, she says, "Perennial optimism is a winning quality. I think you have to believe something can be accomplished in order to accomplish it. This helps you reject immediate defeats and you can take the bumps in the road as they come. This helps you to go on and get beyond until you reach that smooth road."

Karen Caplan, president and CEO of Frieda's, Inc., the country's most well-known speciality produce company, adds, "Be optimistic at all times. I remind myself regularly of my goals and validate them to see if they are still important or achievable. I write them down and talk about them publicly. You have to have a long-term vision and you have to be an optimist."

When I interviewed hundreds of women entrepreneurs, I found that despite differences in race, age, geographic location, political preference, education, financial levels, all of these women demonstrated certain key qualities that were critical to their success as entrepreneurs. I learned that entrepreneurs look at the world a little differently from most people. The late Mary Crowley, president of Home Interiors, told me, "to an entrepreneur, a roadblock tells them one thing: behind the barrier lies a road."

Entrepreneurs find the road, but they find it in their own way. In fact, the only "boss" they are willing to listen to is the marketplace, their clients or customers. Susan Bari explains, "One reason why women choose to start businesses is that it gives you a freedom to pursue whatever your goals in life may be that you don't find when you're working for someone else."

She quotes one of the graduates of AWED's courses as saying, "I certainly don't work any less hard working for myself than I did when I worked for corporations. But if I'm going to work 12 hours a day, I get to choose which 12 hours those are."

One consistent trait of the entrepreneur is that she follows her own counsel, even when others are saying, "Do it this way, not that way!"

Mary Kay Ash, president and founder of Mary Kay Cosmetics, definitely did it her way. In 1963, when she began the company, she had three things: a product, sales experience, and an idea that women, if given the opportunity, could go as far as their own determination could take them. She gave each woman sales representative of her company training and product support, while allowing each woman to control her way of doing business. As reward for their bottom-line successes, she not only paid high commissions but also created incentives for even greater achievement. She did all this in the face of economic recession, negative attitudes toward women in business, and naysayers who insisted that business just couldn't be done this way.

By maintaining control over her product and her vision, Mary Kay Ash not only built an empire, but also created a corporate culture that empowers and rewards the women who work for her. Her best counsel to women considering business ownership: "The only difference between successful people and unsuccessful people is extraordinary determination."

How do you get this "extraordinary determination" and a "positive belief system?" Is it learnable? Can you practice it until you have "it"? I believe you can by tapping into a heritage you may not even realize you have.

When I was on a trip to Budapest, a woman asked me, "How are American women so sure? How can women in your country suddenly walk away from a good job to start a cookie company? How do they know anyone will buy the cookies?" I didn't say research or marketing or intense preparation. I told her the great secret: that we are scared to death half the time, but we just do it.

As Americans, our heritage reflects people who were the ultimate risk-takers. They either came to this country because they were in fear of their lives and wanted something better, or they were wrenched from their homeland and forced to learn how to survive in whatever way they could in a hostile environment. In a sense, they were all entrepreneurs looking for opportunity in the face of very real and brutal challenges.

So it doesn't really matter if you do not currently have one entrepreneur in your family to teach you the ropes or serve as a role model. If you are interested in stepping up to the entrepreneurial table, you can take encouragement and inspiration from the men and women who have pioneered before you.

Sheri Poe, founder and CEO of Ryka, Inc., a manufacturer of women's athletic shoes, had to conquer her emotional fears before she could move ahead with her business goals. As a teenager, Poe was attacked and raped. She developed bulimia and other health problems as a result of the rape. When Poe formed Ryka, she knew that she wanted her company to not only make the best athletic shoes for women but to reflect Poe's desire to have an impact on society in a positive way.

Two years ago, Poe and Lady Footlocker started the Rose (Regaining One's Self-Esteem) Foundation to help educate and aid victims of violence. Poe is a spokesperson for the Rose Foundation on the subject of violence against women. Ryka is now a $14 million company and Poe, who once lived on welfare and food stamps, credits her business success to her ability to find a need and fill it. To speed her recovery from bulimia and heal herself emotionally, Poe turned to meditation and exercise. She was upset to find that there was little available in footwear for the woman who wanted to work out or who was an avid athlete.

Poe faced challenges every step of the way. Money ran out, and there were endless production and quality problems. Despite the critical financial problems, Poe persevered and created Ryka and Rose, marrying her dream of owning a business and helping victims of violence.

Diane Graham, CEO of Stratco, took the entrepreneurial path after her father died. "I had been working as a secretary for him. After college I really didn't know what I wanted to do. My father bought a controlling interest in the company he had worked for for 18 years, Stratco Engineering Corporation. Stratco licensed technology to refineries worldwide, and were perceived as an equipment supplier. Two years later, my father had a fatal heart attack, I was pregnant, my mother had cancer and my husband and I separated. My mother died and my husband served me with divorce papers one week later."

Although Graham owned 17 percent of the company after her father's death, the new president was not interested in keeping her on. "I could not understand it. I was in my twenties and even though, between my brothers and me we owned a controlling interest in the company, the president didn't want us. I told him I would take any job and he hired me as the receptionist."

Graham had her foot in the door, but the leadership in the company did not encourage her to become more involved. She asked to go to seminars on refining, to learn more about this then 53-year-old engineering company, but she was turned down. She went to the public library and began to read everything she could about the industry. She learned a lot about Stratco's competitors. "Even though we had a better and safer environmental process, the big companies were outdoing us in just about everything," she says. "No one knew about us, but our competitors were very well-known."

Within three months, Graham had become so knowledgeable about Stratco and its market, the president promoted her to be his personal secretary. The real challenges began when Graham found out that her investment proposal for the company had been presented to the board without crediting Graham. The idea was a good one and Stratco began to turn a profit.

Graham, however, made a decision to leave the company. "There was so much pressure on me from this man that it was hard to come to work each day. Fortunately, I realized that if I ran away from this conflict I might not be able to solve whatever was waiting for me somewhere else." Graham convinced her brothers to vote their stock, exert control and name her chairman. Shortly after that the president of the company died, and Graham was elected president in June of 1981.

"It was a volatile time," she says. "We had lost our engineering reputation and were just known as equipment suppliers, but we didn't even manufacture the equipment. I didn't think it was a very stable position to be in. I wanted to regain our reputation and make my Dad's dream come true."

She began moving toward that dream by picking up the phone and calling people from her father's Rolodex. Every one of the men Graham called agreed to see her. Graham's mission was to announce that Stratco was alive and well and ready to deliver the best in service and equipment. She asked a lot of questions, and based on the replies, was able to tailor services and provide new equipment to a growing base of customers.

Just Do It

Graham hated making calls when she sold insurance and she did not enjoy calling any better when it was for Stratco. "It was very difficult for me," she says, "to get on a plane and see strangers but I knew I had to do it if Stratco was going to grow."

Open Leadership Style

Graham does not thrive on confrontations and will avoid them as much as possible. She believes you can side-step a negative confrontation by being honest with people in the first place. "If I have an offer from someone to buy the company, I tell the employees. I want them to know what's going on at all time. I communicate with them on everything that has the potential to impact their lives."

As a woman in a nontraditional industry for women, Graham had to fight the status quo. The company had always been run by engineers. Graham was a woman and young as well. If she were going to succeed, she would have to convince the employees to join her team and help her through. "The vote to make me president was not unanimous," she says. "I knew the only way to turn attitudes around and have a profitable company was to give equal opportunities to both men and women. Opportunity and responsibility."

Graham remembers when she was denied time off to go to the hospital when her child was ill. "I didn't like the way that felt, so why would I do that to someone else? What else do you need but the Golden Rule? If you wouldn't like it, don't do it to someone else."

Graham's advice to would-be entrepreneurs? "Surround yourself with good people. Get involved and never say die."

Do I Really Want To Be an Entrepreneur?

What does it take to step up to the entrepreneurial table? Smarts are important, but not necessarily the kind that you get with a degree. Growing up in a family business can be helpful, but most new business owners do not have such direct experience. A longitudinal study of U.S. women business owners explored the relationship between "strategic origins," i.e., business skills, education and occupational experience, and "business growth." It concluded that previous occupational experience in the area of the venture, strong financial skills and higher educational levels were key factors in discriminating growth from non-growth businesses.

What this means is that if your new business is based on a current area of experience you have an advantage. If you have graduated from high school, you have an advantage. If money and budgets and planning is not a totally alien concept, you have an advantage. You can learn anything you need to know, but, if you already know it, you're ahead of the game.

On the other hand, you can have a Ph.D., tons of money and great contacts, but if you have developed the wrong product for the wrong market, all of those pluses disappear. Markets change, as do the ways in which those markets do business, so the dictum should be: Never stop learning. The great thing about the marketplace is that it is neither for you nor against you until you give it a reason to move one way or the other.

If you wonder if you have what it takes, you may want to look at some of the qualities successful women entrepreneurs demonstrate. These are key attributes but no one, no matter how successful, demonstrates all of them on a daily basis. However, as we go through these qualities, if none of them seems applicable to you, you may want to reconsider the entrepreneural table.

ACTION STEP: Evaluation

High drive and high energy.

Would you describe yourself as someone who has unlimited energy or drive?

YES _____ NO _____

Before you answer this question you may want to first consider the following:

You've been working all day. You finally get home and your in-laws or relatives have called to say they'll be staying with you for a month. How do you feel?

ENTHUSIASTIC _____ OR SUDDENLY TIRED _____

You've been working all day. You finally get home and the White House calls and invites you to a state dinner. How do you feel?

ENTHUSIASTIC _____ OR SUDDENLY TIRED _____

If you don't think of yourself as a high-energy person, and you do not have a physical reason for fatigue, perhaps you are spending too much of your time doing things you are not enthusiastic about.

When you decide to commit to something, do you always follow through?

YES _____ NO _____

If you drop the ball halfway through, you were never truly committed in the first place. Think through the next time. Where are you committing your energy and drive?

Would you consider yourself a procrastinator _____ or a self-starter _____?

Again, it is important to really focus on what you put off doing. Look at what you like to do and what you do under duress.

What is your reaction when others try to tell you "it can't be done"?

Therese Shaheen says, "My particular talent or secret success trait is tenacity. You can be intelligent and talented, but if you are not tenacious you are definitely not going to succeed. In my company, we just don't take no for an answer. Our business is dependent on foreign entities feeling comfortable with us and trusting us to deliver the service. So when problems arise, we have got to be there. Excuses, no matter how valid, just won't work. So we stay in the country until we have delivered on all our promises. So many companies that are like ours think they can just go over to Asia and do the deal and then leave. We never do that, we are always there, working things out to the client's satisfaction. Tenacity means you never spend time coming up with the reason why you didn't deliver."

Shaheen doesn't believe there is anything magical about her company's success. "Really, if you are totally committed you will succeed. Totally committed to me means understanding that the fax machine will never replace the value of a face to face meeting. In order to always 'be there' to deliver, to prevent a crisis, you have to be persistent which brings us right back to tenacity. And tenacity means that I never let anyone tell me, 'it can't be done.'"

Dr. Lillian Beard, who in addition to running her practice as an entrepreneur, is an associate clinical professor of pediatrics at the George Washington University School of Medicine and Health Sciences, an assistant professor at the Howard University College of Medicine, and a consultant to Carnation Nutritional Products Division. She says, "I have always been confident that I have certain skills and talents that will always serve me well. I know I have the ability to be tenacious and not to give up. That's something that I remember from my earliest experiences in childhood. It was instilled at the dinner table and every opportunity at home and growing up."

Beard's mother was an entrepreneur and attending school at the same time. "I went to her graduation. I remember my mother getting her diploma when I was about three years old. I watched her struggle to get her business going and I also saw her being successful. I grew up in a household with a woman who managed to do all this and I thought to myself, 'Gee, I could do this too.'"

In most cases, telling an entrepreneur, it can't be done, is like waving a red flag in front of a bull. Entrepreneurs enjoy finding the way it can be done.

"My mother taught me early on not to give up," says Lillian Beard. "In fact she would not tolerate the words, 'I can't.'"

The interesting thing about drive and energy, they are your natural resources and should not be exposed to harsh elements. For example, a day spent letting others push your buttons is emotional and energy draining. Women have been accused forever of taking things too personally, of overreacting.

That was the general stereotype and reflected in the old joke: Ask a man where he bought his steak and he'll answer, "Joe's meat market." Ask a woman and she'll answer, "Why? What's wrong with it?" Entrepreneurs do not spend a lot of energy-depleting time asking "What's wrong with it?" They do spend a lot of time making sure it's right in the first place.

What are your top three energy depleters?

1. _____
2. _____
3. _____

If you find the fun in what you want to do, you'll have all the energy and drive you need.

Now, can we reconsider the question?

I have the potential to be a high-energy person if I change the following in my life _____

_____

I will take the following steps to move to that high-energy level:

1. _____
2. _____
3. _____

Answer the following questions:

What am I waiting for?

When will I stop waiting?

One last word on energy and drive. You can't demonstrate either if you let the little things get you down. You really do have to take the high road, the leader's road to get to this seat at the table. Forget or avoid those who disappoint on a regular basis. Travel light and get rid of the baggage of jealousy, self-doubt, feeling unworthy or resentful. All these bags, even half full, can really make you tired and stop you dead in your tracks.

QUALITY: CONFIDENCE

According to all the experts, self-confidence is the central core of the personality. It keeps us moving through change and unknown territories with a belief that we will arrive safely on the other side. Self-confidence lets you move forward on your dream when very few will help.

It's Coco Chanel saying, "I am here to make a fortune."

It's Estee Lauder saying, "There is no such thing as bad times. I keep telling myself, there is no such thing as bad business. Business is there, if you go after it." Lauder, who never finished school, had enough self-confidence for a room of business owners. She was never intimidated by her advisors, who all had the degrees she never obtained. "Accountants and lawyers make great accountants and lawyers," she said. "I need them. But I make the business decisions."

Can you build the self-confidence to be an entrepreneur?

You can, even if you've never had it before. It comes with the vision for your company, your product or service. It starts with small steps. A friend of mine, Carey Stacey, president of Dialogos, a company that provides translation services worldwide, works with Russian women entrepreneurs. She told me that the last time she was in Moscow, one of the women said to her, "When you ask Americans, 'How are you?' They always say, 'GREAT.' I realized that 'GREAT' is the right answer for my new life. Before, I would have answered with all the problems I have. Now, I just say 'GREAT' and I feel a lot better. Also, I get more business because people do not think I have so many problems, so I must know what I am doing."

The interesting thing about this Russian woman's response is that it is not typical of the Russian people in general. A recent survey showed that the majority of Russians, when asked if life was better now or before their new free-market economy, said, "before." The entrepreneurs who view change as equal to opportunity choose "now."

In 1980, when financier Warren Bennis interviewed 90 successful men and women to determine what qualities of leadership they all had in common, he called their entrepreneurial leadership traits the Wallenda Factor after Karl

Wallenda, the famous tightrope walker. It seems that in all the years Wallenda walked across the tightrope, his confidence and concentration never wavered. His focus was always on a successful walk. After his fatal fall, his wife said, he had been talking constantly about falling. It seemed to her that for the first time he was putting all of his energy into not falling instead of walking across the rope.

Bennis concluded that successful people, leaders, entrepreneurs, never think about "failing"; they build their confidence by thinking only of their ultimate goal.

What "failing" thoughts do you repeat on a daily basis?
Any of these?

> This is a terrible time to start a business.
>
> No one is our family has ever made it financially.
>
> It will take too much time.
>
> Whatever made me think I could do it?
>
> What if I fail?
>
> What if I succeed?
>
> What if I lose?
>
> It will take too much time.
>
> I won't be able to get a loan.
>
> This is too selfish of me.
>
> My family needs me.
>
> It's probably a bad idea.

Self-confidence means that you have taken the time to slowly develop a quiet belief in yourself and your judgment. I remember a few years ago, when I was on a show hosted by Linda Evans, who at that time was starring in "Dynasty." She was beautiful, thin, articulate, rich, successful and very smart. After the show, we had a chance to talk privately and she said that all of her life she'd had to work hard to believe in herself. It wasn't too comforting to tell herself she was beautiful. After all, she said, this industry is full of beautiful women, "I had to invent the self-confidence others thought I had, in order to move ahead in this business."

I can't tell you how many women, successful women, have echoed what Linda Evans said. The next time you see a name in the news, a woman who you admire, remember she is not superwoman. She has her own demons to deal with no matter how confident she looks, how fearless she seems to be. You can reference her achievements and be inspired, but you would be mistaken to think that the achievements were obtained without a struggle, without a challenge, without overcoming personal doubts and fears.

Barbara Gardner Proctor, from the wrong side of the hill in Black Mountain, North Carolina, conquered the roadblock of prejudice to become a successful entrepreneur. Proctor, who couldn't find a mentor in Black Mountain, looked up to Lena Horne. "She stood for something positive, quality and dignity. Because of the positive influence she had on my life, I would like to think that I might serve as a positive role model for some child growing up today. My firm, Proctor and Gardner must reflect good images, strong values, not negative messages."

Proctor, who received the first service loan ever guaranteed by the SBA, started her advertising firm with a clear set of values. "I knew from the beginning that I would have certain standards regarding who I would or wouldn't represent. I did not want any client with a product which would adversely affect the black community or that would portray blacks in a negative way. I would refuse to advertise a company that portrayed blacks in a stereotypical manner." As an entrepreneur and Chicago Advertising Woman of the Year, Proctor says, "Know where you stand and what you think."

Women entrepreneurs want to be financially successful but they also want value-centered success as well. The desire to accomplish or achieve is coupled with a strong desire to make a contribution. This combination is unbeatable for starving fear and feeding self-confidence.

Patty De Dominic, CEO of PDQ Personnel Services, Inc., says, "I value the ability to help others grow and really believe that the Golden Rule is a key to living a balanced life." De Dominic, a successful entrepreneur, is a leader in the National Organization of Women Business Owners, an organization that a majority of women entrepreneurs credit with helping them succeed in the marketplace. "I believe that entrepreneurial success is based on optimism. I also believe that the most positive aspect of my success is the ability to help others and to make positive changes in my company, my industry, my networking groups and the community."

MaryAnn Van Dongen, president of Express Visa Services, started her company based on an observation that travelers were not getting the service they needed when it came to quickly expedited visa service. Van Dongen has built a successful corporation with offices throughout the U.S., based on filling a need and raising it to a new personal-service level.

In her spare time, she is owner of M Designs, a company that provides couture style at affordable prices. M Designs grew out of Van Dongen's own appreciation of quality fabrics, beautiful design and affordability. Recently, on a leisure trip to Venice, she discovered beautiful Fortuny-like scarves which she is now making available to her U.S. customers.

How Do You Get Self-confidence?

How do you get self-confidence? Practice, practice, practice. Cross off a few items from your fear of failing list. Start putting more choices on the self-confidence list.

The Very Big Secret

We are all constantly re-inventing ourselves or trying to improve on what we started with. We just never share this information with anyone else. Self-confidence is not a destination it's a lifelong trip.

Marsha Sands, owner of Camelions restaurant in Santa Monica, says, "You want to know the secret of self-confidence? You get up in the morning and you move your feet, one foot after the other." Several years ago, when Sands discovered she had breast cancer, the first thing she did was book a cruise on the Sea Goddess. She figured that as long as she was headed down the road of chemotherapy, she might as well fill her head first with visions of beautiful vistas and the Aegean Sea. She felt that holding these visions would help her move confidently through the bumpy waters that lay ahead. And they did.

These entrepreneurial qualities do not stop working for you when the work stops. They help you through all kinds of challenges, personal and professional.

Self-confidence can save your life. Studies show that if you walk with a strong stride and your head held up, and you look as if you are heading for a specific destination, as opposed to just wandering around or being lost, you are less likely to be attacked. On the street those who appear unsteady, tentative and unsure are in danger.

In business, you must also avoid the "victim walk." If you act like you mean business, you will get business. If it appears that you're doing well, you will! It is critical that you be a silent cheerleader for yourself. Walk strong, feel good, give yourself credit.

ACTION ITEMS:
1. **This week I will monitor what I say and what I read. I will avoid all articles that warn me, if I achieve success, I will be doomed to a loveless and lonely life.**
Therese Shaheen does not read the articles that tell her she can never achieve

in Asia on the same level of her male counterparts in eastern countries. She says, "I never consider that I cannot add value in a given situation. If you approach a challenge like water approaches a rock, you can always go around or over it even if it is impossible to break through it."

2. **I will not set myself up for a self-confidence puncture by voicing my doubts and fears.**

Preparation is critical to business success. Confidence comes from knowing that you know what you need to know.

3. **I will learn everything I can about the business I am about to enter. I will talk to everyone who can give me information, I will call and meet with anyone who can lead me to the next important information or contact.**

Georgette Mosbacher, author of *Feminine Force* and president of Georgette Mosbacher Enterprises says, "I was successful for the same reasons that other people are successful: I trusted myself and I did my homework. Look at your own life. Most of the things that you have accomplished have happened because you believed in yourself, because you put the time and effort into making a solid plan, and because you were unrelenting in the pursuit of your goal."

"I read constantly," says Mosbacher. "Where is that next idea coming from? Where is the next opportunity coming from? You have to keep up with your world. I didn't know I was headed for the cosmetic industry. That just grew out of moving from one job to another and keeping my eyes and ears open to take advantage of the opportunities within the job."

When I met Georgette Mosbacher she had just arrived in Washington, D.C., with her husband Robert Mosbacher, soon-to-be Secretary of Commerce. The town went wild. She just didn't fit the mold of what a Washington "wife" was supposed to be. Of course she didn't, she was and is an entrepreneur and entrepreneurs refuse to fit anyone's mold.

While the media was focused on the color of her hair or the jewelry she was wearing, Mosbacher kept focused and bought a company, La Prairie. At the same time, she was generous with her time advising women to move toward their goals, to learn on the job, to move out and up, and reach out to people.

As a member of the Board of Governors of the Alliance, she opened her home to host programs with CEO's and senior-level women, candidates for corporate board positions. Like most entrepreneurs, she has no time for negative people or those who constantly chant, "It can't be done."

"Life should be exciting," she says, "for anybody, anywhere, anytime. It is really up to you. This may sound like a cliche but it is a cliche because it is true: You have the power to decide if an event is either an opportunity or a setback."

Run the Race Against Yourself

"When I am on track, I really believe my main competition is the clock. And myself." Bonnie Blair, five-time Olympic Gold winner.

This may be the hardest challenge you face in your goal to reach a seat at the entrepreneurial table. And it is this: to put the blinders on when it comes to comparing yourself to others and their success. You have to find your race and run it.

But, but, what about? It isn't easy. As a business owner you have to know where your product or service ranks in the marketplace. Where you rank requires a very different measurement approach. The truth is that it is easier to run someone else's race. We get to stand back and critique, undermine or resent and sometimes even sabotage. In the meantime, the road to our goals never gets used. It takes a lot of discipline and courage to keep your eye on your own ball.

Measure your success against your own achievements. Where were you last year at the same time? Is your "game" improving? Are you making headway? Are you measuring up to your own goals and objectives? Have you gone beyond your goals and are just coasting? Have your goals changed?

"I think you need a strategic plan for yourself," says Susan Bari. "The same way you would for a business. You need to make an appointment with yourself to review your goals and objectives and your progress toward them at least on an annual basis, if not more frequently."

I Am Not Jane Fonda

Sharlyne Powell, who is a very large woman, went to many exercise studios in an attempt to lose weight. She was surrounded by women who were already fit and thin and who did not welcome her to their exercise routines. Powell finally decided she'd had enough of trying to be someone else. The leotards didn't fit. The workout clothes were made for people who were already trim. There was nothing for her or for others like her in the marketplace.

Realizing that others must have the same need, she created a chain of exercise studios for the extra-sized woman called Woman at Large. Following that success, she designed an exercise clothing line, produced exercise videos and created workout products. Powell didn't waste time bemoaning the fact that she was not Jane Fonda. She found the winner in Sharlyne Powell and marketed her unique vision. Find your race and run it. Find the seat at the table that belongs exclusively to you.

When I was in Hungary a few years ago, conducting the first workshops for women considering business ownership, I was told this joke that underscores the problem of competitiveness run amok, of focusing on others rather than yourself: There are two farmers whose farms are adjacent to one another. One farmer has a great thriving farm. The cows and horses and chickens are healthy. His produce sells first in the marketplace. He is successful. The other farmer cannot make ends meet. His farm is not bountiful. His produce is inferior. One day, an angel appears to the poor farmer and says, "I will give you one wish. Anything you want." The poor farmer says, "I've been waiting for this day all my life." And the angel says, "I know what you want, and it is yours. You want a farm as good or better than your neighbor's." "Oh, no," says the poor farmer, "My wish is that you will just take his farm away."

Once you stop competing with yourself and begin to focus on the next person, you begin to lose. Your slice of the entrepreneurial pie is very big. If you worry about the size of your neighbor's slice, you won't have time to enjoy yours.

Lorraine Spiess, one of the first women venture capitalists in China, says, "In China, when you resent someone else's success, they call it the 'red eye' disease." Spiess believes it is more likely to occur in former communist countries, because "when the government dictates how much someone can earn, or achieve, or grow, the pie is really perceived as a very small cookie. If someone else 'wins', it means you lose. There is only a finite amount to be had."

In our own culture, we remember the phenomenon known as "keeping up with the Joneses." The only redeeming quality about that activity is that we didn't want to take away what they had, we just wanted the same things or better. We found that participation only led to a dizzying spiral of one-upmanship and collecting things we didn't need and probably didn't want.

The danger of competing with someone else's success is that it tends to zap our self-confidence and leaves us very little time to focus on our own road. The question you have to ask yourself is: "Would I really be better off without my chief competitor, or would another entrepreneur come along and take her place with a better product or service?" If so, then why am I not providing this better product or service now?

What's important is to find out what your ideas are, what your position is and how well they fit you and what you're trying to accomplish.

Marilyn Hamilton was hang gliding and the wind failed. She and the hang glider crashed. When she came to, they told her she would be permanently paralyzed from the waist down. She tried to be as mobile as possible, but she felt that her wheelchair was holding her back. It was heavy and hard to maneuver. She began to envision a wheelchair made from strong but lightweight materials. That vision resulted in her new company, Motion Designs, which produced the first custom folding chair with modular frame construction, an innovation in hang gliding technology.

Hamilton not only founded a successful company, she reframed the word disabled. She spells it disAbled, with emphasis on abled. She should know. Marilyn Hamilton continues to win sports and business challenges.

"Challenge yourself to go after your dreams," says Hamilton. "Don't compare yourself with anyone else or you will work to someone else's limits instead of your own. Focus your attention only on those things you can control, instead of wasting energy on things you cannot influence or change."

"Through accepting my individuality, which I can't expect everyone else to recognize and pat me on the back for, I shape my goals and desires. I am not compelled to be a victim of unknown forces in myself. I am not compelled to be simply a creature of others, molded by their experiences and shaped by their demands." Carl Rogers.

Risky Business

"All serious daring starts from within." Willa Cather

Women have been told as long as time that this is the one thing they are not very good at demonstrating: taking risks. Nothing could be further from the truth. Of course we take risks. Who do they think traveled across the country in all those covered wagons, who was left to keep the homestead thriving when the men went off to shoot whatever they needed to shoot? Women have been taking risks since time began but mostly on behalf of others, family, husbands, children. Now we are finding out that this heritage of risk-taking is serving us well as entrepreneurs.

Do you consider yourself a risk-taker?

How many serious money bets have you made on horses, cards, elections in the last year?

1 _____ 2 _____ 3 _____ 4 _____

If your answer is more than one you may want to get help. This is not the kind of risk-taking we are talking about.

What is a Definition of a Risk You Have Taken Lately?

The following qualify:

Mortgaged house to start new business.

Hired another staffer.

Made a presentation on new business development.

Made the appointment to talk to the loan officer.

Quit job to devote full time to enterprise.

Gave a speech to potential investor group.

Gave a speech.

Signed lease on new space.

Borrowed money from bank to finance acquisition of smaller company.

Made decision to grow the company.

Made decision to stay small.

Estee Lauder said, "I'd risk the rent, but if it worked I would start the business I always dreamed about. Risk-taking is the cornerstone of empires."

Entrepreneurs are willing to take a chance. When they are faced with choices they don't always take the easy one. A winning strategy regarding risk-taking: Don't be immobilized by your fear of failure. Don't be afraid to begin.

Georgette Mosbacher agrees and advises, "I take calculated risks. There is no other way to stay in the game. And I am going to let you in on a little secret. The difference between a calculated risk and rolling the dice can be expressed in one word: homework."

For some, the fear never goes away, but you learn to put it on hold by looking at risk as not just one chance to win or lose, but more as a necessary requirement, a ticket that puts you on the train to your next goal. We have learned a lot about the risk-taking process and the concept of winning and losing through athletes.

Psychologists, who work with world sports figures, help them win by dealing first with their fear of losing. The process involves meditation, refocusing on goals, learning from what we term "failure" by not dwelling on "losses." "Getting in the zone" is the term used to describe the ability to wipe all the potential negatives from your mind, focus on the goal and enjoy the process as you move forward.

Jim Loehr, a sports psychologist, was quoted in *The Washington Post*: "In Dan Janssen's story is the entire message: Out of great adversity can come the greatest triumphs. As painful as they are, in the right context, mistakes should not be marks of great frailty, but of great courage, because these are the people who have put themselves on the line. That's what it takes to be successful."

The next quality we will look at may be the key to the entrepreneurial personality. I am not sure if this is teachable. It may require you to change some core beliefs about your world and your position in it.

WHAT DO YOU THINK OF YOUR WORLD?

A.   It's directed by an unseen but maniacal despot intent on preventing me from getting ahead.

B.   It's run by men intent on preventing me from getting ahead.

C.   It's a jungle out there.

According to a national survey of successful men and women entrepreneurs, the feeling is that the universe is not unfriendly, that if you do work hard and smart, success is possible. They believe that events in their lives are self-determined and ultimately their responsibility. They believe that "success like failure, lies within their own personal control and influence rather than being determined by luck or other external, personally uncontrollable events."

The interesting thing about this attitude is it indicates again the control entrepreneurs need over their lives. They will not even give up their own failures as someone else's fault or responsibility. Is this you?

I know women business owners, who when faced with a real business challenge will say, "What is the good in this situation?"

If you still feel that the entrepreneurial table is for you, it may be valuable to take a tip from America's women entrepreneurs: Find out what your good at doing. It is probably something you love doing already. Spend a lot of time doing whatever it takes in your mind to be the best. Establish a standard of performance that is high, yet realistic. Learn to compete with yourself and discover the real power of being yourself, then you are not only positioned to look at other tables but to help others in the process.

BASIC ACTION PLAN: TAKING CARE OF BUSINESS

If you seek to fill the CEO's seat at the entrepreneurial table, we'll assume that you have an idea, that you've surveyed your market and believe the idea has a chance, that you have confidence in yourself at this point and are ready to begin. Where do you start?

Entrepreneurs who succeed have done their homework. Yes, first the dream, the imagination, the vision, the excitement of: Wouldn't it be great to own my own company? Without a dream you will not even get started. However, the dream is the vision that hovers in front of you, always a little illusive, always one step ahead of where you are.

The dream has to be reinforced with the grunt stuff. The unglamorous day-to-day, how do I make this work? Who can help? Where does the money come from? How do I know they want what I'm going to sell? (They don't.

You have to find out what they want to buy.)

Sheri Poe, founder and CEO of Ryka athletic shoes for women, spent many weeks talking to women in aerobics classes, working out in gyms to find out that there were a lot of complaints about footwear available to women. She learned that women were not being fitted properly. They were basically buying shoes that had been modeled on the much larger male foot. She posed as a graduate student and surveyed department stores and athletic gear shops querying customers about the kind of shoes women want.

Although Poe began with an idea and a dream, she knew she had to find out if the dream would be validated by the marketplace.

THE BUSINESS PLAN

The best way to begin is to imagine you are talking about your idea to a potential backer. What would that person want to know? Have you researched the marketplace and determined you would be filling a need that doesn't exist? In what way? How much will be needed to capitalize your venture? When do you anticipate you will make a profit? What personal resources will you commit? What kind of time commitment are you prepared to make. How will you let others know about your product? How much will that cost? Are there vendors involved? What kind of payment schedule have you worked out with them?

Just basic questions. The ones your mother will ask you anyway. Why are you doing this? Who are your partners? What is your backup plan if the economy takes a dive again? Who are your customers? How do you know? Just look at the first three years: where are you now and where do you plan to go? The plan can, and will, change as you and your business change, but you really do need to develop a tentative plan to serve as a map on your journey toward your goal(s).

IDENTIFY YOUR RESOURCES

Resources are family, friends, contacts and money. As an entrepreneur, you are going to need to create an environment in which you will succeed. You need to know that your backing, financial and personal, is in place in order for you to reach your short-and long-term goals. One resource you might want to consider is Capital Rose, Inc., a multi-dimensional corporation that solves problems for women business owners. The most pressing need identified by female entrepreneurs is access to capital. Capital Rose created The Capital Rose Perpetual Fund, Inc., a nonprofit corporation with a $40 million fund, which finances economically viable, women-owned businesses.

Capital Rose is a company created by women, with women and for women. The Fund provides capital to a balanced mix of women-owned businesses representing new ventures, established companies, management buyouts, franchises, and professional corporations. Your ability to obtain funds from Capital Rose will depend on your business plan, the existing climate in the marketplace for your product or service, and other financial considerations. A financing minimum of $50,000 has been established.

For women entrepreneurs Capital Rose has an added flexibility to act as a laboratory for character-based financing, which is a goal of many institutions, but which is restricted among traditional sources because of the current regulatory climate. You can find the address of Capital Rose in the Resource section of this book.

REVIEW SHORT- AND LONG-TERM GOALS

All this means is that now is the time to set your priorities. The short-term goals can be as short as what you're going to do today, and they give you great satisfaction and a sense of forward movement, every time one is crossed off the list. Long-term goals, such as "take over the cheese market in Switzerland" need not be consulted every day, but the short-term goals should take you toward the long-term goal, so you want to check occasionally to see how much headway you are making.

MAKE THOSE CALLS. TALK TO PEOPLE. PUT DOWN THE BUSINESS PLAN AND GET OUT AND AROUND

Every day should involve some type of reaching out to touch someone, whether to actually sell your product, network about the need for your product. Nothing beats finding out for yourself what's out there. You should resolve to make at least one call a day that puts you closer to information, people or that loan you need for start-up. One entrepreneur I know makes 10 marketing calls every day, no matter what else she's doing. It may help to know that statisticians tell us that for every 100 marketing calls, you can expect to find 10 people who are interested, and one person who will buy.

SCHEDULE THREE APPOINTMENTS A WEEK

If touching base by phone is a good idea, meeting face-to-face is even better. You know the ones you really need to talk to, but you're afraid of getting a "no."

Rehearse what you need to say and practice saying it while smiling. Don't be tentative. There is life after "no." In fact, some of the best deals start with a definite "no."

And, even if today's visit does end in a definite "no," next time you approach this person, he'll have a face to put with the voice on the phone; or, though he may not be able to use your product or service, he might know someone who can. No personal visit is ever wasted.

GET VISIBLE

No matter what your goal, you will be advised by people in your chosen field to "get visible." You do not have to do this all at once or in one day or even a year. You do need to develop a long-range plan that you consult frequently. A plan that will allow you to write a certain number of articles a year or speak to key groups. Or serve in a leadership position for a nonprofit organization, or get involved with a political campaign and develop an article on an issue you care about. Join a business organization of men and women leaders, offer to take on a project and complete it beyond expectations.

Diane Graham says, "I looked at our company and realized we had been in Kansas City for 50 years, but no one knew who we were. So the first thing I did was make sure that everyone in the company became involved in the community."

PRO BONO

Decide what you can afford to give away in hope that business will come back to you. Most entrepreneurs give back to their community in some way. The problem can be choosing how. How many projects are you involved in now, because you thought it would be good for business? Was it? How much time have you contributed free in the hope that recipients will hire you later? Did they? Are you getting the visibility and return you counted on from organizations you've joined or are you a faceless member of the crowd? It is especially important for entrepreneurs in a service business to evaluate how much time they spend on projects that may never result in business and, in fact, take away from time needed to focus on business goals.

Identify a cause or issue you really care about and decide how much you are willing to spend, either in time, in-kind services, or financial commitments. Stick to your plan for a year and review your pro bono commitment on an annual basis.

Graham has institutionalized volunteer activity within Stratco so that employees can do their volunteering during office hours. She credits her involvement with pro bono activities with raising the her profile and that of her company.

VISUALIZE SUCCESS

This is not mumbo-jumbo. A recent study of women in senior management, who were having difficulty making it to the next level, showed that they really didn't see themselves in that top-level executive position. So, if you are the CEO of your extraordinarily successful enterprise, be a leader. Encourage yourself to build an inventory of positive traits with realistic and inspiring goals. See yourself seated at the table.

CREATE AN ADVISORY BOARD

Identify five people whose expertise you respect in fields other than your own. You probably do not have a budget for directors' fees, but you can ask them to meet once a quarter and host a catered lunch. It is important that you plan these meetings ahead of time and provide your board with an agenda. Since this is strictly an advisory group, there is no liability connected with their serving.

Having a board increases your outreach. You may have all the drive and energy in the world, but you can't be everywhere at once, or know everyone. But what's in it for them? You would be surprised how much talent and expertise is out there, ready to help, but no one ever asks. Perhaps one or two on your board have recently retired from their own businesses, corporations or associations. Most people, whether men or women, take pride in nurturing a new enterprise to a successful level.

When you have five names, call them and tell them exactly what serving on your advisory board will entail and why you have chosen them. If they agree, send a letter outlining how long you would like them to serve and how much of their time will be required. Offer to pay for parking expenses. If money is a problem, try to provide other compensation that is important to them. It may be recognition through a press release to your local paper. It may be just remembering their birthdays with a gift or card. Stick to your quarterly schedule, set a definite amount of time for the meeting, then begin and end on time.

"I depend on my advisory board a lot," says Diane Graham. "Each person has been a mentor to me. I compiled the board by consulting with an attorney friend of mine who advised, 'find people who do not just give good advice but who truly want you to succeed.' My board is constantly encouraging me. They send me articles I may not have had a chance to see. They spend valuable one-on-one time providing me with the sounding board I need. And they all help me with community projects. We have the women helping women golf tournament that raises money for underprivileged girls and women."

Strengthen Your Commitment

Women commit to family, husbands, lovers, children, friends, and society. The first promises we break are those we make to ourselves. Therefore, women, who would be entrepreneurs, must not only commit to the idea, but must find a way to meet their other commitments as well.

First, identify those in your life who will be affected by your commitment to be an entrepreneur. Think of them as the rest of your team. What benefits will accrue to the team if you succeed? How can you relate these benefits to them, so that they will become cheerleaders instead of naysayers? Are their others who have a stake in your success? How can they help you strengthen your commitment? Fit this all into the puzzle before you set your sights on the entrepreneurial table.

Linda Collier, owner and president of Triad International Freight Forwarding, Ltd. of Canada, did just that. Less than one percent of freight businesses in Canada are owned and operated by women. There are over 1,000 freight businesses. Collier started working in the freight forwarding business with Emory Air Freight right after high school. She started in a junior position, in customer service and learned from the ground up about the U.S./Canada transporter business. After several senior jobs in the industry, she decided at age 25 that there wasn't anything she was doing for the company that she couldn't do on her own.

Because of the relationships she had developed with various airlines over the years, she was able to establish immediate credit and terms for her fledgling company. Her clients, Fortune 500 corporations paid her within 15 to 30 days, which resulted in a positive cash flow. Collier was able to do this strictly on the value of her personal relationships. In fact, in all the applications for credit with any airline it says in big, bold letters: **DON'T APPLY UNLESS YOU HAVE BEEN IN BUSINESS FOR ONE YEAR.**

Relationships, trust and rapport launched Collier's business. "All business is personal," says Collier. "Never burn a bridge. In my business it is very cut-throat. You'll see people move hundreds of thousands of pounds of freight over to another freight forwarder for two or three cents a pound. There isn't a heck of a lot of loyalty and your reputation is based, literally, on your last shipment and how well it worked."

Collier admits she did not have a B.A. or M.B.A., but credits her people working skills over her lack of education, although she took courses specific to her industry. As she began to run her business she learned that freight forwarding has more to do with lawyers, auditors, marketing and sales than the actual freight forwarding. She shares with other successful entrepreneurs the commitment to keep learning about her industry and the market.

"It is important you carry yourself like a winner," says Collier, "but you don't have to talk about your wins. Sometimes the guys brag about their success and that can turn people off. If you are going to have a seat at the table as a business owner you have to know where you are going. You have to have values."

6

TARGET TABLE: THE CORPORATION

"I find when I work an 18-hour day, I get lucky."
ARMAND HAMMER

"Senior women executives have made monumental gains in both their professional and personal lives over the past decade. They are beginning to exercise choices that appeared unthinkable just 10 years ago."
RICHARD FERRY, CHAIRMAN AND CEO OF KORN/FERRY

Recent studies underscore that women (and men) do not want to work an 18-hour day. They want a seat at the table, but they want the opportunity to have a life as well. In the case of the entrepreneur, who may be working those 18-hour days, we know she regards the work as her life, not something apart. If the company is a family-owned or a home-based business, the line between a separate life and work is blurred even more. For striving for a seat at the corporate table, there are many routes, but all involve hard work.

A study conducted by Korn/Ferry International, the executive search firm, indicated that among executive women, a majority were not planning to remain with the corporation until retirement. In fact, many top-level women in the corporation are leaving to start their own companies. They are not all leaving for the simple reason of "the glass ceiling."

In fact, many of them have broken through the glass ceiling and are receiving salary, title and benefits similar to their male counterparts. And they are not leaving to work fewer hours, because as entrepreneurs they may be working even longer. What they are leaving for is a chance to shape their own business creations, to breathe life into a personal vision. The question is: Can the corporation provide these talented women with the autonomy they crave and deserve, the professional and financial rewards, and the recognition required to keep them?

The jury is still out. According to a study by *The Wall Street Journal*, which surveyed employment records of companies filing reports with the U.S. Equal Opportunity Commission from 1982 to 1992, "Women held less than a third of the managerial jobs in the 38,059 companies that reported to the EEOC in 1992." True, women have made gains since 1982 when they held 21.7 percent of all managerial jobs compared with 30.5 percent today. And they are in the pipeline, poised to move to those top positions. And they are succeeding in specific industries: Allied Signal, Sears, Xerox, Johnson & Johnson, USX, Tenneco, Monsanto and General Motors all have female treasurers, a job just below chief financial officer and not that far removed from chief executive officer.

Jacques Nordeman, chairman of Nordeman Grimm says, "The lines of least resistance within the corporation seems to be finance. The new treasurer of Westinghouse is a woman. Seagram's has a woman treasurer. What this means is that when it comes to intellect and ability, a keen financial mind is more important than gender and more and more corporations are understanding this across the board."

The Korn/Ferry International study showed that there is an increasing trend of women joining the upper ranks of large corporations. Carol Scott, a professor of marketing at the UCLA graduate school of government, conducted the study which offers good news and bad news. The good news is women are slowly gaining seats around the corporate executive table, but the bad news is they are not necessarily enjoying it. A majority (75 percent) do not want to work at this level until retirement. Many of them are eyeing the world of the entrepreneur and have plans to start their own businesses.

Although they cite stress, juggling home, family and job as reasons to look at other ventures, they may indeed stay on until retirement because they are receiving more money, recognition and perks than they did 10 years ago. "The average salary of senior female executive has doubled in 10 years to $187,000, but women earn two thirds of what their male counterparts earn and men still outnumber women by 3 to 1 at the executive vice president level."

Ten years ago, women executives were clearly deciding between achievement in a corporate career and marriage and family. Fewer than 50 percent of top female executives were married and only 39 percent had children. The 1992 survey shows that 69 percent are married and over half have one or more children.

The Decade of the Executive Woman study of female executives, company vice presidents or higher in the country's largest industrial and service companies shows that she:

❖ Took short maternity leaves with no effect on career.

❖ Took career risks to gain visibility or move up fast.

❖ Is married and has children.

❖ Is sought after by corporations.

❖ Expects to be part of senior management in their company by the year 2000.

Of the women surveyed, 39 percent said that sexism was the greatest obstacle to their success.

And in *The Wall Street Journal,* Joann S. Lublin says, "Some big companies are trying to break their glass ceilings. They're putting out the word that only women need apply for some of their top jobs. That's a turnabout from the recent past when women were recruited last, if at all for senior posts, executive recruiters say."

One key example of this is Avon Products. "Avon is an organization where women's leadership style is ingrained in the management structure, " according to Gail Blanke, a senior vice president of corporate affairs and communications at Avon Products. "That shouldn't be surprising, since Avon is a company that makes products mostly for women and distributes them through some 1.7 million independent Avon representatives around the world, almost all of whom are women. Quite simply we're a women's company. And that's reflected in our management structure. Five of the nine people who report directly to the chief executive officer are women. We have five women on our board of directors. Going down in the ranks, about 75 percent of our managers are women."

Blanke adds, "In other words, the thinking of women is understood to be a crucial part of top-level decision-making."

That's a great example, but the generic advice to women who want a corporate seat at the table: Do not wait until the corporate culture is ready to accept you. You may be waiting a long time. First, understand the corporate culture and second, figure out how you can not only fit but thrive within that culture. As you acquire power, you can begin to impact the culture. Corporate America may be willing to meet you more than half way. As Lublin indicates, business and industry is trying to attract women to top slots and they are reviewing their internal policies to determine what may be keeping female executives out of the picture.

In *Neanderthals at Work,* Dr. Albert Bernstein asks, "When it comes to rising to the top of a company, what is the 11th commandment?" The answer: "No one will tell you the other 10." Many women and minorities within corporate structures would agree. The annual report may speak of empowerment and diversity, but if the message is not demonstrated in real terms, the end result is a clear line between reality and the brochure. Who gets promoted in the company? What is their promotion based upon? What kind of behavior is being rewarded? What does it take to get ahead? Does the company provide real support and encouragement? Is it possible to be offered challenging work and visible assignments? Are there training and developmental opportunities?

In England, Unilever is now recruiting almost equal numbers of men and women because of its highly rated graduate management-trainee program. Prior to the program, Unilever was losing 75 percent of its "rising star" women within a five-year period. The women were leaving for reasons directly linked to the culture of the organization. The loss to the company was dramatic, apart from the impact on moral, there was a high financial loss equal to four times initial salary costs.

Bill Morin, chairman and CEO of Drake Beam Morin, the world's largest career transition and career management company, says, "The answer to revitalizing employee/employer relations is in values. Corporations express their values by treating employees equitably; by enabling employees to strike a balance between their professional and personal lives; by contributing to their communities; and by understanding that the more they invest in their workers, the more their workers will produce."

Barbara Krouse, who achieved her vice presidency at the youngest age of any executive in Stouffer Foods, headed the team that developed Lean Cuisine. The president of Stouffer at that time, Jim Biggar, wanted to ensure that other women in Stouffer/Nestle were encouraged by Krouse's success and so he established the Women's Advisory Committee. The purpose of this committee, which was among the early groups of its kind within the corporation, was to help women make better use of their talents working for the company and to create an aggressive program to attract other women. This was a bottom-line decision. Biggar believed that many more commercially successful ideas such as Lean Cuisine could emerge and profit the company if women were given a chance to lead.

As companies downsize, employees are being asked to work even harder and longer hours. Not everyone is willing to do that. If you are one of the ones who are, your opportunity to negotiate for what you want and have a seat at the corporate table may be better than ever. You will also have to work smarter, be stronger, make decisions faster in a less secure job. If your performance impacts the bottom line in a positive way, the culture will bend to you.

"Despite decades of management fads, U.S. businesses essentially have practiced military, chain-of-command management," says Bill Morin.

This is not a style guaranteed to provide comfort level to women at either entry or senior level. This style also has affected how women are perceived in the workplace.

As reported in *PR Reporter*, Brouillard Communications surveyed male and female executives on the following: If the majority of CEO's of the top 1,000 corporations were women, how would business change?

❖ 71 percent of female and 36 percent of male respondents believe employee relations would improve under female leadership.

❖ 37 percent of women and 27 percent of men think general communications would improve.

❖ 41 percent of women and 18 percent of men say marketing would become more innovative.

❖ 38 percent of women and 24 percent of men believe that the overall reputation of U.S. business would become better.

❖ 13 percent of women and 26 of percent men believe it would make the U.S. less competitive internationally.

❖ 18 percent of women and 7 percent of men believe U.S. business would be more competitive.

The only way to change this stereotypical thinking is for women in corporate America to begin to be as visible as their counterparts in small business and track financial success, due to their performance, for their companies.

There is no doubt then that you will be rewarded, but will you value the rewards and do they balance against what you must commit? In Judy Haberkorn's case the answer is "yes."

Judy Haberkorn, vice president of consumer markets for NYNEX Telecommunications Group, grew up believing that "beauty is as beauty does" long before Forrest Gump made this phrase a national cliche.

"I never for one moment believed that old maxim, 'men are what they do and women are what they look like.' Fortunately, for me, neither did my mother," she said. "I grew up thinking that if I did what I said I was going to do, that if I produced the result, that would be good enough. The focus was never on being liked for how I looked or didn't look." Haberkorn's result-oriented approach led her directly to the corporate world right out of college.

"I was the first kid to ever be hired with no work experience for the job of supervisor for the traffic department at C&P Telephone Company in Baltimore, Maryland. My job was to supervise a group of operators. They all knew I had no previous experience as an operator and that I had not worked my way up the ranks through the company. It was a tough situation," says Haberkorn. "The level above me to whom I would be reporting were all former operators who had been promoted. The women below me were currently operators. There were a lot of bets that I wouldn't last through the week. In fact, the smart money said 'she will succeed with one group or the another, but not both.' 'This kid will soon be out of here.' Everyone was surprised when it worked out."

GUTS AND SKILL

It worked out primarily because Haberkorn kept her eye on the larger goal: a decision-making seat somewhere in the distant future around the NYNEX table. This long-range goal gave her the courage to take the risks she needed to take in order to move ahead. Risk-taking alone was not the only quality she needed to succeed in the corporate environment. Risk-taking enabled her to say "yes" to a job where her chances of success were not high. The key quality that sustained her was an ability to work her way through the tough times. Her long-range vision, knowing what she wanted, enabled her to make a commitment, no matter how tough the assignment, to see it through.

"You can call it risk-taking," says Haberkorn, "but it really is a combination of skill and guts. You need both parts of the equation. We all know people who may be brilliant intellectually, but they may not be able to make decisions in a timely way. A combination of talents is required to succeed in a corporation, not just one. And each corporate culture is different. You need to know who you are and for whom you are working."

Eventually the operators realized she was willing to work hard not only on her behalf but on theirs as well. She was a leader who could be part of the team.

If you are currently working for a corporation, have you had a chance to move consistently throughout the company, increasing your skills and enhancing your reputation as a person who can deliver? A person who can make a difference to the bottom line?

MOVING THROUGH THE CORPORATION

Judy Haberkorn's success attracted the attention of senior-level executives and a decision was made to test her again. When she left the largely female-oriented operator services department, she was promoted to the plant to oversee the heavy-duty outside work. This meant she would be managing the men who climb the telephone poles. Again, she faced a chorus of doubt. "Everybody said, 'She's not technical. She's not even an engineer. How will she manage this? These guys are so tough,' " remembers Haberkorn. In addition to the lack of a vote of confidence, there was a more vocal group of men who thought they should have been promoted to the job. It was soon clear that the men did not want a woman in the department.

"I would go home and for weeks have no dial tone because in the parlance of the business, it was 'pull the coils' on me," said Haberkorn. "But in the space of a month those tricks stopped and they began producing results for me better than that operation had ever produced. It just took time for them to understand that they weren't going to scare me away. I was not there to fluff my petticoats. I was there for the duration."

In that situation, Haberkorn believes that she needed guts to stick it out, but she also needed the skills to be an effective manager. Lacking one or the other she never could have stayed. "It was a rough month," she admits. "But within that time it was clear that the only person or persons who would be leaving, would be those who could not work with me. Once that was established, my dial tone returned," she laughs.

Have you been faced with a situation recently that required "guts and skill"? How did you handle it?

WINNING RESPECT

The tests Haberkorn passed proved to NYNEX that this young woman was a winner and one they wanted to encourage. In order to enhance her ability to manage and lead and eventually impact the corporate bottom line, it was necessary for her to understand every aspect of the company and the industry.

Her move up the ladder included the following various assignments:

Real Estate Operations, New England Telephone

Operator Services, New England Telephone

General Manager, Special Services New England Telephone

General Manager, Access Markets, Marketing and Technology,

Vice President, Materials Management for Telesector Resources Group. This position required her to oversee the centralized purchasing and logistics for two telephone companies, New England Telephone and New York Telephone.

In 1992, she was promoted to Vice President for Marketing and Sales, New York Telephone

In January 1994 to Vice President, Consumer Markets, NYNEX Telecommunications Group.

As we view Judy Haberkorn's various seats around leadership tables within NYNEX, it is clear, that as she mastered one management or leadership challenge after another, her skills were recognized. Throughout her 26-year career, she received tangible and intangible signs that she had a future with NYNEX. Women, who have achieved within the corporation, advise that it is important to be realistic about your chances achieving a seat at the table.

It is critical to develop goals and milestones for yourself, to have a vision of your own future and to "cut the cord" if your vision has little chance of realization.

Are you receiving tangible and intangible signs that you are moving toward your seat at the table within the corporation? If not, what is blocking your rise? A vision of your future without action, is a vision that will never be realized. What can you do to get your career on the seat at the table track?

"I think what takes you into the leadership realm are first, being extremely focused and being very decisive," says Andria Jung, president of marketing at Avon Products. "And I have felt all along that those two things have probably made my career propel at a speed faster than others, perhaps, just because I've been very committed to being very focused with every group of people I've led. Every single one of them, hopefully, can spell out the same direction or understand where the train is going. And also being able to make decisions in a timely manner. That is another thing that can really hold management back. Speed is of the essence today. Speed in everything, but speed in decision-making most of all."

Jung adds, "And the other thing is, it's not a skill and it's not a talent, but it's a passion for the business. I think that been the differentiator. I think I've always had a tremendous amount of passion for the vision of the business. And that unless you can take that passion and have it become infectious to your organization, you don't become a leader; you're still a manager."

Judy Haberkorn, who is described by men and women who work with her as fair and straightforward, is an example of a woman who has "made it in the corporation." In the last 20 years, she has seen a big change in the corporate arena. "It is so gratifying," she says, "because finally, women are getting promoted now. Not because someone says, 'We need a woman,' but because at the middle-management levels our competence is so clear. The vast majority of women in the corporation are doing an excellent job."

Patricia Higgins, group vice president of NYNEX, agrees. "Judy and I connected well in a partnership when I was at AT&T. At that time there were very few women at senior levels and it was perceived as unusual that two top women were working, partnering and teaming together so well and bringing results doing it. Eventually we both wound up in the same Harvard Advanced Management Program. Out of 160 people in the class, there were only six women. When NYNEX was looking for someone to help them frame strategies in the market, run the business unit and have P and L responsibility, Judy recommended me for the job. She knew from our working relationship that I could develop strategies to deal with the new group of competitors coming into the market in various forms. That I could anticipate new competitors and the new alliances that they might develop. She knew that I had a track record of looking very carefully at the factors impacting our ability to retain or grow market share."

Higgins, who worked for AT&T for 16 years before joining NYNEX, adapted well to the corporate culture, where if you performed well and demonstrated leadership capabilities in a fairly short time, you were guaranteed promotions.

If you didn't achieve the goals, you did not remain in the company. Higgins, who was a high school teacher, never talked much with her corporate peers about her teaching experience. She felt it had no significance in the business world. Lately, however she has realized how teaching enabled her to be successful from the standpoint of communications, organizing planning, and selling. "Once you understand the corporate culture, you can develop the skills that are rewarded within that culture," says Higgins.

Haberkorn sees more and more women like Higgins moving into positions formerly held by men. "In our company, the logjam is broken," she says. "Women have gotten to levels where the managers that are really capable of judging talent see that talent very plainly. In the past, you had less talented people in the middle ranks suppressing women's rise up the ladder. They had the bright women working like dogs for them and they were taking the credit."

The challenge that is specific to women, she thinks, is a lack of feedback on performance. "It's so important," she says. "I see young men coming through the business, who may give a less-than-successful presentation, taken by the arm in the company or on the golf course by a senior male executive, and in a non-threatening way way, coached about how to make a better presentation next time. It's similar to a father-son coaching and it is a very positive thing.

Women never, ever get that kind of coaching. So those of us who somehow get to the top, have to be sensitive on our own to the clues. We have to seek our own feedback in many different ways. We watch for signs, for body language, a tone of voice, because no one every tells the woman."

"I try to get back to everyone who works for me, or who may give a presentation, or takes a strong position in a meeting, and provide them with feedback," she says. "I say, 'here's what I think was terrific,' 'here's what I think could have been better.'"

She feels it is unfair to save feedback for a performance appraisal when it can affect salary. By the time, the appraisal is scheduled, it is too late to effect positive change. Most of the time, the employee has no idea what the supervisor is referring to. "Feedback works when people are convinced you have their best interests at heart," she says, "and you are not just venting or having a bad day."

If you want a seat at the corporate table, Judy Haberkorn advises:

Find the fun:

It should be fun. Find something you like to do and you'll be successful at it by and large.

Do the work:

It will be hard work.

Read and study and spend a lot of time knowing as much about the subject, the service or the product as you can. Haberkorn reads three newspapers daily, 10 magazines a week.

Build relationships:

That means, customers, suppliers, your subordinates, your peers, those who are higher up in the corporation. Understand that every interaction that you have with a human, is a chance to make a fan or create a foe. People go away from an encounter with you either feeling better or worse about themselves. To the extent that you understand as you're working in business, the possible impact you have on customers, on suppliers, on shareholders, on people who are going to make the corporation run, and if you choose to make that a positive contact, you will be successful.

"What counts in this business as in life, is when your name is mentioned, do people's hands go up or do they look at their shoes?" says Haberkorn. "It is something so simple and so basic, yet I can't tell you how many people I have known in our business who are very driven to get to the top, so much so that their focus is all upward. Those who are already high up the ladder probably think that they are wonderful people, that is they always return a phone call in a snap. But what are they like to work with as peers? I always tell people, you better be as concerned about how you treat your peers and subordinates. You shouldn't treat the guard at the door any differently than you treat the president of the company."

Don't get bogged down in company politics:

"I see a lot of people jockeying for my time and attention. I feel like saying, 'Sit down, be quiet and do something good for the business and your customers. Don't worry about me. I'll like you if you do the right thing.' "

But...be politically astute and aware:

Understand your environment. Understand the culture. Then you can make your choice, and live with your decisions. Haberkorn says she would never advise anyone to try flattery as a way up the ladder nor would she advise against it. Understand what your values are, she counsels, and choose your behavior. Then if you are unsuccessful in the environment, don't blame the environment or the culture or life, but come to terms with the reality that you may have made a wrong choice. You may be in the wrong environment, one in which you are not comfortable. You may belong somewhere else.

Have a life:

Although Haberkorn works very hard at what she does, she believes it is critical to be connected to something or someone outside of your specific industry. She is a member of both The Committee of 200 and The Financial Women's Association of New York. She also serves on an advisory board to The Enterprise Foundation, whose mission is to enable underprivileged men and women to find affordable housing.

As a director on the board of the Stanhome Corporation, she makes recommendations to the company regarding qualified people, who happen to be women, for corporate board appointment. "One of the greatest pleasures of my life was getting one of my Harvard classmates, a woman, on the Stanhome board. It is great to look across the table and see her there." Haberkorn continues to serve as a mentor to women at entry and senior levels and believes we must get rid of the idea that if a woman fails, even if we have recommended her for something, it is somehow a failure for all women. "I am pleased when a recommendation of mine is accepted, but if the person makes a mistake, it is her problem and not mine."

Practice saying, "I am responsible":

"One core thing that is more important for success in business, and I believe in life as well, and happiness, it is the day you look yourself in the mirror and say, "I am responsible." Whether it's your career, your health, your life. It doesn't matter," says Haberkorn, "that things don't happen that are not within the realm of your control. But as a cancer patient, if no other experience ever taught me the extent to which I am responsible, that one did. Nobody is looking out for your health care and making sure that all those pieces fit, you are responsible. The day that you decide that, it can make all the difference in the world. I see people day in and day out blaming everything from the weather to their parents for the results they are getting or not getting in life, in work, in relationships. Claim your successes and claim your failures. And learn from both."

THE CORPORATE ENTREPRENEUR

In order to have the best of both worlds, the structure and resources of the corporation and the freedom to think entrepreneurially, you have to bring a lot to the table. Or, as Beth Bronner demonstrates, the willingness to demonstrate "out of the box" thinking. Prior to accepting her current position with AT&T, Bronner was president of Revlon Professional North America. From Häagen-Dazs to Slim Fast to Revlon, Bronner was an innovator, reading the market and market needs correctly.

At Slim Fast, she launched a complete line of desserts that were 90 to 99 percent fat free. At Häagen-Dazs she led the team responsible for the introduction of the Häagen-Dazs Ice Cream Bar. Following that in less than three years, she was instrumental in the development of five new product lines, which today account for over 50 percent of the Häagen-Dazs business. She acquired a reputation as a turnaround virtuoso when she led the company to new levels of profitability.

PROFITABLITY = PORTABILITY

Beth Bronner, vice president and general manager of the consumer communications services group at AT&T, believes her corporate success is based on the ability to anticipate and satisfy the needs of the customer. Until just a few months ago, Bronner was responsible for total operations and profit of all aspects of Revlon Professional North America, a $150 million dollar business. She managed a staff of over 500 and was responsible for two manufacturing and three distribution locations.

Bronner did not have a clear career goal when she graduated from Vassar in three years in order to get married. "My husband was in law school in Chicago and I didn't really want to go to work so I went for my M.B.A. at the University of Chicago Business School."

Unlike many girls her age in junior high school, Bronner loved hearing the stories of the robber barons and the captains of industry. "I knew I was never going to be a teacher or a social worker. However, my degree from Vassar was in urban studies. I was very naive. I thought I was going to build model cities and save the world," she laughs. "That's why when I interview young men and women for jobs now. I am so impressed at how self-directed and goal-oriented they are. When I was 20, all I really knew was I wanted to wear a pair of jeans and long hair and dangling earrings and make sure that everybody voted for McGovern."

Bronner finished her M.B.A. in marketing and finance. She admits she had no specific goal other than she thought she might be good at marketing. Her first interview was a disaster. "They told me they couldn't possible hire me because in six months I would walk in and tell them I was with child. I didn't even know what that meant."

Eventually she received two offers. One was from Quaker Oats in product management. Bronner took that job because it paid $3,000 more than her offer from an advertising company. "In retrospect, Quaker was a very good experience. I'd had a protected background and had never really worked. I learned a lot but it was a very tough year."

Quaker started Bronner with other new M.B.A.'s in the pet food division. She was the only woman among a group of new marketing assistants and had no idea about corporate structure, corporate politics or an understanding of the hierarchy.

MAKE YOUR MOVE FOR THE RIGHT REASONS

In 18 months she left Quaker and went to Standard Brands. Her salary was not as good but the title was better. She was now assistant product manager and that was very important to her. Bronner had learned about titles in the corporation.

In 10 years she moved through the ranks at Standard Brands, which later became Nabisco and then RJR Nabisco. Bronner believes that because she was a woman, she was given a certain leeway, not expected to fully understand the corporate structure, in fact not expected to fit the corporate mold. "It was great for me," says Bronner. "It allowed me to balance the kind of classical skills everyone had with a little bit of flair and an entrepreneurial spirit."

During her stint at Nabisco, she held almost every marketing title available until she was promoted to department head. Although Bronner had survived Standard Brands transformation into Nabisco and RJR, she was ready for a change. Again, she made a move for less money in exchange for a chance to move up with what she believed was an exciting energy-packed job. She joined Häagen-Dazs, a subsidiary of Pillsbury, as a director and within six months was vice president of marketing for the entire company. Within five years she was senior vice president and general manager of the entire Häagen-Dazs shop division.

Beth Bronner's initial meeting with the president of the company did not go well. When she called her father to cry on his shoulder he told her, "Well, you don't have to take that. Just go in and tell them exactly what you think."

And that's what she did. It was a turning point in her career. The president became her number one mentor. Bronner believes that men, who are fathers to daughters, are great bosses. Others at Häagen-Dazs became her mentors as well. "I really found that I am most successful working as a member of a team and I realized that I could accept the support of friends in business."

While at Häagen-Dazs, she increased volume by 8 percent per outlet, as well as system profitability by over 100 percent. She created a second brand strategy to leverage store delivery system to enhance the company's position in the total ice cream market. Record market share was the result of Bronner's marketing efforts for Häagen-Dazs.

Go for What You Want and Go When You Don't Get It

Bronner's performance for the company was measurable in dollars and cents terms. She turned around Häagen-Dazs within an 18-month period, and put together a plan to eliminate the division as a separate entity and integrate it into the rest of the company. In the process, she eliminated her own job. Bronner wanted the position of head of North America for Häagen-Dazs, but it was made clear to her, despite her great successes, that she wasn't going to get it. She resigned and accepted another job. Häagen-Dazs then offered her the job she wanted. Bronner told them she needed a week to think about the new offer. "In hindsight, I may have cut off my nose to spite my face but I told them, 'Listen, if it was to be, you would have offered me this job before I resigned. I've made a commitment. I've accepted another offer. Let's get on with our lives.'"

Hurt and disappointed, although she wanted the Häagen-Dazs job, she wanted to keep her self-respect even more. She took a job with Slim Fast as president of a division and built the division for them. But she didn't feel as if this was going to be a good fit, a long-term relationship.

"Then, Jerry Levin, one of my mentors, who had been chairman of Häagen-Dazs became CEO of Revlon." Beth Bronner started at Revlon as a senior vice president and very quickly became executive vice president, and then president of a division.

Recently, she resigned to become vice president and general manger at AT&T in the Consumer Communications Services Group. Again, Bronner's track record — entrrepreneurial energy, which translates into bottom-line dollars for the corporation combined with her corporate marketing background make her an ideal candidate for senior-level corporate positions. Her move from a $1.4 billion company to a $75 billion company is a big one. She will be running a $4.5 billion business within AT&T. Why did she make this move?

VALUES AND SATISFACTION

"At the end of the day," says Bronner, "when all is said and done, if you're really true to yourself and you know who you are, that's when the satisfaction comes. It took me 20 years to figure that out. Money's important but you get to the point where you ask yourself, 'Are people going to be working with me as a team? Am I going to like them? Will we respect each other?' If the answer is 'yes' then you have something."

TIPS AND TACTICS

- ❖ Get work experience before you go for higher-education credentials such as an M.B.A.
- ❖ Be focused, keep your eye on your goals but don't lose your flexibility.
- ❖ Be willing to take chances or as Bronner says, "Get out of the box."
- ❖ Be willing to move from industry to industry.
- ❖ Have a strategy but be willing to move on faith and trust.
- ❖ Enjoy the trip!

TIME AND MORE TIME

If there is a common denominator among senior-level women in the corporation, it is the time they commit to the job. Similar to women entrepreneurs, corporate women at the top, in seat at the table positions are not 9 to 5'ers.

Dinah Lin Cheng, vice president of worldwide development at Burger King says, "I put in 11-12 hours every day, five days a week. On top of that, I spend 5 to 6 hours over the weekend with the reading file I bring from the office."

Part of the reason Cheng does this is habit. She believes as does Haberkorn, that there is no substitute for hard and smart work. "I really do believe that if you are going to have a seat at the table you must put in the hours. There is no shortcut. Most of us have learned our business lessons the hard way, trying to understand the corporate environment or maze, the corporate structure, what corporate politics are all about. If you are adaptable and flexible, have a great deal of determination to succeed you will, but there is no getting around it, you will work hard."

A key trait that Dinah Lin Cheng believes is critical to corporate success is perseverance. "But perseverance with a twist. You must persevere but you must be flexible, so if something doesn't work, you can change your method or approach." Cheng believed she could enhance her success-rate by returning to school and adding an M.B.A. in finance and business economics. She believes you should never stop making deposits to your talent bank. "Keep it growing," she advises, "whether through a degree program or courses specific to your industry or public speaking seminars. Keep improving."

TABLES: CORPORATE, GOVERNMENT, CORPORATE

Unlike Judy Haberkorn, who has moved up the ladder in NYNEX over a period of time, Dinah Lin Cheng has moved up by leaving and learning and starting in new companies and industries over the same period of time. There is not one way to tackle corporate success. The important fact is to understand what your comfort level is, to research what is available and how high you can rise and to be willing to take risks within and without in order to achieve your vision for your own career.

Do you like change? Can your current job or position offer steady challenges? Can you accomplish what you want and need within your current environment or is it time to consider something different?

Haberkorn satisfies her entrepreneurial bent and need for challenge and risk-taking by taking on different assignments and titles within NYNEX. The corporation is large enough to afford Haberkorn a wealth of experience without getting bored. Her career continues to be a constant learning process at higher and higher levels of difficulty.

Dinah Lin Cheng has taken another route to climb the corporate ladder. Cheng, who is Asian-American, started in banking in Hong Kong but returned to the United States in 1980 to get her M.B.A. She surveyed various industries and decided that the banking and consulting field were suffering from a glut of M.B.A.'s and didn't need another one. Instead, after researching various companies, she decided she could make her mark in nuts-and-bolts manufacturing, the hard and heavy industries. These were not industries typically targeted by women and Cheng believed this improved her chances. The company that seemed most favorable to her goals and vision was Union Carbide.

THERE'S A COMPANY THAT NEEDS ME!

"I was very interested in strategic planning but there was just one thing wrong with my interest, typically corporations do not hire new M.B.A.'s to come in and develop a strategic plan for the company. You have to have been a part of the team for almost 10 years. So, I kept persevering, but I changed my tactics and joined the company investor relations department." During this time, Cheng volunteered to help with strategic planning projects and was doing two jobs for three months. At the end of three months, she was offered a strategic planning position at Union Carbide. With corporate experience under her belt, she began to look at small companies where she could quickly gain experience in line management.

TAKING ONE STEP BACKWARDS TO GET TO THE TOP

"I took a step backwards in terms of my title," says Cheng, "but I wanted to have a hands-on marketing experience, which I got. From there I went to another high-tech start-up company in Chicago, a subsidiary of JC Penney, where I became the Director of International Development."

Cheng's table-hopping plan was missing one element, a stint in government. "I always wanted to dedicate a few years out of my career to serve in government and I was gratified to receive an appointment as a senior political appointee with the Bush Administration."

The government position, which included high visibility, brought her to the attention of Burger King.

"I have a variety of background in terms of industry," says Dinah Lin Cheng, "and in terms of functional responsibilities and it's the way I wanted it to be because to me it's more exciting than staying in one place for the rest of your life. My favorite job is one that I've never done before and that no one's ever done. I get to go in and be able to create it. Burger King is involved in 53 countries around the world." Cheng admits that she doesn't have a preconceived approach to deal with Burger King operations in each country. "I will go wherever in the world the company wants me to go. My focus is on major new market entries and expansion of business in present markets."

Doing business in many countries means being aware of cultural differences and how they impact business relationships. Cheng's biggest challenge so far has been dealing with a sensitive situation in South Korea. According to a survey of 300 executives, South Korea is known to be the most difficult country in Asia. Cheng had to steer the project through legal issues, and then became involved in putting together the structure and framework and budget for a pilot entry into Japan at the same time. She is also focused on China and feels good about the progress she has made so far raising the awareness and appreciation within the company that China is a priority for Burger King.

Cheng believes her ethnicity is an asset and not a liability. She was born in Shanghai and speaks Mandarin and Cantonese. "My background is a help because it gives me a cultural sensitivity. I have a certain instinct for the correct approach and how to do business in China. It is something that someone else, man or woman, who hasn't been to Asia and doesn't speak the language would need to develop."

"I believe the most important quality you can bring to the decision-making table is the ability to get things done. In order to get things done, you have to rely on a great many people. In government, I could issue a policy decision, but if I didn't have the backing of the civil servants and the bureaucrats, my policy decision would not be worth very much. In order to get things done effectively, you must have a vision and be able to communicate that vision to others. If you can't communicate your vision in a few simple sentences, it may not be an achievable goal."

Cheng's self-confidence, combined with education and a proclivity for risk-taking are all part of her corporate style. Although she describes herself as "flexible," she believes everyone has a fundamental style and it can be extremely difficult if not impossible to change it. That is why it is important to pick an environment that will match with your fundamental nature. "I tend to be outspoken," says Cheng. "So, I've learned to be a little more tactful, and to try to say things differently, but my basic style is to put things on the table. I would rather not spend time second guessing someone and having them try to second guess me. So, I express myself as clearly as possible. I have not changed dramatically, but I have made small shifts when I've needed to."

Whether it is in the corporation or a senior-level government position, Dinah Lin Cheng believes it is important to stay focused, to step back and take a look at all the things on your plate and ask: "Which ones are going to be helpful to me and my goals? Whether for this year, or for this company, or as part of my 3 or 5 year long-term goal?"

REFLECTION

You can't step back while you are on the track. In order to review where you are and where you want to be you have to take time to get away from the daily business at hand. The hardest thing, admits Cheng, is to carve out that hour that you spend on your goals and desires. The best time for her is on the way back from a trip. After the trip goals have been met or attended to, Cheng reviews her own goals, her own performance. "I have plenty of time on a 19-hour plane trip from Asia," she says.

POSITIVE BELIEF SYSTEM

Cheng, like Haberkorn, believes in embracing responsibility. She rates "positive belief system" as the most critical quality of success. "My overarching belief is truly that the glass is half full, not half empty. It's up to you how you choose to view a situation. This is a fundamental belief, which anyone can choose to embrace."

HAVING IT ALL

"What a terrible concept," says Dinah Lin Cheng. "What does it mean anyway? If you are doing what you absolutely love doing more than anything else in the world, that can be 'all.' Everyone's 'all' is different. Are you loving 'it?' Are you happy?"

If your goal is a seat at the table, you can achieve it. You will also be making certain choices that have to do with how you are going to be spending your time. There is no way you can be successful and not devote a huge amount of time to the effort. Time is finite. It doesn't take much to figure out that you can't have a seat at the table at the same exact time you are choosing to become a hermit. Somewhere between those two extremes, you can sample quite a lot.

THE BIG CAREER CHANGE

Elynor Williams, vice president of public responsibility at the Sara Lee Corporation, made a career change from education to communications in the private sector, from a not-for-profit organization to a corporation, without having a clear idea of what she wanted to do. But she was confident that whatever it was, she could do it. In her fifth year in the workplace, after considering various career changes including that of fashion designer or buyer for a department store, she decided, "I want to stay in communications."

Williams, who is 47, believes there are many women, especially minority women like herself, started out in teaching as a profession. "We found ourselves in a position with very few options. If you wanted to be respected in the community, the choices were either teaching or nursing. We had no female role models who were doctors. Part of me rebelled against this predetermined choice because all the people in my family are teachers or in education in some way."

Williams' mother, who was an elementary school teacher, had placed her in day care in the neighborhood. Williams spent a happy day playing in the mud until she returned home. Her mother took her out of day care and began taking her to work with her. She then spent her days at the age of three in her mother's first grade class. She learned enough early on to qualify for college at age 15. Following college, she had to wait until she became 19 to get a teaching job.

"I was teaching at an inner-city junior high school and we went on strike for better books and better equipment for the children. Following the strike, the teachers were penalized and in a way so were the children. A woman who was a mentor to me at the school said, 'You need to consider doing some other things.' "

CAN YOU SUCCEED WHERE YOU ARE?

Williams realized that if she stayed in her current environment she would become discouraged and even more angry. She assessed her situation and decided to leave education. Her next career move was a job with General Foods where she started out as the food editor. "I did recipes and minor copy for the packages. Eventually I moved to product publicity which involved more writing. A woman at General Foods, who had her Ph.D. from Cornell, suggested that I had enough potential to be doing a lot more. She believed that education would help me break through the barriers impacting women and minorities."

WHAT DO YOU NEED TO DO TO QUALIFY FOR A SEAT AT THE TABLE?

Elynor Williams applied to Cornell and was accepted and given a scholarship. General Foods gave her leave to go to school. In fact, General Foods offered to pay her salary while she attended Cornell full-time. Williams decided not to accept the offer. "Perhaps it was stupidity," she says, "but I felt it was the only honest thing to do. I wanted to be free to choose where I would go after I received my degree. If I accepted their offer, I would be obligated to return. At that point I didn't really know what I wanted to do in the future."

Williams vision for her future was so strong that it sustained her through the months of poverty, living over a garage, going to school, relying on family and friends for food. "The difference, between me and those men and women who are surrounded by poverty for a lifetime, is that I saw the light at the end of the tunnel. I knew I was going to move on. At that time I couldn't buy shoes and if

I couldn't pick berries from the bush next to the garage, I didn't eat. I shoveled snow in the winter time to help pay my rent and kept the vision for my future in front of me through those tough months."

GET OUT AND GET VISIBLE

Williams credits her involvement with the Public Relations Society of America, and the International Association of Business Communicators with providing her with the professional networking and skills improvement she needed. She has a track record of long-term volunteering for the National Women's Political Caucus and the National Council of Negro Women and Women in Communications. She is a founding member of the Spelman College Corporate Women's Roundtable and the Executive Leadership Council, and a member of the board of directors of the National Coalition of 100 Black Women. She is a member of the International Women's Forum. In 1992 she was selected by *Ebony* magazine as one of the Top 50 African-American Executives in Corporate America.

Williams has a history of meeting the right person at the right time. People, who are impressed with her abilities and character, want to help her achieve success. Following graduation she returned to the south and accepted a job as communications specialist for the Agricultural Extension Service at A &T State University. While in North Carolina, Williams joined Leadership Greensboro, a community organization. Through Leadership Greensboro she met an executive who was impressed with her fundraising skills on behalf of the organization. He offered her a job with Western Electric.

"I learned that I had a lot to learn about thriving in a corporation. You must understand the culture before you can begin to see where you fit in. I learned and quickly moved from community relations to public affairs and then to external communications, which included media. I had three different jobs; each year I got a promotion." Williams also had set her sights on the political table and ran for public office for the House of Representatives. She lost by 20 votes. She continued to remain active politically and chaired the National Women's Political Caucus. This involvement provided her with a government relations link for her company.

It also provided her with high visibility and it wasn't long before she was one of the most important women in the three-county area. Sara Lee Corporation, which was then The Hanes Group, hired her as Director of Corporate Affairs. Her first action item as director was to meet with every senior-level person in the corporation and ask the question: "What is my role?"

"What they wanted," says Williams, "was for me to be the media spokesperson. In order for me to do that job effectively I needed to put together a full-fledged department, look at the product mix and focus on women. This was a market-driven company and I had to show how my short-term and long-range plans would positively affect the bottom line."

What is the Corporate Culture? Do you fit in? Can you make a difference?

Williams was soon promoted to the corporate office in Chicago and named Director of Corporate Affairs. She is one of the main reasons that Sara Lee focused on women. As a corporate officer and vice president of the corporation one of her first tasks, in 1990, was to create the Public Responsibility Department with a long-range plan and an annual operating budget.

"I am very excited about what I do. In a $15 billion company, this is no small department. I find my job stimulating. Our mission is to manage, interpret and define public expectations and perception and then provide strategic planning for the corporation to respond and to be accountable for our major constituency. We truly are a catalyst and a resource."

Williams has a seat at the foundation board table and is executive secretary and staff liaison of the Board Committee of Employee and Public Responsibility. She also works on the Diversity Task Force. (Under her leadership, there is a focus on human resources.) Sara Lee is the largest American corporate employer back in South Africa with 4,700 employees. Sara Lee is active in supporting South Africa's emerging democracy and a new day of how employee/employer relations can be conducted.

Williams' top list of winning qualities include:

Sincerity

Belief in what I am doing

Ability to work with people

Ability to listen

Ability to lead

Compassion

Positive belief system

Ability to learn from failure

A strong sense of who I am

Ability to differentiate between good and bad criticism

Ability to be flexible

Williams calls this her "survival skills" package. She also recognized that she would have to learn to project her voice and be more succinct in her verbal communication. "I came from a family of soft-spoken females and lesson number one was realizing that not everyone was going to love me as my family did, or listen to me. Many of my challenges were connected with gender and race. It was critical for me to improve my skills, but just as important for me to develop a support system externally and internally. This system would keep me from folding when I faced certain barriers or challenges or 'glass ceilings.'"

Williams achieved several seats at various tables within the corporation, women's organizations, community and professional organizations. All of these entities provided not only outreach to information and knowledge, but also an opportunity to interact with various publics. Her network and high visibility networking has enabled her to bring something of value to the leadership table.

One of the clearest examples concerns minority advertising. When Williams assessed Sara Lee's advertising, she realized they were missing a comprehensive way to reach minorities. She organized a task force of the vice presidents of marketing in all the personal products groups, including Hanes, L'Eggs and non-food entities. When they looked at the demographics, it was clear that they were missing one billion dollars just in the Hispanic and African-American communities alone.

Williams knew that the campaign could not be driven by the task force, so she talked to the president of the company and suggested that the new outreach needed a real focus. This was the genesis of the ethnic marketing initiative.

Elynor Williams has made a difference at Sara Lee and through the Frontrunner Awards program, she has made a difference in the lives of many women and organizations that help women. Sara Lee provides a $25,000 grant to four women annually, who have made a difference in business, arts, government and the humanities. It is now considered one of the most premier awards for women in the country. Williams also works with over 200 organizations and individuals providing funding and other resources.

THE VISION

Williams, who has been called one of "Chicago's most powerful women," says, "I think our challenge is to get the best and the brightest for business within the next generation. One way to do this is to look at public responsibility issues, including diversity and try and create an environment within which everyone can do well."

WHAT ARE THE BENEFITS OF WORKING WITHIN A CORPORATION?

NYNEX is a $27 billion corporation. Burger King is a $6.7 billion dollar corporation. Sara Lee Corporation is a global packaged food and consumer products company with annual sales of $15.5 billion. Avon Products is a $4 billion corporation.

Resources. In terms of budget and access to the departments and materials, you need to make things happen. Even in this era of downsizing, you will have people, vendors, contacts, who are eager to help you, because you are connected to a top corporation.

Access. Doors open more readily for the corporate executive than they do for the start-up entrepreneur. You will have immediate access to nonprofit organizations dealing with those issues of interest to you. Your involvement can be at the leadership level if you choose, backed up by a commitment to deliver corporate funds or in-kind gifts.

Security. Although a corporate career may not be as secure as it once was, it is still a place where benefits and salary and perquisites and title are just the beginning of an executive package that you can negotiate.

Stimulation. You will be surrounded by bright and ambitious people, who can provide the excitement and energy, you need to be inspired.

Experience. After your stint with the corporation at a leadership level, you will now be positioned to consider where you next want to take your expertise and experience. Your contacts and network formed, while working for the corporation, can provide you with a base for the future.

A seat at the corporate table is not for everyone. Understand who you are, what you are willing to commit and where you want to make this commitment. Women who have achieved in corporate America are this country's best and brightest. They are a resource for our future and deserve the titles, the money and the perquisites. They are 100 percent committed and they have changed the face of business and industry. They are also potential entrepreneurs. Their impact cannot be minimized.

Do you want to be one of them?

7

TARGET TABLE: THE CORPORATE BOARD

"It's totally different now. Companies are very wary of having an uninformed board. The boys' club has broken up. There's too much risk."
BEVERLY SILLS GREENOUGH, DIRECTOR OF AMERICAN EXPRESS, TIME WARNER. (*WHO'S IN CHARGE? CEO'S AND BOARDS SHUFFLE POWER* BY RICHARD M. CLURMAN)

"Henry Ford II at first screamed and hollered like a banshee. He wasn't about to have a woman on the board. It'll spoil the club. But he changed his mind and finally invited me on."
MARIAN HEISKELL, DIRECTOR OF MERCK, FORD, CON-SOLIDATED EDISON. (*WHO'S IN CHARGE? CEO'S AND BOARDS SHUFFLE POWER* BY RICHARD M. CLURMAN)

The days of banshee screaming are over and for all the right reasons. Corporate America needs more qualified people to serve on corporate boards. Beyond the requisite impressive resumes, companies are looking for directors who are connected to community, customers and the marketplace. Leadership in this country's most successful corporations has acknowledged that in order to compete effectively in this changing marketplace, nationwide and worldwide, more tuned-in and independent talent must be seated around the corporate board table.

So, if your goal is a seat at the directors' table, you could not have picked a better time. Since 1992, half of the top 500 companies have had at least one woman director in 1993 and 76 percent of the leading 500 companies have one or more women on the board. In 1995, the National Women's Economic Alliance Foundation's publication, *Women Directors of the Top 1,000 Corporations*, reported that of the top 1,000 corporations, 825 director seats are held by women, compared to 357 seats in 1985.

Of the top service and manufacturing companies, the industries with the highest concentrations of women serving on their boards are:

90 percent of the top 50 largest manufacturing companies.

88 percent of the top 50 largest utilities companies.

74 percent of the top 50 largest commercial banking firms.

62 percent of the top 50 largest retail companies.

50 percent of the top 50 largest financial companies.

48 percent of the top 50 largest life insurance companies.

The important thing to remember about these statistics is not that the glass is half-full or half-empty but that companies are viewing the glass in a new way.

The search is on for truly qualified people to serve as outside directors and increasingly those qualified people are women.

Can we say this too much? I don't think so. Women really need to begin to read their collective press releases.

If you were running a company in today's marketplace and you heard that a specific group of people were achieving in the workplace at higher and higher levels of responsibility as chief executive officer's of their own companies, and as political, business, community, academic and government leaders, wouldn't you want this talent around your table?

Smart chief executive officers and nominating committees understand that women have taken a different road to get to the top, and because of this different road, may be better positioned to deal with a changing marketplace of diverse customers and customs.

Women have been in the workplace at executive levels for a relatively short time. The gains we have made have been based on our ability and willingness to learn what we didn't know in order to succeed. In the process, as a group, we built a reputation of which, collectively, we can all be proud.

The momentum may be proceeding at snail's pace but it is going in the right direction. When Regina Herzlinger, a professor of business administration at the Harvard Business School, started teaching at Harvard in 1972, women comprised two percent of the M.B.A. class. Four years later, 15 percent of Harvard M.B.A. degrees went to women. By 2000, predicts Herzlinger, female chief executive officers of Fortune 1000 corporations will be commonplace.

In 1980, 35 percent of the female officers in Fortune 500 and service 500 companies held the title of vice president or higher compared with 83 percent today. In 1975, women received 11.7 percent of M.B.A. degrees granted, today they receive 33 percent of all M.B.A. degrees.

Frances Hesselbein, president and CEO of The Peter F. Drucker Foundation and former executive director, Girl Scouts USA, says, "Future-focused companies, understanding rapidly changing demographics, appreciate the significance of a healthy representation of women directors on corporate boards today. The year 2000 work-force projections require inclusion now for market and work force share later."

If the corporate board of today and the future is going to be filled with the best and the brightest, the inclusion process must begin now. A group of British corporations including British Airways, Cable and Wireless, and Kingfisher, are sponsoring an organization called Prowess to groom potential candidates for corporate boards. The companies designate younger executives with management potential to serve in non-executive positions in other companies or in the public sector. The goal of Prowess is to increase the pool of potential board candidates, while providing critical experience now to young executives, including women and minorities.

Marketplace research in Britain shows there are few women directors although women make more than 90 percent of purchasing decisions. Prowess will also identify leaders in the charity or nonprofit sector for board grooming.

What extra qualities do qualified women bring to the corporate board? According to a recent study by Covenant Investment Management, a Chicago-based management company, it may be an ability to see and identify new opportunities in the marketplace. Covenant monitored 1,000 of the largest companies and assessed their records regarding advancement of women against stock performance. The top 20 percent of these companies performed better than the market by 2.5 percent; the bottom 20 percent, companies that did not have a strong track record promoting women, were outperformed in the market by 8 percent.

William James said that "Genius means little more than the facility of perceiving in an unhabitual way." Women, who historically have not been part of the leadership or status quo, can bring a fresh way of looking at things, of doing things that can enhance what already works or improve what hasn't worked in a long time. The ability to perceive in an "unhabitual way" can be a valuable asset to any corporate board.

Other key qualities nominating committees look for in a director include integrity, honesty and reputation. Bill Alley, president of American Brands, puts these three qualities at the top of his list when looking for a director. He also looks for management acumen, experience, expertise and qualifications in an area such as international business or consumer products. He values independence; strength of character; a decision-maker with mature judgment; a candidate who demonstrates willingness to get the facts and take a position. Independence is valued, but also of value is the ability to be compatible with existing directors, to be able to relate to a board of peers.

While women as a group do not have a lock on integrity as a quality, studies indicate that women are perceived as more ethical and tend to ask more questions of corporate management. Women are also perceived as more connected to community and, therefore, more aware of how a corporation can profitably respond to community and consumer demands.

These qualities alone do not represent a magic management formula, but when they are combined with bottom-line effectiveness that is a dynamic combination that can't be ignored.

ONE SIZE DOES NOT FIT ALL

The one-size-fits-all board of the past — all male and all white — can send an unintentional and negative signal internally to employees. The message: If you don't fit the mold, you need not aspire to decision-making seats around the power table. To employees, this message underscores the true culture of the corporation, no matter what the annual report says about diversity.

Through proxy statements and annual reports, the corporation communicates its policy externally as well. Many women shareholders, asked to vote on board nominations, are returning proxies with notes asking, "Why are there no women on this board?" An all-male board may trouble consumers and investors concerned that the corporation is existing in a different world from that of its customers or market. And that is a disconnect no corporation can afford.

CHANGE CAN BE AN ALLY

The corporate board does not exist in a vacuum, neither does the corporation. In order to thrive, these entities must be prepared to meet the demands and needs of a changing marketplace, educated consumers, concerned community leaders and involved shareholders. There is always opportunity during a period of great change for the man or woman, who can look ahead and see what doors, previously closed, are now open.

Why are there not more women being tapped for directorships?

1. Women, who can qualify, don't understand the process.

2. Chief executive officers, who influence the process, don't reach beyond their traditional sources.

Let's focus on **1.**, and we will be better placed to change **2.**

For 10 years, through the National Women's Economic Alliance, we have worked to help corporations identify qualified people, who happen to be women, for corporate board directorships. The corporations are always very clear about the potential candidate. For example, they might ask for a woman who has experience at the chief executive officer level, or a background in international marketing, or senior-level business experience combined with community outreach at a leadership level.

Recently, I received a call from a company who was very specific: "We want a woman who is a partner in a major law firm and she needs to have Pacific Rim retailing experience."

Or a corporation may need someone who brings an in-depth understanding of a government process, nationally and internationally. Someone like Lynn Martin, former U.S. Secretary of Labor, who understands key employment and glass-ceiling issues facing management today, who is also familiar with regulations impacting specific industries. Board-level perspectives on government are a practical asset in corporate governance. When that perspective can be enhanced with an informed and intuitive imprint, the board benefits.

The increased numbers of successful women business owners, women leaders in science, academe and nonprofit organizations have provided a pool of talent from which qualified candidates for boards can be identified.

In addition to the resume specifics required, every board candidate, male or female, must have a track record of achievement, there are also a list of intangibles, equally important.

Does this sound like you?

Are you an independent thinker?

Do you have a reputation as a team player?

Are the strengths you bring to the board critical to the whole?

Can you get along even when you don't go along?

Do you have a sense of the company and industry issues?

What is your reputation regarding judgment?

Richard Clurman, author of *Who's In Charge*, cites James D. Woods, chairman and chief executive officer of Baker Hughes, as a chief executive officer who has high board expectations. Woods asks that his board rate one another on an annual basis in 15 categories of performance and contribution, on a scale of 1 to 10. If they fall below 7.5 they may not be re-elected to the board. The board also rates Woods.

"Corporate America has more often based board membership on business contacts and social acquaintances with a chief executive officer or other board members," said Woods, "than on a process that objectively attempts to represent the interests of the stockholders."

In an effort to further define the qualities an effective board member should demonstrate, the United Kingdom's Institute of Directors and the Henley Management College in 1994 issued a special report: "Good Practice for Boards of Directors." The report featured a list of 29 qualities nominating committees should consider when reviewing candidates for corporate boards and measuring the effectiveness of current directors.

LEADING QUALITIES

At the top of the list of leading qualities a successful director must demonstrate were integrity, business sense, ability to deal with change, a reputation for judgment, independent thinking, an ability to analyze and solve problems.

But these essential characteristics now will need to fit new molds of corporate governance and this can mean more and better entry opportunity for qualified women board members. One example is the corporate need to respond and relate to new, organized investor groups.

As shareholder dynamics have shifted to institutional investors, the interest and involvement of these groups is recognized by corporate boards.

This is not just one more management fad that will peak and fade away. Institutional investor groups are now getting lists of potential board members from chief executive officers and providing input on the selection process. They are also asking for and getting a significant role regarding consultation on director nominations.

According to the New Foundations Working Group's report, "Improving Communications Between Corporations and Shareholders-Overall Findings and Recommendation," "This process can result in a positive interaction with investors and in valuable suggestions for new board members. Using this process can engender a more responsive relationship between shareholders and board members over the long-term and promote enhanced communication in the future."

Often cited in assessing the current and coming role of boards is America's largest corporation, General Motors. After a high-profile display of board power, General Motors issued a guideline on the role and composition of directors, underscoring that decision-making power would rest with the board and not the chief executive officer.

The guideline affirms that all directors will have "complete access" to the management of General Motors. This frees the board from going through the chief executive officer. Key to the report is the stipulation that the board is responsible for selecting its own members. The General Motors guideline (which has been called a "magna carta for U.S. directors") drastically changes the ground rules and demands accountability both from directors and the chief executive officer. Anne Armstrong, former U.S. ambassador to Great Britain and Ann Dore McLaughlin, former president and chief executive officer of the New American Schools Development Corporation currently serve on the General Motors board.

New Routes Open

What this means to the woman, who is interested in serving on a board, is that now there are many routes of recommendation as opposed to the past, when the chief executive officer in a search for a new board member rarely ventured beyond his closed circle of other chief executive officers.

Change has resulted in two positive aspects for women: Corporate America is slowly realizing that women bring something of value to the table, and the process is becoming more open. At the same time, more is expected from the director, man or woman, who serves on today's board. Directors can no longer enjoy the prestige of serving without concern for responsibility, capability and legalities.

The director of the '90s and beyond must be an independent thinker committed to the company and connected to community. The role of the board has become more important than ever before.

Directors face complex management and financial decisions and challenges such as environmental assurance, industrial crisis prevention and management, industry and corporate restructuring, global competition, social reforms, deregulation, technological shifts and liability issues.

Global economic shiftings have created more opportunity for contribution by women in the private sector. Walter Wriston, former head of Citibank, says, "Those of us who do not fear change and are able to view the entire world as a market for goods, services and ideas, now have as our allies the men and women who know that a global economy is here. Companies who access the talent and business acumen represented by women in the work force will be the winners in this global economy."

A good example of corporate board experience is set by Jean Sisco, a partner of Sisco Associates, a global consulting firm, who serves on the boards of Chesapeake and Potomac Telephone Company; Chiquita Brands International, Inc.; The Growth Fund of Washington, Inc.; K-Tron International, Inc.;

McArthur/Glen Realty Corporation, Neiman Marcus Group, Santa Fe Pacific Corporation, Textron, Inc., and the Washington Mutual Investors Fund, Inc.

Sisco, who first started as a director in the '70s, says, "Today's board must be independent groups, who represent not only the shareholders, but the stakeholders. The stakeholders could be the customers, the employees or the community in which the company operates. All of these people now have an interest in corporate governance."

Change Provides Opportunity for the Prepared

There is opportunity. Corporations are seeking qualified women for corporate boards. Executive search firms call the Alliance daily for recommendations, and directors, such as Jean Sisco, are actively helping identify qualified candidates. What can you do now to get into the process that puts you at the board table?

Let's assume that you are at a place in your life where you have a strong resume, leadership-level responsibilities in your field and a list of potential endorsers as the result of people having witnessed your effectiveness.

Why do you want to serve?

❑ Board service is senior-level problem solving, dealing with national and international management, trade and competitiveness issues.

❑ Board service offers an opportunity to help steer the corporate ship profitably and safely, benefiting shareholders and consumers.

❑ Board service will put you across the table from your peers in business, industry and government and provide an opportunity to work with the best and the brightest on behalf of a company, its employees and shareholders.

❑ Board service offers prestige and remuneration. Outside directors of top companies average $36,556 in annual compensation, according to a 1994 study by Korn/Ferry International.

❑ Board service provides an opportunity to bring your talents to the table and effect change.

These are a few reasons candidates give for seeking the director's seat. What is missing is your personal involvement. Why do you want to serve on this particular board? Why do you want to be affiliated with a specific corporation? What draws you to the seat at one corporate board table over another?

The other factor to recognize is that the corporate board selection process is not an annointment. Potential candidates need to have a strategy that keeps the objective, getting a seat at the corporate board table, constantly moving forward. Does having a strategy seem contrived? Having a strategy provides you with the focus you need to move forward toward a goal. If you want to be a doctor, you need a strategy for getting into medical school. If you want to start a business, you need a strategy or a business plan to identify how you are going to pull together your resources.

Your strategy will include specific goals and objectives, such as identifying corporations on whose boards you would be proud to serve, understanding the marketplace issues impacting the corporation, learning and preparing as much as you can to qualify as an excellent candidate for a board seat. A strategy is not a campaign. In the words of one woman director, "You can't really seek a board membership. It's more a question of being in the right place at the right time."

Being in the right place at the right time should be part of your strategy.

Jean Sisco emphasizes this point from personal experience. "It is important that you not stand away and wait to be asked. You should be ready. I used to have a old boss who said, 'You know there is a lot of luck out there and there's a lot of ability out there, but unless you're ready at the right time it ain't going to be.' You need to know what you can bring to the board."

Bonnie Guiton Hill was elected to the board of Hershey because she was in the right place at the right time. She accepted an invitation to speak at the annual Directors Choice Awards program, hosted by the National Women's Economic Alliance in Washington, D.C., which honors directors and leading chief executive officers and attracts an audience of over 400 men and women business leaders throughout the country.

Richard Zimmerman, the chief executive officer of Hershey who was attending the event, had an opportunity to hear Guiton Hill's presentation and was impressed. Hershey was looking for a female director with a varied background and Guiton Hill fit the bill. Her resume included private-and public-sector experience at the leadership level and a history of strong community involvement.

During the awards ceremony, Richard Zimmerman not only had an opportunity to listen to Bonnie Guiton Hill, but also read all about her accomplishments and experience in the Alliance program.

Zimmerman said that Hershey's nominating committee was looking for a woman candidate with "personal qualities that are extreme." These qualities included high ethics, integrity, a sense of well-developed values, respect for others and an open mind on policy issues. In addition to these requirements,

Hershey wanted a director who had a track record of demonstrating a broad rather than a narrow view. Someone with the ability to communicate the company's views, to articulate positions and the ability, willingness and inner strength and independence to take on and maintain difficult positions.

"A professional sense is very important," says Zimmerman, "combined with an understanding of business problems and the challenges a corporation faces. We value the ability of the director to challenge conventional thinking from a business point of view."

For Hershey, it was important that the candidate have in-depth consumer affairs experience coupled with an accounting background. Experience in the human resources field was deemed important, as was government experience.

The consensus among the chief executive officers we surveyed indicates that they are not necessarily looking for Ph.D.'s; however, academic achievement is valued. Equally important is the candidate's ability to articulate and create a vision for the company. Zimmerman asks the potential board member, "Can you describe your vision in terms of geography, in terms of people, in terms of product? What market niches do you plan to fill in 10 years, 15 years, 20 years?"

For Bonnie Guiton Hill, the right kind of visibility led her to the Hershey board. For Jean Sisco, it was community work that led her to her first corporate board appointment. This is a route common to many women who serve as directors.

A recent Alliance survey found that more than 90 percent of women, who currently serve in a director capacity, believe that their involvement at a leadership level on one or more nonprofit boards was directly responsible for their appointment to the corporate board.

Barbara Grogan, president and CEO of Western Industrial Contractors, Inc., serves on the boards of Deluxe Corporation and the Federal Reserve Bank of Kansas-Denver branch. She says, "The most instrumental factor without a doubt in my appointments was 'being out there', knowing the players and having them know me. When a board opening came up, I am certain they decided they should be looking for a woman. Two of the directors knew me, one through the U.S. Chamber and one through the Federal Reserve."

THE VOLUNTEER ROUTE

Grogan underscores that the volunteer/community route can get you in front of decision-makers. "Be the best person you can be. Excel at what you do and give back to the community. Be involved. Follow your passions and lead, lead, lead."

"My first three boards were due to the fact that I was only either on United Way or the National Conference of Christians and Jews or had done some things where people could see that I could conduct meetings," says Jean Sisco. "And that I knew something about financials, that I was a person that had some sense of consensus building, and that I could work well with others on a board, whether corporate or nonprofit."

In addition to her corporate board service, Sisco serves as chairman of the board of the National Association of Corporate Directors and as vice president for Global Affairs of the International Women's Forum. She has a national and international network based on friendship, good will and excellence. It is not surprising that she is in demand as a director. Whether on corporate or nonprofit boards, she brings the same high-level of excellence to every commitment.

The volunteer route led to two board positions for Rae Forker Evans, vice president of national affairs for Hallmark Cards. "Brinker International had been looking for a woman director for a number of years and I had been involved in the Komen Foundation 'Race For The Cure,' an event for breast cancer awareness." Norm Brinker, president and CEO of Brinker International, had a chance to observe Evans in action as she organized the Washington, D.C., race involving leaders from the Congress and the Administration. Further, Evans' public policy background and her credentials in Washington dealing with legislators was of value to Brinker in his roll as a restaurant and business owner.

Evans met Brinker through his wife, Nancy Brinker, founder of the Susan G. Komen Foundation, which sponsors "Race For The Cure." Evans and Norm Brinker had a chance to discuss many small-business issues, such as minimum wage, health care and tax policy. According to Evans, "There were a lot of synergies between the legislative issues they were facing at Brinker and the issues we are concerned about at Hallmark."

YOU'RE ALWAYS BEING INTERVIEWED

Whether Evans knew it or not, her dialogue with Brinker constituted an "interview" process, just as important as formal interviews conducted in the corporate offices. Informal interviews, where information and business and political views are shared, weigh heavily in corporate executives' decisions regarding board selection.

Chief executive officers will list the qualities they are looking for in a director but it is impossible to list the intangibles, talent plus experience, plus personal values. Talent and experience show up on resumes but personal values and traits (which will show through at the board table) are not so readily ascertained. Personal interaction, exchange of views through dialogue between the candidate and the corporate leaders, can make the difference.

Do you think she will be a good director? Will she be a productive and collegial member of the team while still maintaining her own independence? Who is she? What is her philosophy? What does she value? It is often far easier to ascertain the answers to these questions in a relaxed social setting as opposed to the formal interview. So be aware, you are always being interviewed.

Evans performance on the Brinker board won her high marks and this led to a seat on the Haggar Apparel board.

Nancy Brinker was not thinking of corporate boards when she founded the Susan G. Komen Breast Cancer Foundation to raise awareness about breast cancer and the need for early detection. She tragically lost her sister to breast cancer and continued her work following her own bout with breast cancer reaching out not only to women vulnerable to the disease, but to families, decision-makers, members of Congress and the President. The Komen Foundation is the country's largest breast cancer organization, having raised more than $24 million. Through her efforts and outreach she has saved thousands of lives. In the process, she has learned a great deal about breast cancer, medicine and health care. Her outreach, visibility, and growing expertise made her a valuable candidate for the Caremark International board.

GET OUT OF YOUR COMFORT CIRCLE AND GET VISIBLE

In order to get the recognition you need, it is sometimes necessary to pop out of your comfort zone of friends, co-workers and begin to demonstrate your talents and expertise on behalf of something new such as a nonprofit program, a political campaign, a community initiative. Evans, who on a daily basis, interacts with political leaders on behalf of her company, utilized her impressive organizational skills on behalf of a national volunteer efforts for the prevention of breast cancer. Her achievements were noticed not only by the leadership in her own corporation, but across the board with chief executive officers who were involved in sponsoring the "Race For The Cure."

Perhaps it is time for you to consider another table of interest outside of your day-to-day current commitments. You can only win. You will come away from the experience with new insights, new contacts and the satisfaction of having contributed your talents and expertise for a good cause. In the process, your horizons will be broadened as well.

STRATEGY CHECK LIST

The following questions are starters to help you develop a strategy that makes sense for your goals. If you apply these steps to a personal strategy, you will have a better understanding not only of the corporate board process but also of the corporations on whose boards you wish to serve.

ACTION STEP:

1. I have identified the corporation on whose board I want to serve. I have identified industry groups where I can make a contribution.

This may seem to be an obvious and easy "yes" but many women who do want to serve as a director have not identified a specific company or industry group.

YES _____ NO _____

2. I have a clear idea of why I want to serve as a director.

YES _____ NO _____

Please write out your statement:

_____

_____

_____

_____

Sample reasons: You have expertise in the field — consumer goods, telecommunications. You admire the chief executive officer and the company's performance. You love the product. You understand some of the challenges facing the industry as a whole. You see yourself as part of the team of directors and you know where your area of contribution will be.

3. I know what personal and professional qualities I bring to the table specific to this corporation.

YES _____ NO _____

List them here:

A. _____

B. _____

C. _____

D. _____

E. _____

Jean Sisco explains: "You need to know what you bring to a board and that becomes very important if you can bring organization, if you can bring knowledge of the community. But more than that, they are looking for the person who brings a basic skill and this skill can be one of many disciplines. If you have financial acumen that can be very helpful. If you are a successful entrepreneur, that is of value."

4. I have spent time researching the corporation and the industry and I would be proud to serve.

YES _____ NO _____

If you hate cigarettes, do not seek to go on the board of a cigarette company with an eye on abandoning the product. If you are an activist for a specific political or issue agenda, you should seek another table, other than the board room, to express your views.

"To be a one-issue candidate is totally wrong," says Sisco. "You are not elected to a board to represent only women or to represent minorities. You're elected to the board to represent shareholders and the stakeholders and that is a very broad base."

5. I have sent for an annual report.

YES _____ NO _____

This is an easy first step. You can go to the library and review Standard and Poors, but the annual report will give you a feel for the company. Check the community programs they support, identify key issues relating to the product, in addition to the financials, what kind of a company is it in regard to women at the top of the management ladder?

Read the following example:

Annual report: Toys "R" Us

Board of Directors: 10, 9 men, 1 woman

Among all the 83 directors, officers, general managers of Toys "R" Us and Kids "R" Us, 8 are women

Sales: $8 billion in 1993.

Outreach: National and international and growing

Corporate citizenship: Improving healthcare needs of children; hospital play-room program; leading purchaser of products from minority-owned toy companies; toy safety program; elimination of look-alike toy guns; literacy promotion through Books "R" Us; books to children in homeless shelters.

6. I have identified the current directors and the industries they represent.

YES _____ NO _____

Beyond bemoaning the fact that your target company may not have any or many women or minorities currently serving as directors, you should know what areas of expertise are represented by the current crop. Are they all chief executive officers? What industries do they represent? Is it a well-balanced board or do all the board members bring the same experience, title, areas of expertise to the table? What need could you fill if you were asked to join the group? Which board members are slated to go off the board?

7. I have looked at past proxies, analysts' reports, press clippings.

YES _____ NO _____

Is all this really necessary? Don't search firms and individuals look for you? They do if you have very high visibility or were recently a member of the president's cabinet. But even if this were the case across the board, it takes time to be considered. Why not use this time to take control of the process and learn as much as possible about your chosen companies?

Then, when and if you do get a call for any board, you will have a grounding in the process and the terms and will be that much more comfortable in the interview. You will understand how the company has handled crisis in the past. Is the leadership perceived positively? What do consumers think of the company regarding specific issues: price, environmental issues, value? What questions do you have about the company? Have you done your board membership homework? What directors are up for nomination? Who is going off the board? Who do you know?

PROXY STATEMENT TOYS "R" US

If you look at the proxy statement for Toys "R" Us and review the list of directors you will learn that:

Reuben Mark, chairman and chief executive officer of Colgate-Palmolive, has been a director of Toys "R" Us since 1990 and that he serves as director of Time Warner Inc., the New York Stock Exchange Inc., and Pearson, P.L.C. He is 55.

Shirley Strum Kenney, president of Queens College of the City University of New York, has been a director of Toys "R" Us since 1990. She is 59.

The other nine directors range in age from 46 to 84, they are all male. This board held six meetings during the company's last fiscal year. The board of directors has an executive committee, a nominating committee, an audit committee, a management compensation and stock-option committee and an operating committee.

The executive committee of the board has all the powers and authority of the full board of directors, subject to certain exceptions. The proxy tells us that the executive committee took action twice by unanimous written consent during the company's last fiscal year.

Effective January 1994, the board of directors designated a nominating committee, consisting of three board members, all male. This committee recommends candidates for election to the board. It has the authority to recommend the individuals to be elected as directors to fill any vacancies or additional directorships.

The proxy tells us that the company's by laws provide that nominations for the election of directors may be made by any stockholder in writing, delivered or mailed by first-class mail to the secretary of the company, Toys "R" Us, not less than 14 days nor more than 50 days prior to the annual meeting.

The proxy tells us that directors receive $20,000 per annum for service on the board and an additional $1,000 for attending any meetings of the board and any committee meetings held on a date other than the date of the board meetings. Each non-employee director was granted options to purchase 1,000 shares of common stock under the company's non-employee directors' stock-option plan.

Reading proxy statements and annual reports, current and past, will give you valuable information about the company and its culture. What kinds of directors have they appointed in the past? Have they all been chief executive officers? When they choose a woman director is she always from academia, or business, or industry or government? What is the mean age level of the board? Are new directors older or younger than current directors? Are there women on the nominating committee? What outside projects or programs or causes does the company support? What is their reputation in this arena? How are they perceived in the financial press as compared to their annual report financial statement?

8. I have read the annual report and the proxy statements and have learned the following:

A. _____

B. _____

C. _____

D. _____

E. _____

9. I have questions about the following:

A. _____

B. _____

C. _____

D. _____

E. _____

10. I am still _____ or no longer ____ interested in serving as a director for this company.

11. I have identified the current chief executive officer, chief financial officer and chief operating officer and the current board of directors. I have listed the companies represented by the outside directors.

One name leads to another who knows someone you may know. Before you can move forward with your strategy you have to know the players and the supporting players. Is the chief executive officer visible in the community? Does he or she chair the same event each year? What nonprofit cause is the corporation involved with?

For example, Jim Renier, former CEO of Honeywell, is personally involved with an education program for children in the inner city, as is Reuben Mark, CEO of Colgate-Palmolive. Jim Preston, CEO of Avon Products, supports women's entrepreneurship. Preston has also invested his company's resources in the fight against breast cancer. What is your passion? Where do you want to serve? What do you want to contribute?

12. I have identified what I can "bring to the table" specific to each corporation. Let's do this one again.

A. _____

B. _____

C. _____

D. _____

E. _____

This is not the time for false modesty. At this point you should have enough background information about the company and the industry to zero in on how your talents and expertise will be of value. It is important to write this down and be clear about it in your mind. When you do have an interview, informal or formal, you won't be surprised or awkward when the question is posed.

Your stance is of course not one based on arrogance: "Put me on the board and I will save the company." It is and should be an expression of your commitment to be a diligent board member, one that is well informed and poised to be an independent thinker and a member of the team for the benefit of the shareholders.

13. I am aware of the liabilities of serving on a corporate board and aware that directors' and officers' insurance may not fully cover potential financial liability.

You can be sued. You can be "fired" by the shareholders. According to Raw-leigh Warner, who served as director on the board of American Express and is a director on the boards of Time and Chemical Bank, "You wouldn't go on a board unless you were thoroughly satisfied that the directors' and officers' insurance was adequate. There's no major personal liability except for criminal malfea-sance. What really concerns you is looking like a fool and having your name tarnished as somebody who has been duped by the management. You're sup-posed to be involved. Of course, you've got to be careful about the kind of company you go into."

Now, Who Do You Know That Can Help?

"Do your own bridge-building because it is very, very important," says Sisco. "Reach out to anyone you can within discretion and without losing their friend-ship to contact those they know that you know or need to reach." Don't restrict your search to the Fortune 1000. Sisco advises that one route to a top corporate 1000 board is to first get nominated to a capital formation board for a new com-pany. Research the new company to make sure it is everything it is purported to be. Fees are usually paid in equity.

Identify organizations involved with the corporate board process. Research which one(s) can be most helpful to you. For more information on corporate board placement, you can write to the following organizations:

> Directors' Resource Council/NWEAF
> 1440 New York Avenue NW, Suite 300
> Washington, D. C. 20005
> 202 393-5257
> Contact: Elise Garfinkel

> National Association of Corporate Directors
> 1707 L Street NW
> Washington, DC 20036
> 202 775-0509
> Contact: John Nash

> Catalyst
> 250 Park Avenue South
> New York, New York 10003
> 212 777-8900
> Contact: Sheila Wellington

Note: There is an extensive resource list in the Appendix.

EXPAND YOUR LIST TO INCLUDE:

International Law Firms

Corporate Attorneys get involved with various transactions that are ongoing with corporations and are board knowledgeable.

Local and Regional Organizations

Don't ignore the regional or local level. Where is the corporation located? How visible in the community is the corporation through its regional offices? Review the businesses in your area, locally and regionally. Get to know the local or regional chief executive officers, who are on the boards of local or regional companies. Identify what good causes within the community these chief executive officers support.

Nonprofit Organizations

Identify where your interests lie. If you are committed to helping in the fight against breast cancer, why not identify the leading organizations where you can contribute your time and expertise. At the same time, research the corporations and chief executive officers, who contribute time, money and energy. Beyond your resume, who are you as a person? What do you believe in? Where are you putting your time and commitment? Work hard and work smart and target the nonprofit board that matches your interest and also has the interest of the corporation on whose board you would be willing to serve.

THE UNCAMPAIGN

Now what? Do you call everyone and tell them you want to serve on a board? How do you activate your strategy? You don't want to look as if you have a "campaign." You certainly should be chary of the "campaign" model of some would-be political appointees where the aggressive office seeker leaks his name to the press in an attempt to lock in his early, front-runner position.

If you were to launch this kind of campaign, aggressively sending out letters with your resume attached, you would not win marks for good judgment, a key quality for any director.

SO WHAT ARE YOU SUPPOSED TO DO?

Work Smarter Not Harder

At this point, you have identified the boards and the corporations. You have done your homework on the industry and the issues, you know who the key people and stakeholders are. You are confident you have something of value to contribute.

Now let's consider some action steps in an uncampaign to move you toward board service.

Get Visible: One to One

Create a core group of mentors. No more than three people who become your corporate board guides. Tell them your goal, ask for their counsel and follow their advice. Be of value to your core group. At this point in your career you are networking on the high end and you will want to keep the relationships equal by looking for ways to provide a return on the investment of your mentors' time and good counsel.

Many women directors are helpful as mentors. Jean Sisco meets with potential board candidates on a regular basis and gives them a realistic assessment of their chances of serving, ways to avoid dead ends, and advice on improving their route to the boardroom.

Follow-up your mentor meetings with an action report back to your mentor and move the project forward. Keep your goal alive by being an active participant. Ask for an introduction to someone you have identified that can help, someone your mentor knows. Take both of them to lunch or breakfast. Make it easy for everyone to meet with you.

Research and Follow Through

Create a tickler file on each corporation. Clip articles pertaining to the industry and especially profiles of the chief executive officer.

Read the trades and keep up with pending legislation that may have an impact on the industry as a whole.

When appropriate, send a note on letterhead or personalized card to the chief executive officer with your comments and the article enclosed.

Does this work? Let me ask you. When you write an article and someone takes the time to send you a copy with a congratulatory note, how do you feel about the sender?

Remember

As you develop your outreach consistent with you own style you are not asking for anything. You are seeking first to meet the decision-makers, understand their issues, zero in on what they need, make the most of opportunities which you create and respond to, position yourself for consideration.

Stay Visible

"Women can get in front of opinion or decision-makers by knowing the field on which they plan to speak, being articulate, thorough, and knowledgeable about the facts, good humored and quick with responses. It is an asset to have important pieces of writing in *The New York Times* opinion pages and other notable places, where the fact of her work being published will draw her attention to the decision-makers," says Dr. Claire L. Gaudiani, president of Connecticut College. Dr. Gaudiani serves on the boards of Southern New England Telephone, Municipal Bond Investor Association, American Council On Education, American Public Radio.

Visibility: Writing

Writing, getting published in journals, trade publications, magazines or newspapers, is a way to show your exceptional qualifications. If you don't yet have it, begin now to create a file of articles you author on issues you care about that are relevant to the corporation. These articles will highlight your base of experience, the expertise you can bring to the corporate board table.

Visibility: Speaking

Stand up and deliver. Make your opportunities for contributing a valid and useful perspective on private or public sector topics. specifically, write three speeches that you can deliver before key industry audiences, decision-makers, and chief executive officers, your identified target groups. Steadily, build a reputation among these groups as an expert on an issue of significance.

Carol Brookins, chairman and CEO of World Perspectives, Inc., is an agricultural issues expert. She publishes a trade briefing paper for her international clients and is a frequent speaker on agri-issues and trade before national and international audiences. This year, she was asked to serve on the board of Terra Industries, Inc. Decision-makers in the company had attended a trade conference where she was the keynote speaker. They were impressed with her knowledge and expertise, her ability to communicate and think on her feet. Brookins is a very caring person who is also a relationship builder. She is an active contributor with time and money to the D.C. Orphans Home.

If you are a neophyte speaker, join Toastmasters and work to develop this critical skill.

Volunteer as an expert in your field for interview by the media. Establish yourself as a resource on a specific issue to the media, print and broadcast. What issues currently being debated in the press, on television, provide you with an opportunity to respond?

During the debate surrounding the North American Free Trade Agreement, the media interviewed small business owners, corporate representatives, politicians, environmentalists, trade experts. This national debate provided a good opportunity for those prepared to talk about the issue.

Stay Visible

The board process takes a long time. You need to keep the momentum moving by doing something daily. Every day work your plan to meet either a decision-maker or those who can impact the decision-makers.

A Seat at the Board Table Check List

If you can answer "yes" to the following statements, your chances of obtaining a seat at the corporate board table are much better than average.

1. I have identified the corporation on whose board I wish to serve.
2. I am clear as to why I have chosen this corporation.
3. I have spent time researching the company and the industry and I would be proud to serve.
4. I have sent for the annual report.
5. I have identified the current directors and the industries they represent.
6. I have looked at past proxies, analysts' reports and press clips.
7. I can name the chief executive officer, chief financial officer and chief operating officer.
8. I have identified what I can bring to the table.
9. I am committed to allocating the time and preparation required to be an effective board member. The average director spends up to 125 hours, more than three full work weeks on board business each year, according to a survey by Korn/Ferry International.
10. I have increased my visibility by getting involved in organizations, events, projects that I truly care about and that are supported by the decision-makers I need to reach.
11. After I obtain my board seat, I will actively help qualified women to take their seats around the corporate board table.

8

TARGET TABLE:
THE POLITICAL TABLE

"You talk about the 'year of the woman', but it was the 'year of opportunity' that women seized."
HARRIETT WOODS, PRESIDENT OF THE NATIONAL WOMEN'S POLITICAL CAUCUS, 1992

"This may sound very old-fashioned and nineteenth century, but women have a lot of leeway to make up. When we have done that, then we will help the men to solve the problems of the twentieth century. Plainly, they can't settle them without us. But for the time being it comes to this. The men must paddle their canoe and we must paddle ours."
CHRISTABEL PANKHURST, 1913

Woods is right. In 1992, more women than ever before were elected to Congress because long before '92 as individuals, they built on a vision, a seat at the political table, went to work and not only seized opportunity but created it. Today all issues are considered women's issues and our canoe must travel the main tributary, not the sidestreams, if we are going to get our canoe to Congress.

The political arena is not an environment for the faint of heart. Joan of Arc was burned at the stake, Eleanor Roosevelt was vilified and Hillary Clinton, as she struggles to create a new model for the role of First Lady, suffers through peaks and valleys of voter approval. When Marilyn Quayle tried to break out of the mold and practice law while her husband was the vice president, the hue and cry was deafening.

The truth is that new women political leaders are creating their own rules and while sometimes they stumble, they are bringing fresh voices and views to the process. Whether you are a Democrat or a Republican, you have to recognize that Mrs. Clinton is a top player in the game of politics. She knows the issues, she knows the personalities, and she doesn't blink when the going gets tough. Margaret Thatcher, Golda Meir, Indira Ghandi, represent the variety of women who reached the top of the political ladder.

The common denominator that links these diverse personalities is a belief that they can fix what's wrong. A passion for change. Dolores Ibarruri believed in the need to overthrow Franco and establish a Republic in Spain. At great risk, she continued to hold meetings throughout the country to get support for the Republic and became known as La Pasionaria. Without this passion or commitment, you cannot last very long in politics. If you have an opinion on practically everything and an idea how to fix things, this may be just the arena for you.

Politics offers so many opportunities for women to get involved and ultimately arrive at the leader's table. For a long time, it was like golf, a place where men dominated the green, had fun and made power deals. Like golf, women have learned to play and in the process discovered, they love the game.

Politics offers something for everyone, but be careful, it is addictive. You may start by getting involved at a local level with the party of your choice. Perhaps, you volunteer to work the polls on election day, or host a fundraising event for the candidate in your home. Before long, you will will be observing the candidate up close and saying, "I can do that." You will have jumped from behind the scenes to the main scene.

If running for political office holds little appeal, you may want to focus your sights on the finance side and become known as a fundraiser for the party and the candidates fielded by the party. Women are discovering that finance offers a good way to get in front of decision-makers, interact with business leaders and, at the same time, sharpen their knowledge of issues.

Experience in finance can propel you to forming your own PAC (political action committee) in order to determine who gets the money. Nine years ago, Ellen Malcolm, founded Emily's List (Early Money Is Like Yeast, it makes the dough rise), which supports pro-choice Democratic women. Today, Emily's List has 34,000 members and has raised over $5 million for candidates. It has provided a concept for other PACs which followed, including; the Wish List (Women In the Senate and House), founded by Glenda Greenwald , which supports pro-choice Republican Women; RENEW, founded by Karen Roberts and Margaret Mankin, which supports Republican women candidates at the state and local level. The Women's Campaign Fund and the National Women's Political Caucus are bi-partisan political organizations, which provide training, research and support candidates. Wish List and The Hollywood Women's Political Commitee, a pro-choice Democratic candidate group each raised over one million dollars for women candidates in 1992.

Not all PACs target Congressional candidates exclusively. Liz Bergman founded the L.A. List to help women get started in politics. The L.A. List supports pro-choice women, who are candidates for any kind of elected office, including school boards and city councils. Bergman's goal is to help women get "a seat on the dais." The women candidates supported by the L.A. List receive checks, large and small, from women throughout California. Bergman believes support is critical at the earliest levels. Without financial help, many of these women would not go on to run for Congressional seats.

More of these organizations are being formed. Women make up 52 percent of the population, but hold only 10 percent of the seats in Congress. If that number is going to change, many more women are going to have to run for office.

After years of working for candidates, stuffing envelopes to get out the campaign message, serving as volunteers and being behind-the-scenes cheerleaders, women know they can run as candidates in their own right. A record number of women have been elected to the 103rd Congress.

Although Congress has 90 percent male members, the total of women serving has jumped to 55 from 31 in 1992. We can bemoan the fact that there are too few women in Congress, but at the same time more women are being tapped to serve on corporate boards, the numbers of women being elected to local and national offices are increasing.

Who are these women?

There is no one profile that fits today's female candidate. What they have in common is the conviction that they can make a difference. This was the motivating factor for Lynn Martin.

A SEAT AT THE TABLE: THE CANDIDATE

For former Secretary of Labor Lynn Martin, the trip to the seat around the table as a member of the President's Cabinet began when she ran for the Winnebago (Illinois) County Board in 1972. In just 20 years, this former high school teacher had landed a seat at the most powerful table in the country.

Let's look at the route she took.

TARGET TABLE: EDUCATION/PUBLIC SERVICE

Growing up on Chicago's North side, she graduated Phi Beta Kappa from the University of Illinois in three years. Right after graduation, she married and eventually had two daughters. Up until the birth of her second child, she taught high school English, economics, and government in several public and parochial school around Chicago. Her time out from teaching to care for her children offered her a change and choice in her life. The break from teaching gave her an opportunity to follow the issues confronting the Winnebago Country Board. The "aha" moment occurred when she said, "I can contribute something here."

TARGET TABLE: COUNTY BOARD COMMISSIONER

In 1972, she was elected to and served on the finance and public works committee. The road supervisor was upset, he believed that women had no business "messing around with potholes and sewage." Martin felt at home around the political table. She knew the issues and she enjoyed working with people and trying to address their problems. She wanted to be a catalyst for positive change. She had a vision and she was able to connect with both men and women, who admired her straightforward, no-equivocating approach to issues and answers.

TARGET TABLE: ILLINOIS HOUSE OF REPRESENTATIVE/ILLINOIS STATE SENATE

In 1976, she recruited her daughter's junior high school class to help her campaign for the Illinois House of Representatives. She won and two years later, she was elected to the state Senate. All this was occurring at the same time that Martin's marriage ended.

TARGET TABLE: U.S. HOUSE OF REPRESENTATIVES

In 1980, she won a seat in the U.S. House of Representatives. Her political style, a combination of head and heart, gave her a reputation as a politician who voted her conscience. Her ability to be tough on issues of government spending, but compassionate toward those in need appealed to Illinois voters.

TARGET TABLE: VICE CHAIRMAN, HOUSE REPUBLICAN CONFERENCE

Martin, who remarried in 1987 to a U.S. district judge in Illinois, became the mother of five children, two of her own and three from her husband's previous marriage. This did not stop her momentum on the political scene. She continued to move up the political ladder and was elected vice chairman of the House Republican Conference, a policy-making caucus. Her reputation increased among Democrats and Republicans, when she temporarily took over for the ranking Republican on the budget committee and proved to be an able negotiator. National visibility occurred when *U.S. News and World Report* name her one of the "Ten Rising Stars of American Politics."

MISSED TARGET TABLE: U.S. SENATE

In 1990, she challenged Illinois Senator Paul Simon for his seat in Congress. The party wanted another Republican in the Senate, so Martin gave up her seat in the House to run. She lost by more than a million votes. She really believed her political career was finished and began to focus on spending more time back in Illinois with her husband.

TARGET TABLE: THE CABINET

In 1990, President Bush chose her to be Secretary of Labor. Her nomination was endorsed by several leading Democrats, including Senator Paul Simon.

Martin won high marks as Secretary of Labor. She got out of her impressive office and talked to men and women in the work force. In effect, she was a one-woman town hall, constantly getting input. Martin led the charge against the glass ceiling in corporate American by using a carrot-and-stick approach. No more labor contracts for corporations, who did not have women in middle-to senior-level positions.

She cleaned house in the Labor Department to ensure that qualified women and minorities would have opportunities for advancement. She obtained training for labor department employees on issues ranging from sexual harassment to cultural diversity. "I believe that women have a different kind of agenda," says Martin. "We are willing to risk change, we are willing to leap beyond color or gender."

TARGET TABLE: CORPORATE BOARD

Following George Bush's defeat, Martin has continued working to improve the status of women in the private sector. She chairs Deloitte and Touche's Council on the Advancement of Women. She serves on the board of directors of Ameritech, Harcourt General, Dreyfus Funds, Ryder Systems, Inc., and Chicago's Lincoln Park Zoo. She also has assumed the Davee Chair at the J. L. Kellogg Graduate School of Management at Northwestern University.

What enabled Lynn Martin to move from high school teacher to Secretary of Labor?

Education: According to Martin, being able to finish college provided her with the preparation to take advantage of opportunity when it did come. Her early goal of becoming an educator gave her a change to see firsthand how effective she could be inspiring and teaching students.

Drive/Push: She was never just a casual observer. Her point of view was always coupled with an action. Her drive to make her local community better was the same drive that led her to try and improve the national community.

"I realize now it is the style to say 'Let's let people be what they want to be,' but I think that misses the point of people later in life being all they can be. I wish people had said, 'You can do it, you will do it, and you can do it sooner rather than later.'"

Affirmation: "I had so much help and support along the way," she says. "My neighbors who came out to vote for me, the people who helped me raise money when others said a woman couldn't win, my father who kept telling me I could do anything, and a memory of my mother and her quiet strength all made a difference," she said. "Unlike many young people today, I was surrounded by the kinds of love and imperative to try that made a difference." The key thing here is apart from Martin's immediate family, her commitment, sense of purpose served as a lightening rod to others who wanted to be part of whatever Martin was going to accomplish.

Willingness to move up: A key factor in Martin's climb from county to country is her willingness to learn what she needs to know in order to step up to the next level. She never refused to open the door to the senior position. Putting aside self-doubts, she leaned into opportunity and did not waste any time learning everything there was to know about her new environment.

Identification of the table: Martin always kept her eye on the leadership table wheverever it was. If action and real work were on the pothole committee, that's where she headed. She took on the tough assignments in Congress and came through. As her reputation for follow-through increased, she also was careful to build relationships. Similar to Judy Haberkorn, Martin does not have one style for senior people and another for entry level. She is consistent with everyone.

❖ ❖ ❖

Harriett Woods, president of the National Women's Political Caucus, has achieved in both the private and public sectors. She began her career as a journalist and documentary film producer. She ran for office and served as city councilwoman, state senator, and lieutenant governor of Missouri, but was defeated after being nominated for the U.S. Senate. After leaving office, she led a public policy institute.

Throughout her various careers, there was always one constant: a concern for social justice. Her concern motivated her to build a solid area of expertise on the problems of the elderly and community development, through research, and hands-on community involvement. In order to build on her base of political knowledge, she took leadership positions in a number of policy-related groups.

These included the Missouri Municipal League, the National League of Cities, the League of Women Voters and the National Women's Political Caucus. Today, as part of her work with the Caucus, Woods works with leading corporations to encourage corporate women executives to become politically involved.

"The most important thing I had to learn in order to succeed," says Woods, "is that satisfaction comes in different ways in the private sector than in the public sector. In the public sector, for an elected official, it's the voters, plus a complex of interest groups. In the private sector, it can be a limited group of persons or even a single employer, or just your self." Whether private or public sector, Woods believes any list of winning qualities should include: Taking principled positions; integrity; a willingness to take calculated risks; listening and really hearing others; honesty at all levels; mentoring to assure successor leadership; willingness to make decisions.

What Are Your Chances of Winning?

"Winning may not be everything, but losing has little to recommend it." Senator Dianne Feinstein

RENEW sponsored a poll conducted by Public Opinion Strategies which surveyed 800 adults nationwide. The poll indicated that Republican women candidates led Republican men candidates in such traits as middle-class empathy, trust, and leadership. And that Republican women candidates appealed to a critical and fast-growing portion of the electorate, independent voters. The voters surveyed were "split sampled," so that half were read a description of female Republican candidate and half a male Republican candidate. The hypothetical candidate was a prototype Republican with business experience and community roots interested in Congressional reform.

After hearing the description, which covered experience, business background, the candidates attitudes about Congress, a common sense approach to government and reduction of spending and waste, respondents were asked how likely they would be to vote for the candidate. The findings of the poll reflect that the Republican woman had a slight advantage overall, but more important a 15-point advantage among independent voters over the prototypical Republican male.

Previous surveys show that women candidates, Republicans and Democrats, score highly on the "trust" scales. Democratic voters in particular rate the women 20 percent higher with regard to trust.

The trend established in 1992 continues in 1994. A record 110 women ran for the House and according to early election results, 46 had won. Women hold 47 of the 435 seates in the House of Representatives. And with the election of

Republican Olympia Snowe of Maine, the Senate gains one woman, making the total eight.

Just as women discovered their own entrepreneurial skills and talents for business success, more women are running and winning elections by playing to their strengths and not by becoming male candidate clones. That's the good news. Reality is that politics is a blood sport and though more women are entering the arena, they are finding out that the going can be rough, as evidenced by Govenor Ann Richards, who lost her bid for re-election, and U. S. Senator Dianne Feinstein, who narrowly won a tough and very expensive re-election bid. In the process, women are learning that although initially they may be perceived as more ethical than men, they must also be perceived as more competent and able to hold their own in the hurly-burly political environment.

In order for women to win and compete against male candidates, they need money and endorsements. RENEW has created a survey form SHOULD I RUN? in order to help potential candidates determine if the candidate table is one they should target.

Answer the following questions:

Why are you running for this office?

Why should voters elect you?

What is the salary and term of the office?

What are the legal requirements for the office?

What was the political environment when the incumbent was elected?

Do you think the political environment is favorable to your election? If so, why?

Who will be your core supporters?

Where are your three strongest precincts?

Where are your three weakest precincts?

Where are your swing or target precincts?

Do you have a group of close supporters or friends who will serve as your advisory or steering committee?

Do you have a group of close supporters or friends who will serve as your finance committee? Will you be able to ask them for contributions?

Will you be able to ask a stranger for a contribution?

How much money will you need to raise to win the election?

How much of your own money will you be able to contribute?

Will the campaign require time away from your job? Have you discussed this with your employer?

Do you have any activities outside of work which may be neglected?

Have you discussed the time requirements with your spouse? Your family? Are they willing to pitch in to help you?

How many hours must you put in the campaign on a weekly basis, in order to win?

How will the campaign affect your spouse and children?

How will elective office affect your spouse and children?

Do you have anyone with whom you can discuss the prospect of running for office?

Is there a mentor you can call on at any time to discuss ideas or you can help guide you through the campaign?

What are your greatest assets?

What are your weak points?

What will be the most important issues you will concentrate on in your campaign?

What issues will your opponent concentrate on?

Who will be the one person who will help you develop the day-to-day campaign strategy?

Are you a better speaker in a small group? A large group? One or one?

How will you feel about going on the offensive in a campaign?

How do you feel about talking to the press?

You can add your own questions to the list. The point is to really be clear about why you are running for the office and what you are willing to do to win. RENEW warns that women are still facing attacks that they are not "tough enough." The antidote is to stick to your message, answer attacks but get immediately back to your message. Do your homework and do maintain a professional and cool demeanor.

"While it is important for a woman candidate to demonstrate her strength, appearing to be what voters perceive as 'strident' is detrimental. It may seem old-fashioned," says Karen Roberts, co-founder of RENEW, "but while voters want women candidates to appear strong, their femininity is still an important part of the evaluation process."

TABLE: POLITICS/FUNDRAISING

On the fundraising side, women are taking leadership seats around the finance table in local and national campaigns. Barbara Hackman Franklin held a series of key finance positions in the Bush-Quayle campaigns of 1988 and 1992. This ability as a key fundraiser, delivering measurable results, weighed in positively when added to Franklin's impressive resume as she was considered for the position of Secretary of Commerce.

The ability to raise large amounts of money is an attention-getter that no candidate can afford to ignore. As more women fall in this category, we will continue to not only see more women candidates but also more women appointed to senior-level positions in government.

On the Democratic side, Pamela Harriman created PAMPAC and supported Democrat candidates through 12 years of Republican administrations. Her home became a magnet for candidates who needed funding and who could count on Harriman to put together the kinds of events that would attract contributors. Today, Harriman serves as U.S. Ambassador to France.

There are unlimited opportunities to step up to the fundraising table. The reason for this is so few people really enjoy asking others for money. Successful fundraisers believe in the candidate, what the candidate stands for, and that the candidate makes a difference. Women are very good fundraisers. If in the past we have not been credited with writing the big checks ourselves, it is time to acknowledge we excel at convincing others to do it. So much so, that many of the top political events companies are owned by women.

Raising money is a measurable activity. Whether your candidate wins or loses, you can win if you meet your goals and deliver what you said you were going to do. Meeting goals wins respect. Winning respect helps you beyond the political arena.

How do you get a seat at this table? Make a decision and run for office or get involved with a campaign. In order to win, you have to get in the race. Contribute to the WISH LIST, which gives money to pro-choice Republicans. Get involved with Emily's List which provides funds to pro-choice Democrats. Try RENEW which gives money to Republican women with no litmus test on the choice issue. Wherever you are in the political spectrum, there is an organization tailor-made for your beliefs and commitment.

POLITICAL APPOINTMENTS

Women have moved rapidly in politics from behind-the-scenes to front-and-center stage, not only as candidates but also in the cabinet. "It is now possible," said HHS Secretary Donna Shalala, "for a major policy issue to move through the government process without it ever touching a man's hands until it reaches the President of the United States."

In the Clinton Administration, in addition to Shalala, there are women who have a seat around the cabinet table. Of the top Administration positions, 47 percent are women, with 32 percent in senior policy positions. Prior to Clinton, President Bush had broken the record by appointing women to 20 percent of Senate-confirmed, top-level positions.

Whether as candidates or senior-level appointees or as fundraisers, women have discovered politics. You may not want to run for office just now but you can still aim for a seat at the political table. Since we are the majority of voters in every state, it makes sense to identify what is available in terms of appointments on a county, state or national level.

A Seat at the Table: Boards, Commissions Councils

There are thousands of boards, commissions, councils, and committees on which you can serve without giving up your day job, but you will have to lobby for them. Before you are ready to lobby you will have to do what candidates for corporate boards, or nonprofit boards have to do, your homework. If your idea of a seat at the table is a presidential or state appointment, you will need a strategy and a political resume.

You can build a political resume very easily. Identify a local or national campaign. Locate campaign headquarters and pay them a visit. Ask a lot of questions. If you volunteer to raise money, you will be accepted immediately. However, if you say you want to travel with the candidate and help her give speeches, you will probably not get a call back, unless you are a recognizable celebrity name.

Your campaign involvement on the finance side will bring you in contact with people who not only have an opinion, but who are willing to back it up by raising money. Whether your candidate wins or loses, the people you meet in fundraising have the potential to be friends for the long term. Since these folks are usually from the business community, you will find you have a whole new network of men and women who think on similar political lines and who have the potential to help you professionally.

Following the local campaign, you are ready to identify the commission or board on which you would like to serve in your state. Do not approach a key decision-maker with the query, "I'd like to serve on something. What do you suggest?" Just like the corporate board or anything else worth trying for, you have to take the responsibility for getting to your goal. Take time to do the research. Understand what is available and realistic for you to apply for. Just because you once met Colin Powell does not mean you are ready to be appointed secretary of defense.

That may sound ludicrous, however if you have lived in Washington, D.C., a long time and have become very familiar with the positions that are available, you might be indulging in heavy duty daydreaming on a regular basis. In which case, a reality check may be in order.

Match your talents, goals, convictions, experience with the position you want. For example, if you are an entrepreneur and you are personally involved in supporting tax changes to benefit small business owners, you may want a seat around the National Advisory Council table, which is a organization under the aegis of the Small Business Administration. Men and women from every geographic area in the country sit on the council. Find out who is on the council now and what your chances are for joining the group. Council members usually remain throughout an Administration's term, however people resign and drop out for various reasons within the four-year period and slots open occasionally. Many of the national boards and commissions are duplicated at the state level, so don't ignore these opportunities.

If you are looking at the federal level, your strategy for a seat at the political table should be a long-term game plan. There is fierce competition for all spots. Primarily because most seekers do not do the research, there are a great number of people going for the obvious positions, such as secretary of commerce or under secretary or deputy under secretary. These are all full-time jobs and require top-level endorsers and a stellar political resume in addition to a stellar professional resume.

If you do not want to give up your life as you know it, aim for a board or commission or council. These meet quarterly or annually and usually do not provide an honorarium or fee.

Let's look at the boards and commissions available on a national level, realizing that many of their counterparts exist on the state level. On a national level, there are full-time regulatory commissions; approximately 300 part-time presidential commissions including 1,500 appointments. These appointments are made by the president and tend to be more global in nature than the federal advisory committees. There are approximately 1,000 federal advisory committees, including 22,000 seats. These appointments are made by agency heads or secretaries and tend to be more technical than the presidential boards.

Boards and commissions are created by executive order. They are created by the president and can be abolished by the president, or they are created by agency and department and can be abolished by the specific agency or department. Or they are created by public law. Congress can create boards and commissions which can only then be abolished by law. However, Congress might not allocate the funds for all the commissions it has created so while a board may exist technically, if there is no money available to fulfill its mandate, it becomes nonexistent.

You can go to the library and request the Annual Report of the president on Federal Advisory Committees. This is released annually by the General Services Administration and lists many of the federal boards and agency staff members dealing with boards and commissions. Another publication is the U.S. Government Manual, which is available from the Government Printing Office. This book discusses the larger independent regulatory commissions as well as some of the other boards and commissions and provides a brief description of their work.

Get the Plum Book, officially known as the United States Government Policy and Supporting Positions, printed by Congress. It lists some of the boards, the current seat holder, the expiration date for the appointment and the party designation. I used the Plum Book (so called because of the color of the cover and not because all the appointments are "plums.") to learn more about the President's Export Council, on which I eventually served.

Members of the President's Export Council are appointed by the president and serve under the secretary of commerce. The council is a resource to the president in an advisory capacity, identifying ways to help American business compete more effectively in the export market. Currently, 15 percent of American business is doing 85 percent of all the exporting. There are many reasons for this, but the number one factor is "fear of exporting." The council looks into ways to help American business move more effectively into the export market by providing information and services through the Department of Commerce.

Identify the position you want. Know why you want it. List the qualities or experience or talents you have that will contribute to the appointment.

Your next step, once you have identified at least three appointments you would be happy to take, is to get your resume organized, provide a short cover letter identifying the three appointments you would like and send this to Presidential Personnel. The White House will assign you a number and your official file will be born. It is up to you to feed it and keep it alive by checking on the progress of your appointment status.

Eventually, you will hear from the White House and be asked to fill out forms which will be given to the Secret Service. Try to list people who are still alive for them to contact. If the position you are aiming for is Senate-confirmed, you will go through an extensive FBI check and financial disclosure.

If your party won the last election and you worked on the campaign in some way, you are in luck. Most of the appointments go to the party in the White House. However, there are boards and commissions that must by law consist of both Democrats and Republicans.

Next, develop your endorser list. (Have you noticed that no matter what seat you are aiming for, you will need the help of friends and their friends to help you?) This list should comprise men and women leaders from business, industry and government, who will write endorsing letters for you. You will also need help from your member of Congress. In fact, whoever you can get to weigh in for you, helps to build your file in the right way.

It will also be helpful if you can fill your file with articles you have written or speeches you have given on the subject connected to your appointment. I was appointed to the Small Business Advisory Council, and chaired the International Committee. Articles I had written, supporting the North American Free Trade Agreement from the viewpoint of a small business entrepreneur, were a factor in my appointment.

As you conduct your uncampaign, writing articles, giving speeches, keeping your file up-to-date, you can call presidential personnel to check on your status.

Now is the time to develop a second tier of endorsers. In addition to the personal letters, you will want to have letters from organizations. Do you belong to any women's organizations? If so, get a letter from the president endorsing you for the appointment. It helps if you write the letter and make it specific and have the president sign it. A strong letter is needed to indicate the writer really knows you and is wholeheartedly backing you. A lukewarm letter is a clue that this is one of many letters that had to be written but there is not real commitment behind it.

When I was seeking my appointment, I asked the following groups I'm a member of to write to presidential personnel: The National Italian American Foundation, The National Women's Forum, Women In International Trade, The Women's Political Caucus, and The National Association of Women Business Owners.

After a year, I was appointed by President Bush to the President's Export Council and by Administrator Pat Saiki to the Small Business Advisory Council. Under President Clinton, I was appointed to the Services Policy Advisory Committee.

Too often, in our zeal to get what we want, we forget that getting and giving is an equal equation. As you plan your strategy, which includes asking a great many people to help you, try to identify why they should support you for the position. As with the corporate board process, you will guarantee and then follow-through by doing the best job possible once you are appointed. You will give everyone credit for helping you get your commission or board or appointment seat. You will be helpful when you can to those who supported you.

And finally, if you are in a political position, you remember that you serve at the pleasure of the president or the cabinet secretary. This means that you are loyal, you don't repeat confidential information, you don't go negative to the media or to your peers. If you disagree, express yourself within the board room and if things do not change to your liking, resign quietly.

One key rule of political involvement: When the applause dies down and your party loses, continue to be active politically. Support local politics, raise money. The glory may be in presidential campaigns, but the real reward is working at the grassroots level and understanding that it is there in your own community where you can truly make a difference.

And don't get used to titles or appointments. They disappear when your party loses. Remember why you wanted the appointment in the first place: to do a really good job and make a difference. Barbara Hackman Franklin, former secretary of commerce, is now helping to build the Republican party in Connecticut. This is a far cry from her leadership days at Commerce, working with heads of state on trade and international monetary issues. Now Franklin is building a party from the ground up, raising money, developing resources. She has her own company and serves on several corporate boards, but she decided it was payback time for the party.

You can get your seat at the political table by becoming involved and supporting candidates or issues about which you care deeply, or by running yourself. In the process, you will refine daily what you really think, you will stay current on issues that impact people on a daily basis; trade, health care, the economy, crime, education. You will find yourself reading more than ever before, just to stay on top of the issues. Your appointment is a really a by-product. The real product is a stronger democracy because you took a leadership role.

9

TARGET TABLE: PROGRAMS FOR THE PUBLIC GOOD — IF THEY DON'T EXIST, CREATE YOUR OWN

Rather than ask yourself if you want to contribute time and talent to a nonprofit or volunteer organization, consider the following:

1. Is there an issue about which you care deeply?

2. If you had all the money in the world, and could use it for a good cause (other than yourself), do you know now what that cause would be?

3. Is your current position giving you a chance to use all your talents and ideas?

4. Do you get up in the morning and ask yourself, "Is this all there is?"

5. Is your volunteer time distributed among many organizations or are you targeting a leader's seat with one specific group?

6. If you are involved, is it still as worthwhile to you as it was when you first joined?

7. Does your current nonprofit or volunteer activity provide you with visibility among the leaders you want to know?

8. Does the organization enjoy a reputation for achieving goals?

9. Do you feel personally and professionally rewarded by the work you do with the group?

10. Have you made a difference to this organization?

11. Are you being challenged by this organization to do work at higher and higher levels of responsibility?

12. If you had to give up your volunteer work, would you miss this activity in your life?

13. Is it time to take your time and talents to another group?

Wilhelmina Holladay is an art collector, who began to wonder why there were no museums featuring work by women artists? Why, she wanted to know, was it so hard to find out about the paintings she owned, which were painted by women? Why wasn't there a central place where one could learn more about women and art? Holladay not only wondered, she did something about it. That something is now the National Museum of Women in the Arts located in Washington, D.C., and sponsored by leading corporations and not so well-known individuals who believed in Holladay's vision.

Step-by-step Holladay realized her dream, but the first step was recognizing that if it were going to happen, she would have to do it. Today, Wilhelmina Holladay has expanded the scope and goals of the museum and is rewarded by seeing how the women artists of the past and those of today continue to inspire others, including young women and men in the inner city of Washington and throughout the country. The museum stands as a testament proving, what can and can't be done, when one volunteers one's time and energy and passion on behalf of the greater good.

Nancy Gracey didn't target the activist table as a career goal. In fact, as the mother of nine children living in Belfast, Ireland, her plate was quite full. All of this changed when her son was shot in the leg by gunmen of the Irish Republican Army. The bullet was supposed to have hit the base of his spine, preventing him from ever walking again. The gunman's gun jammed and the second shot never came. When Nancy Gracey visited her son in the hospital, she met another mother who was there because her son had been shot as well, only by Protestant extremists.

At that moment, Gracey knew she had to do something and formed Families Against Intimidation and Terrorism (FAIT) to help families and individuals threatened by extremists on both sides of the political spectrum in Ireland. FAIT, which was formed in 1990, now has a volunteer core and an annual grant from the government.

Gracey put herself in harm's way when she formed FAIT. Her visibility increased as she worked with newspapers and broadcasters to identify how both Irish Catholics and Protestants were being victimized and terrorized by thugs hiding behind ideology. Stories began to appear that confirmed what Gracey had been saying, citizens were being beaten and shaken down for protection money, threatened to contribute, banished or killed if they didn't. FAIT succeeds by shining the light on terrorists' tactics. Gracey says that at least 200 people a year are forced to leave Northern Ireland because of threats. Gracey believes that the only way anything changes is for "ordinary people who hold the key and have the power" to act.

Gracey like Candy Lightner, founder of Mothers Against Drunk Drivers, and Nancy Brinker, founder of the Susan G. Komen Foundation were moved into action as the result of a cataclysmic event, a personal tragedy. The nonprofit organizations they created were meant to ensure that the memory of their loved ones would not be forgotten. In the process, through loss, they created new entities benefiting others.

What these women have in common is a desire to persuade others to work together to effect change. Whether that change results in more money for more research to determine the cause and prevention of breast cancer, more laws and education to prevent drunk drivers from taking the wheel, or a community coalition to stand as a blockade against terrorism and blackmail, the goals are clear.

Marilyn Van Derbur, former Miss America, served for 16 years as the only woman guest lecturer for General Motors and won accolades as an outstanding speaker. But five years ago, she went to the Kempe National Center in Denver to establish an adult survivor program. She had been sexually violated by her father for 13 years and could no longer put the long-term effects of incest behind her. The Van Derbur family contributed $260,000 to the program that would also concentrate on research. For two and a half years, more than 500 men and women came to the program every week for 35 different support groups. The meetings were free.

Today, Van Derbur serves as a co-founder of the American Coalition for Abuse Awareness, a grassroots national organization based in Washington, D.C., dedicated to strengthening the laws protecting adult survivors and child victims of sexual abuse.

Last year, she founded One Voice, a nonprofit organization in Washington, D.C., of survivors, therapists, child advocates and local and state leaders, who speak together, to end sexual violation of children through public education and awareness.

Anne Firth Murray founded the Global Fund for Women because poor women in poor countries were not even on the bottom rung of the ladder when it came to receiving grants or help of any kind. Today the Global Fund has raised more than $3 million and benefited more than 400 women's groups in 94 countries. Murray believes that the major problems of the world can only be solved if average people start their own programs. Global Fund's grants have provided computers to women in South Africa, money to women in South Korea to start a center for victims of sexual violence, funds for disabled women, and funds for literacy programs.

"My decision to create the Global Fund was also based on my observation of women's lives. It's not that women are essentially different from men: Their experiences are just different. What struck me was the ability of women in many countries, who lead extremely difficult lives, to be strong and kind and generous people," she adds.

We have a need to feel that what we are doing can make a difference. Often that need is not fullfilled entirely in the workplace. Your volunteer work can provide you with a chance to stop at a few stations while your train is hurtling down the track to your ultimate goals.

For those of you who have no desire to create your own organization, but want to contribute time and resources to existing nonprofits or charities, the opportunity to participate is limited only by your commitment and energy. Volunteerism is part of our national heritage and not matched by any other country. It is something we take for granted, our willingness to give.

Several years ago, as part of a program the Alliance hosted in Hungary, we established a mentor program where new entrepreneurs would be matched with seasoned and successful women business owners. Our challenge was to convince the successful women business owners that these new entrepreneurs would not steal their business "secrets," and to identify in concrete terms what they would get back if they did give their time in this way. The neophyte business owners were just as suspicious. Why, they wondered, would anyone help them except to get "free work for nothing?"

Compare that attitude to the many groups that exist in this country that help women climb the entrepreneurial ladder. The National Organization of Women Business Owners and the American Women's Economic Development Corporation give hundreds of hours of time helping would-be entrepreneurs. In addition to nonprofit groups, corporations are becoming more involved in sponsoring community service programs.

Tony Fay, vice president of Community Relations at Time Warner Inc., created a nationwide literacy program for children and adults. Time To Read began as an employee volunteer program. Chrysler Corporation sponsors World of Work to prepare students for school to work transition.

Rockwell International supports SMART (Science and Math Advancement and Resources for Teachers), a program run in conjunction with the L.A. Educational Partnership. Lod Cook, chairman and CEO of ARCO sponsors ALIVE (Alternatives to Living in a Violent Environment), a program dedicated to stopping the cycle of violence in families and communities.

Jim Preston, CEO of Avon Products has committed Avon to the Avon World-Wide Fund for Women's Health, which has resulted in major breast cancer awareness campaigns. Pfizer Inc., provides a Women and Civic Leadership program for their top women executives inviting them to get involved in volunteer and political organizations in order to have an impact through voluntary leadership.

A Pfizer survey of these women executives indicated that 81 percent were involved in charitable organizations at a leadership level; 97 percent were involved in voluntary health associations at high or medium level, and 95 percent were involved in political activities at the high or middle level; 87 percent were involved in the top levels in civic or professional organizations.

In addition to women in senior-level management, chief executive officers in the country's top corporations are paying more than lip service to community and cause-related programs. Their involvement is significant.

Reuben Mark, chief executive officer of Colgate-Palmolive and an Alliance Excellence In Leadership honoree, says, "My feeling in terms of my own satisfaction is that sitting on a charitable board and approving programs and raising funds is important, but I feel I can personally contribute more by getting involved directly with the kids." Mark and his wife are directly involved in an education program for youths in the inner city.

Dr. James J. Renier, CEO of Honeywell, Inc., chairs an organization called Success By Six, a coalition of Minnesota businesses allied with social agencies to help three-to-five-year-olds in the inner city. Renier believes it is important to support the best interests of both business and society.

Jacqueline Wexler, who serves on the board of United Technologies, is a former teacher and college administrator, who also was a member of the Order of the Sisters of Loretto. Today, she tutors inner city youth at Maynard Evans High School in Orlando. Wexler's lifelong involvement in education and commitment to youth has helped to direct UT's financial commitment to education.

What are the benefits to you directly and indirectly through your volunteer work?

1. You will give other leaders, outside of your daily sphere of influence, an opportunity to see what you can do.
2. You will increase your knowledge base as you learn all you can, not only about a specific issue or cause, but factors or forces impacting that cause. If you are interested in breast cancer awareness, you want to know how Congress works when it comes to health care issues that impact women; you will want

to know as much as you can about the efficacy of early detection, the impact of exercise, environment, and economics on this disease. Your outreach will include doing research on your own about hospitals and care givers and drug companies involved in the fight against cancer.

3. You will have an opportunity to utilize skills such as public speaking, writing, fundraising. In the process you will have increased visibility, and a track record of performance.

4. Volunteering is a no-lose way to try something new and decide what you may want to do with the rest of your life.

5. Your involvement as a member of a nonprofit board can lead to an appointment to a board in the private sector.

6. Increased recognition outside of your sphere of influence can benefit you in a tangible way within your corporate or business or political environment.

7. By becoming involved in something that nurtures your values, your energy and your enthusiasm level will increase, and you will attract new opportunities.

8. Volunteer work provides you with the opportunity to grow into and up toward the next level of responsibliity with no risk to your primary employment.

9. By strengthening ties to community, you bring something of value to your company and to your community. This value is being recognized more and more by corporate America.

10. A leadership role in a nonprofit organization can provide the "extra" you need to make your resume stand out among others of equal professional accomplishment.

11. Your network and your relationships will grow.

12. You will be perceived as someone who gives more than expected, something of value, and in the process your value will rise.

13. Most important, it is the right thing to do.

When the Alliance researched women directors of the top 1000 corporations and asked them, What do you think was the deciding factor that led to your seat on a corporate board? A majority answered, "My involvement at the leadership level in one or more nonprofit organizations." Their leadership involvement enabled them to interact with other leaders from other businesses, who had an opportunity to observe how the person worked with others.

Did they deliver what they said they would do? Did they reach goals in an equitable way? Were they interesting and dynamic to be around? Did they know how to say "no" without humiliating or destroying others' initiative? What interpersonal skills would they add if they joined the corporate board? What did others think of them? How did they work? What made them angry? How seriously did they treat the project? Were they fun to work with?

The chairman of the board of Pitney Bowes learned all of this about Julia Walsh when they worked to gether on a major charity fund drive. Shortly after that event, Julia Walsh joined the board of Pitney Bowes.

Ray Robbins, chairman emeritus of Lennox Industries, remembers a young woman, who was active on volunteer committees throughout the company. Through these committees she became known to far more executives than she would have during the course of her work day. When an opening came up in marketing, it was a unanimous agreement that the position should be given to her. Her visibility was high throughout the community as well. When her promotion was announced, Ray Robbins received letters from men and women leaders in the Dallas area, praising the company for recognizing her talent.

Executive search firm recruiters place a high value on the service work of job candidates. At the leadership level, they want to see a candidate who has the ability to interact and to have outreach with many publics. Someone who can bring added value to the job.

Entrepreneurs have always been tied to community causes. They believe in the cause and they also have a vested interest in supporting any effort that brings positive value to the community. Frequently, these business owners are innundated with so many requests to provide money and resources, they are unable to meet the demands. Instead, they are creating their own tables of giving, tying contributions to issues in which they are committed.

Judy Wicks, founder and president of White Dog Enterprises, which includes a restaurant and gift shop in Philadelphia, believes in business as a conduit for social change. *Inc.* magazine named White Dog Enterprises as one of the best small companies to work for in America. Wicks funds a mentoring program in which White Dog staff work at the restaurant with inner city kids interested in the hospitality industry. She contributes 10 percent of after-tax profits to projects and causes.

Wicks, like most entrepreneurs, has little time outside business hours. In order to achieve her social outreach goals, she brought programs and projects into the restaurant. People come to eat a dinner and get an event as well. Wicks realized that in order to satisfy her social welfare goals, she would have to tie them in to a successful company. She created a newsletter, which lets customers know about specific events that are held in connection with special dinners at the restaurant.

TABLE: PUBLIC SERVICE

Barbara Ferris, a former coordinator for Women and Development in the Peace Corps, is now an entrepreneur bringing her expertise gleaned in the public sector and applying it in the private sector. She has combined a talent for delivery of goods and services, with her ability to manage against the bottom line. Her values and goals are still the same: a passion for public service.

For the past 20 years, Ferris's work has focused on equity issues for women. It has been her passion and contributed to her feeling that she was "dissolved in something complete and great." Ferris, a woman in her early forties, is the oldest girl in a family of five, and the daughter of two working parents. Her peers say her number one talent is a willingness to listen, to be open to new ideas and things combined with a strong sense of values and ethics. She also has a strong sense of self, of who she is.

"I believe you must have a high standard of ethics," she says. "You shouldn't waiver or compromise away your integrity, no matter what the situation. You also need to take responsibility for your actions. Even if people don't agree with you, they can still respect you."

This sense of self was a critical factor keeping her safe as she traveled alone throughout many countries and nights spent in the bush or remote villages. Ferris is prepared for the unknown, but views it as part of life, not something apart and unusual. She says: "My mom was doing double-duty long before anybody talked about it. I think that is what has guided me in my own career. My mother was a career woman, then she got married, quit her job and had five kids. When I was nine, my father got sick. He had a brain tumor. My mother took over and ran the family restaurant and ran the house and ran the family. She was sleeping maybe four hours a night. At a very young age, I recognized what she was doing, really without any help, and I was inspired by her to try to empower women in similar or worse situations throughout the world."

Ferris believes that women have great skill in breaking down cultural, economic, and political barriers and moving toward substance. "Have you ever seen mothers with children in the grocery store, in any country? Other women come up to them and say, 'What a cute baby?' 'How old is she/he?' Then they just launch into this dissertation about kids, without any barriers blocking the communication process. Women look for the common denominator, they try to put people at ease and then they can get to the heart of the matter," says Ferris. "It is an efficient, productive, cost-effective way to exchange information. It can clear the path toward a goal with fewer obstacles than all the games men tend to play."

The seat at the table for Barbara Ferris is one where she can make things happen that will positively influence people's lives or the outcome of a situation. It is also a place where she can have the opportunity to build her own capacity in order to sustain herself.

"I think being the oldest girl in my family, I took on a lot of responsibility at a very young age. I'm very motivated, I take initiative. I think my reputation is, if you want something done, it will get done if I'm behind it," says Ferris "It was important to me to get an advanced degree so that I could combine the human resource side of management and the technical side in order to be a more effective manager."

Ferris was in graduate school and attended a meeting when she heard Governor Mario Cuomo speak. "After I heard him talk so passionately about public service, I knew I was in the right master's program. I had started under international affairs and moved out of that into public administration. It was a defining moment in my life."

Ferris made a decision early in life that she would not put herself in a work position unless she cared deeply about the objectives of the organization. "I look around and I see so many people getting up and going to work without an ounce of passion in their lives for what they are doing. I've truly operated in my professional life with a passion. I have loved my work and I've had a great time."

When Barbara Ferris joined the Peace Corp as Coordinator for Women and Development, the position had been vacant for 10 months. She was faced with the responsibility of supporting Peace Corps volunteers in 80 plus countries around the world. She started by creating a newsletter, which was sent to 7,000 volunteers and staff around the world. The purpose: to let them know their work was important. She established a coordinator in each country and encouraged people to communicate with one another and share information and resources. She facilitated a regional networking process.

Out of these efforts, Ferris gained a reputation for helping people build and strengthen networks. She raised the level of awareness among Peace Corps volunteers. Women in these countries frequently spent 17 hours a day in both household and income-generating activities and therefore workshops would have to be scheduled at convenient times to fit in their day.

TARGET TABLE: BOARD OF DIRECTORS
Ferris's leadership skills were noticed and she was asked to serve as a director on the National Peace Corps Association board.

TARGET TABLE: ENTREPRENEUR

Ferris left the Peace Corps after five years. The longest period one could serve the agency. Out in the job market she reviewed her talents, education, and commitment to specific issues, in order to assess where she would apply these qualities and skills next. The key qualities she identified many years ago, were still the same qualities she valued today. What was different this time was her vast experience and knowledge of people and places. She also had discovered that relationships were very important to her and that the network she had built professionally, was valuable to her personally as well.

"Sometimes you meet a person and you just click. In Senegal in Tambacunda, I met this woman in a bank who was on her way to Morocco and in about three minutes it was as if we had known each other all our lives. That experience is important to me and I value it in the workplace as well."

For Ferris, a seat at the table within a corporation with a rigid hierarchy and an autocratic management culture, would not be of value to her.

Although her work experience was in the public sector, Ferris always regarded herself as an entrepreneur. "I am a big risk-taker," she said. "I will be this way throughout my life."

WEXIS (Women's Exchange and Information Service) is her new company, a company bulletin-board service that provides information about women's organizations, worldwide grants, resources, funding, and scholarships for women. She is also the founder of the International Women's Democracy Center, established to train women outside of the U.S. how to run for office.

"Throughout my life, I have found myself in volunteer situations or work situations that I was interested in but had no background or professional training. I was willing to take the time to learn. To ask the stupid questions until I could identify where I fit, what I could bring to the table."

Ferris continually asks: "What is the goal here? Does this task move me closer to my goal or farther away? I am always doing 'mid-term' evaluations on myself." Rather than view success in terms defined by the popular culture, she believes that success "is going beyond the goals you set for yourself and sharing the achievements with family and friends. The sharing part makes it real so that other people can enjoy and be part of your achievements."

Dr. Lillian Beard, in addition to her role as a pediatrician serves as a national spokesperson on all health issues relating to infants, children, adolescents and young adults. Her nonprofit work in this area led her to a position as the on-air health advisor to Broadcast House Live on WUSA TV, Washington, D.C., and contributing editor to *Good Housekeeping* magazine, where she writes the monthly "Ask Dr. Beard" column.

Beard believes that one key to success is sharing what you know with others. "When I talk to young men and women, I tell them that you can't hold something in your hand so tightly that it will never get out, because in doing that, nothing will ever get in either. You have to be willing to help others succeed. In the process, you will succeed as well."

Beard, like so many other successful women, continues to participate in civic and professional organizations. In addition to serving as Chairman of the National Women's Economic Alliance Foundation, she has a life membership in the NAACP, serves on the board of the Children's Hospital in Washington, D.C., and is a member of the International Women's Forum. She has served as Chair of the Section of Pediatrics of the National Medical Association and also as vice president of her Links, Inc., chapter.

"I sought out groups where I felt that some of my ideas and ideals were already a part of the mission and I could have a role in helping to further them or that I might have the opportunity to bring my ideas to the table. I feel strongly about wanting to be a part of change and effecting change."

Beard has a record of going from member to a position of leadership in most of the organizations to which she belongs. "I started as a student in the National Medical Association and eventually became chairman of the Association's Council on Scientific Assembly. "I was very single-minded about wanting to be a physician and pursuing this course. Today, now that I have succeeded in reaching that goal, I am more diverse and allow myself to go in different directions to give back whatever talent and expertise I have."

Dr. Beard, who completed her training at Children's Hospital in Washington, D.C., was asked to make a presentation to a group connected with the hospital and others concerned about health care. Although her time was booked, she juggled several appointments on her calendar in order to be able to give the talk. "I wanted to do this for Children's because I had completed my internship there and residency and knew many of the people at the hospital and some of the members of the board."

President Clinton and Vice President Gore joined the group at Children's and were impressed with Beard and her remarks. So much so that the president mentioned that he had met this "compelling doctor" in his address to the nation and later extracted her comments in his health security book.

This one "mention" by the president of the United States on national television brought Lillian Beard offers to appear on programs, to host her own show, to work as a spokesperson on health issues.

None of this would have happened if Lillian Beard had dismissed the request from Children's Hospital to speak because her calendar was "full." She made the extra effort because of friendships and the fact that people were hoping they could count on her.

Lillian Beard's phone did not stop ringing for two weeks. Shortly after her presentation to the president, she was asked to serve on the Board of Directors of Children's Hospital.

TABLE: NONPROFIT

When Elaine Chao took over the helm at the United Way, chaos was reigning. Chao became president and chief executive officer of an organization racked with scandal and mismanagement. Chao faced a great challenge. For the first time since 1946, donations to United Way dropped. Local United Way chapters began withholding dues and moral was almost nonexistent.

Chao, who had served as director of the Peace Corps and deputy secretary of the U.S. Department of Transportation, was a graduate of the Harvard Business School with a background in banking. She eventually became the highest ranking Asian-American ever appointed to the executive branch.

What was Chao's overwhelming goal? What strategy did she demonstrate to achieve so much at a relatively young age?

"My first goal is to bring honor to my family," says Chao. The challenges she faced as CEO of United Way were serious, but no more so than the one she faced as a small child of eight immigrating to this country from Taiwan.

Ironically, the Chao's first apartment, when they lived in Queens, New York, was furnished through a United Way funded agency. Chao decided to take on the United Way position in order to restore the agency so that it could once more be effective in helping volunteer agencies ranging from shelters for battered women to the Boy Scouts.

In her role as CEO, Chao instituted unprecedented cost controls and accountablity procedures. She began restoring trust, visiting more than 35 United Way communities and meeting with more than 6,500 volunteers and professionals in her first four months at the helm.

"Americans share a unique sense of volunteerism. It is part of our national identity, our national tradition. United Way represents this unique sense of volunteerism and who we are as a charitable and generous people."

A guideline for your involvement:
1. Choose something that you really care about.
2. Get involved to make a difference.
3. Stay involved until you do.

4. Bring the same high level of professionalism to your volunteer activity that you do to your career.
5. Enjoy the experience.

10

A TABLE AT THE TOP

"What I wanted to be when I grew up was in charge."
WILMA VAUGHT, BRIGADIER GENERAL OF THE U.S. AIR FORCE

"You cannot manage men into battle. You manage things; you lead people."
ADMIRAL GRACE MURRAY HOPPER, U.S. NAVAL RESERVE

"I ran as a woman, as a mom, as who I am, because I wanted to be able to be who I am. Women can be women and be very successful."
SENATOR PATTY MURRAY (D-WASHINGTON)

"To thine own self be true and then it follow like the night the day, thou canst not then be false to any man."
WILLIAM SHAKESPEARE

If 1992 was the year of the woman politically, perhaps the last 10 years of the twentieth century can be designated the decade of the woman as leader. We have seen the emergence of the female entrepreneurial leader and as more women achieve in corporate America we will see new women leaders as CEO's of the top 1000 corporations. Certainly, enough has been written about traditional leadership styles: I leader, you follower, male vs. female styles of leadership, entrepreneurial vs corporate leadership, to confuse everyone.

The leader-you follow school has been in disrepute for some time, especially when applied to anything other than military or emergency situations. However, the leader for the year 2000 and beyond, whether in business or the public sector, will be facing many challenges and in some cases real emergencies.

Is there a one-style-fits-all brand of leadership that encompasses both the "heart and the head?" Or will the new leader choose from a menu of actions sometimes combining these qualities, and other times focusing on one or the other, democratic or autocratic leadership styles?

It may be comfortable to say that heart over head is always the right way to go, but anyone, who owns a business and who is faced with downsizing, understands that leadership means more than just showing up on the good days, it means making very difficult decisions, hard decisions that no one else is eager to make. However, the way, the style, and the thought with which these decisions are made, will ultimately determine how effective you will be as a leader.

Leadership is not for the faint of heart. It requires many of the qualities necessary for a successful entrepreneur: commitment, vision, energy, belief in one's self, the ability to take risks, a talent for communcating, the zeal to get out there, to be accountable, and to take responsibility. Even if we suspect that others may have contributed to failure, we don't affirm the leader who says, those guys did it, it's someone else's fault.

The real secret about leadership is that you don't arrive at a seat at the table and then begin demonstrating your leadership ability. You arrive at a seat at the table because the leadership skills, you've been demonstrating, are now being recognized. So it's important for you, wherever you are, in whatever role you enjoy, employee, housewife, chief executive officer, entrepreneur, candidate, fundraiser, volunteer, to take the leadership reins connected to your own life before you can demonstrate leadership on behalf of your business, your corporation, your constituency, your community.

Women, unaccustomed to viewing their daily lives through a leadership mode, may not even recognize nor give themselves credit for acts that are clearly leader-like. But the truth is there isn't one person today, who is not challenged on the leadership level by daily events. Now, how you react to these events will determine your leadership quotient.

For example, the 1990s patient, who goes to the hospital today, is very different from her counterpart of several years ago. You are more likely to question procedure, to take more responsibility for your treatment or convalescence. You will treat the physician not as a guru with all the answers, but as part of your paid team to help you make the decisions you need to make.

The rise in self-help groups is another sign that people understand that no one outside of themselves has the answer or solution for the problems in their lives. Or as Mary Kay Ash says, "If it's going to be, it's up to me."

Just as the physician or the lawyer or the politician expects to be questioned and challenged, the new leader understands that it is very difficult to move forward without the cooperation of those you are trying to lead. Why should this be of interest to women in particular? Primarily because we are much more comfortable with consensus-based leadership.

We are used to asking, "what do you think?" about almost everything. Whether that's talking to someone about a divorce or starting a business. We talk and ask questions. We talk some more, about anything and everything until we reach the point where we have examined all we need to examine, and we are ready to make a decision. In the process we have involved many people in that decision just by asking their opinion.

Women have been fortunate because it is natural for us to talk and ask for help and advice. We were never forced to put on the mantle of stoic wisdom in an effort to impress our peers. In that regard, men have been carrying a horrific burden personally and professionally. If you are a "strong, masculine" leader, you don't cry, you don't talk, you have all the answers and you follow the rules, whether or not the rules are still working.

Recently, I had to take my daughter to the emergency room at the hospital for a cut finger. While she was being attended to, I took a seat in the waiting room. A nurse was talking to a mother about the latter's teenage daughter. She said, "Your daughter has been taken to the doctor's office. It is a small room and the doctor suggests you may want to wait here."

The mother answered in halting English, "What does my daughter want?"

"What do you mean?" asked the nurse.

"I don't care what the doctor wants," said the mother. "Does my daughter want me to come in the room with her."

"Yes," said the nurse, "she does." And with that, the mother took off down the hall to the room, with the nurse following her.

That's leadership. Identifying the problem, cutting through the extraneous information and taking responsibility for a decision based on the information. In the past, perhaps, that mother would have been cowed by the doctor's preference and sacrificed her daughter's wishes in order to comply with authority. Take the leadership opportunity. As you do, you will find a by-product will be increased self-confidence and self-esteem. Increased self-confidence and self-esteem will enable you to make many more leadership decisions. As this process continues, recognition usually follows, whether at home or in the workplace, among friends and peers.

The most important recognition is internal and you begin to see that leadership means ownership of your life, no matter where you are or what seat at what table you may want to occupy.

Meg Armstrong, as president of The Leadership Group, helps business and public sector CEO's structure learning environments for leaders. She is also the founder of Women in State Government (WISG), the first organization of its kind to bring together women state government leaders. WISG was a result of Armstrong's finding a need in the market and filling it. "I was forming something that I wish I had had when I was in state government. I created the network that I had missed in my professional life."

She says, "True leadership is a blend of having the vision, seeing it and being able to articulate it, and having values which I think goes with influencing people to want to buy into the vision that you see and then taking the action that executes the vision."

Armstrong also counts courage, grit, perseverance as leadership qualities. "The most effective leaders, men and women, have to have a kind of grace about them in addition to a blend of all the other qualities."

Robert Gilbreath, president of Proudfoot Change Management and author of *Escape From Management*, believes that the new leaders are going to come from the "ranks of females, minorities and from outside of industry."

What can you do now to develop the leadership skills you are going to need either in the private or public sector?

VISION

First you have to have a vision for your own life before you can articulate a vision for others. It helps to know who you are and where you think you may be going. Vision is critical but it needs to be balanced with some sense of reality.

Beth Bronner had a vision for Häagen-Dazs and she achieved it. When it became clear that her goals and her vision for her professional life were not going to be met, despite what she had achieved for the company, she left.

If you betray the vision you have for yourself, you will not be effective for long. Your vision will be affirmed in direct proportion to the attention you pay to your needs, mental, physical and spiritual. When any of those elements get neglected, the ego takes over, stress takes over, and your vision can become cloudy.

"Vision," says Meg Armstrong, "is what I value the most in a leader. The ability to have the long view, the wide view. The talent to articulate it in ways that capture the imagination."

What is your vision for your life right now?

What is your vision for your company?

Where do your goals fit in the larger scheme of things? Do

your talents fit what will be required by the corporation of
the year 2000?

What about your product or services?

What are you prepared to commit to ensure your vision
becomes a reality?

Remind yourself everyday, advises Armstrong, What is my goal?
What am I doing? How am I doing it? Why am I doing it?

What are you not prepared to commit?

Will your vision sustain you through problems and
challenges?

Are you a one-person band or have you communicated your
vision to others, key decision-makers, critical publics,
family, friends?

Florence Nightingale, who led the British military services into a new era of
care for the wounded and dying, galvanized public opinion to obtain her goals.
In a letter written to her Aunt Mai from the Crimea she says, "There is not an
official who would not burn me like Joan of Arc if he could, but they know the
War Office cannot turn me out because the country is with me."

In a letter to her father, Nightingale said: "In a difficult life (and mine has
been more difficult than most) it is always better clearly to decide for oneself:
what grievances one will bear being unavoidable; what grievances one will escape from; what grievances one will try to remove."(*800 Years of Women's Letters*,
edited by Olga Kenyon)

BEING YOURSELF

We have spent so much time determining, who we will be and how we will act
in order to succeed, it is ironic that we have arrived at a place where we know
we cannot succeed unless we do it by being ourselves. Leadership means you
are comfortable being in your own skin. It doesn't mean you are not constantly
trying to improve. But the improvements are to enhance what you already have,
not to obliterate your soul and psyche. At some point as more women achieve
the top rungs in the public and private sectors, there will be less emphasis on
male and female definitions of leadership. We will, it is hoped, learn how to
learn from one another. Leaders make decisions. They may involve teams and
consensus-building, but at some point they take responsibility and take one
road or the other.

UNDERSTAND YOURSELF

Leaders work on keeping their ego in check. Ego distorts and sees threats and enemies and competitors even when they don't exist. An inflated ego also leads to complacency, and fulsome self-congratulations. On the other side of the scale, a lack of ego can destroy initiative, pump up self-doubt and undermine risk-taking. The goal is a healthy ego. The prescription to achieve a healthy ego includes a steady diet of friends and outside interests, giving back some of your success, affirming others, working for change and a better company, community and world.

Who do you admire for his leadership style?

Who do you admire for her leadership style?

Are they very different?

What are the leadership qualities you are demonstrating now?

Are you uncomfortable making unpopular decisions?

What qualities would you like to possess?

How do you handle problems?

"I worked with a governor who gave me a great perspective on problems," says Meg Armstrong. "He said he used to wake up in the morning and say 'if it can go wrong, it probably will, and that's what I'm here for.' So when things don't seem to be working in my life, I just look at it as part of the overall picture and probably very normal. Then I can diffuse the charge and get on with working toward a solution rather than wringing hands too long over the problem."

UNDERSTAND OTHERS

Historian James MacGregor Burns said of FDR that he "knew how to persuade one person by argument, another by charm, another by a display of self-confidence, another by flatter, another by encyclopedic knowledge."

The only way to obtain information and insight like this is to be a quiet observer and a conscientious listener. People tell you so much about themselves in what they say and what they don't say. How they walk. Is it a tentative apologetic stride or a take charge get-out-of-my-way-world-here-I-come gait? Next time you are having a conversation with someone observe the following:

What are they saying about themselves when they talk? What does their body language tell you?

"I am a straight shooter."

"I'm not someone who likes to gossip but..."

"I really like Mary Jones but sometimes..."

"May I be frank?"

"Titles mean nothing to me but..."

"It's not the money..."

"We can do it because..."

"It's impossible."

Even if we all know everything there is to know about this stuff, when we are in a conversation even the most controlled person forgets himself when he gets animated or excited about a subject. The reverse is also true. Next time you are leading a meeting take a real look around the table. You will be able to spot immediately the ones who will try to shoot the idea down later, the people who are on your team and enthusiastic about your vision, the ones who are on the fence and need to hear a little more before they can decide.

Meg Armstrong says, "I learned to watch what was going on around me. An abstract list of skills associated with achievement doesn't necessarily work from one culture to the next. What does work is looking, watching, listening very carefully to the people who are effective in your environment."

Leaders not only know how to deliver a speech, they know how to connect. They can articulate a vision and inspire others to come along and help make the vision real. They know this because they have taken the time to listen and understand that what motivates one person may completely discourage another.

Dr. Lillian Beard has another definition for what she admires most in a leader. "Back in my elementary school in Brooklyn, New York, there was a box on the report card where your teacher evaluated your ability to 'work and play well with others.' I think that's an important component for the leaders of tomorrow. Also the ability to be fair. We've all come to our various seats around diverse tables with certain biases that we have brought with us. I believe a true leader works at trying to be objective."

"Nothing great was ever achieved without enthusiasm." Ralph Waldo Emerson

Let's say this again. You cannot be negative and lead. You must be able to communicate your high level of commitment, your belief that this is the right thing to to do, your enthusiasm, if anyone is going to buy into your vision.

Was Lincoln happy and positive about the Civil War? No, but he was positive and determined and committed to preserving the union.

At some point, the leader says, "Here I stand. Here are my values, if you share them, share my vision, let's move forward together." That's why it is important to really understand the vision of those to whom you report or who have dominion over your professional life.

As service becomes king in the U.S., the information worker becomes part of the royal family. This means that the autocratic leadership style, based on military terms, is effective only in the military, or in situations where there are very few options for workers to leave. In *Megatrends 2000*, John Naisbitt says, "The military management model can command authority; business leadership must win loyalty, achieve commitment, and earn respect."

This means that as a leader, you will have to spend a lot of time understanding the personal goals of those you depend on to help you build a business, run for office, achieve within the corporation, head a team of volunteers. Frances Hesselbein, who was named by Peter Drucker as the best manager, bar none, in the United States, had to learn just that when she was national executive director of the Girls Scouts of America, the largest nonprofit organization in the United States.

When Hesselbein took over in 1976, the Girl Scouts were in trouble. Women were entering the work force at greater and greater numbers and the women at home were not being affirmed for volunteer work. In fact, volunteering was viewed as victimizing women, who should be paid for their efforts. Hesselbein cut through the societal negatives, the overgrown bureaucracies within the Girl Scouts and formed a corporate management team.

Her vision was to take the organization where the customers, the girl scouts themselves wanted it to go, to create an organization that responded to their needs. Badges could now be earned for computer science instead of home economics, for environmental projects, for business experience. Through training programs, outreach to minorities and even a new design for the Girl Scout uniform, Hesselbein signaled that a new day had dawned for the Girl Scouts. Her vision or mission was accomplished for all to see through a continuous plan of action steps. Hesselbein gave power to teams and not to hierarchies and in the process reinvented the Girl Scouts.

She called it, "managing for a mission." The mission was "to help a girl reach her highest potential." The mission was the vision. What Hesselbein did is what Lynn Martin describes as leading with heart and brain. Inspiration and the bottom line, not one or the other. Hesselbein began her professional life as an entrepreneur, which enabled her to view nonprofit management with the same discipline one might reserve for a thriving top 1000 corporation.

Today, she is the president and chief executive officer of the Peter F. Drucker Foundation for Nonprofit Management.

Jill Barad, president and CEO of Mattel, Inc., went from a junior executive to the second to the top spot at Mattel based in large part on her ability to create a vision and produce the reality. Barad has kept the Barbie doll alive and well and current. Barad's signature is a golden bumblebee pin which she wears daily. It was given to her by her mother and reminds Barad that aerodynamically bumble bees should not be able to fly.

Meg Armstrong agrees that enthusiasm is a key ingredient for effective leadership. She also adds, "You have to like people and be able to get along with a lot of them. Whatever your skills, the things you can carry with you from one seat at the table to another are what I call bedrock values that people can comprehend. The most important of all these values, in my opinion, is integrity."

As men and women move through a roiling sea of change, it is more important than ever before, that as individuals we identify our leadership skills, strengthen them and then, work with one another to determine how we can complement each other. Business and industry will be more accepting of a diversity of leadership and management styles as long as the leaders lead to a positive outcome for the business entity. Interactive leadership, the style most identified as belonging to women, is just one component of effective leading. It is not a cure-all.

Women are not arriving on the corporate or entrepreneurial landscape with a magic leadership bullet. We bring certain traits and qualities and experiences to the business table. Insofar as we are able to translate these qualities into a vision for the future, we and our teamworkers and our businesses and corporations will succeed. How do we do this? By not worrying so much about feminine qualities and male qualities, by realizing we all have something to offer in our own way, and that we all have something to learn from one another.

Boston Globe columnist Ellen Goodman called General H. Norman Schwarzkopf "caring but, well commanding." This is the knockout combination and it being demonstrated by men and women more and more throughout winning organizations.

"But I don't want to be, you know, 'commanding,' " one woman told me. "It sounds so cold." However, when we looked at other definitions of "commanding" in the dictionary she was willing to identify "deserve and get" as a personal goal, along with "caring" as well.

This is what we are all continuing to do, as women at home, and in the workforce, take the old worlds, the old actions, the old meanings, and redefine, through our own experience and insights, what they can truly mean today. Not only for us as individuals moving toward a goal, but for those who will be following the new paths we have cleared for them.

YOU CAN ACHIEVE A SEAT AT THE TABLE.

START NOW OR START OVER.

YOUR TABLE IS WAITING.

Appendix

Women Leaders' Views on Power, Success, Tactics, Leadership

POWER

Women business owners do not view power as an opportunity to "roar." Overwhelmingly, they view power in terms of "empowerment" and the chance to accomplish goals benefiting not only themselves, but also those they work with and for.

What does power mean to you?

- ❖ Control over one's choices and direction in life.
- ❖ Knowing yourself.
- ❖ Ability to make a difference, to achieve goals.
- ❖ To be able to get what you want when you want it.
- ❖ Ability to influence outcome.
- ❖ Access to people.
- ❖ Having others trust your leadership.
- ❖ Having the resources to shape the future for oneself and others for good.
- ❖ Ability to lead with confidence.
- ❖ Ability to get things done.
- ❖ Respect of people working for you.
- ❖ To be able to communicate effectively.
- ❖ To be able to influence.

❖ Having support and respect which enables you to reach goals.

❖ Being able to accomplish goals not just for yourself but for others.

❖ influence others in a positive way that will improve their lives.

❖ Ability to create change.

❖ Building your talents and strengths so you can sustain yourself.

❖ Should be the greatest servant of the people.

❖ Ability to inspire others to do better than they thought possible.

❖ Ability to use your talents, energy and creative ability to reach personal financial, creative, goals while truly enjoying family and friends.

❖ Power is not something to be proud of. It is only a necessary tool to make good things happen.

Once the idea for the business has been created, the prime tactic for success depends on short-and long-term planning. Women entrepreneurs establish goals and to a person demonstrate persistence and tenacity to achieve those goals.

What were some of the tactics used to achieve success in business?

❖ Set goals and priorities.

❖ Develop a strategic plan.

❖ Keep goals achievable and measurable for long-term.

❖ Develop five new contacts a week, follow up with short notes, read, read, learn everything you can about your business.

❖ Manage time by managing phone calls, play back taped messages at scheduled time, use computer e-mail, develop your plan and stick to it, delegate, delegate, delegate. When your goal is accomplished, celebrate.

❖ World and business is constantly changing and keeping up to date is a challenge. Keep up with new ideas and technology.

❖ Organize yourself and make a strong personal commitment to your goals.

❖ Review your progress daily. Respect planning and target dates.

❖ Set priorities and don't waste time or energy or effort on things beyond your control.

❖ Network effectively.

❖ Visualizing a successful outcome.

❖ Focused flexibility.

❖ Hard work, homework, hang in there.

SUCCESS

The group we surveyed felt the number one quality a leader needed was to have a positive belief system. Under this umbrella, it was then necessary to have the following qualities.

❖ Enthusiasm

❖ Tenacity

❖ Honesty

❖ Intelligence

❖ People skills

❖ Self-respect and self-esteem

❖ Spiritual focus

❖ High energy

❖ Dependability

❖ Courage

❖ Mental analytical skills and intuitive skills

❖ Love

❖ Resourcefulness

❖ Empathy

❖ Straight-shooter

❖ Willingness to work harder than anyone else

❖ Confidence in yourself and respect for others

❖ Credibility

❖ Risk-taker

❖ Humor

❖ Strategic thinker

❖ Fairness

❖ Integrity

SUCCESS

What is your definition of success?

❖ Work hard, but don't put blinders on. Don't be so driven that you lose track of what's going on. Be open and not single-minded.

❖ Happiness with self, in the belief I tried my best to reach my potential.

❖ Achieving your goal, never giving up, no excuses. Being the best you can be at whatever you choose.

❖ The accomplishment of goals: personal and professional.

❖ Happiness and making a difference in my field; helping someone else.

❖ Personal goals: family and children.

❖ Ability to get up every morning looking forward to doing what you are doing that week and to be in a position where you are able to earn a living doing something you would do even if you weren't paid.

❖ Satisfaction with achievements, feeling of fulfillment. Having fun with what you do every day.

❖ Security: emotional, financial and social.

❖ Having no trouble accomplishing goals and financial security.

❖ Health, wealth, love and the time to enjoy it all.

❖ Independence to take on challenges as they arise and the ability to walk away when it is not fun any more.

❖ Having the life you want and feeling terrific about it. Knowing you are doing it for yourself and not trying to keep up with anyone in society. Joy and fulfillment.

❖ You have got to be happy with yourself. Achieve your goals and be comfortable with your achievements.

❖ Achieving deserved recognition as leader in your chosen pursuit. Making a real contribution in your field.

❖ Being in control of your life.

❖ Developing tomorrow's leaders.

❖ Success is fun, but my family is first in my heart and although the success is mine, my life would be lonely not to share it with my family.

❖ To be happy with yourself and be able to look at yourself in the mirror every morning and every night and be able to say that you've done the best that you know how to do.

LEADERS KNOW HOW TO "NETWORK": RELATIONSHIP BUILDING

"Networking in the '80s meant being in the pipeline, but networking in the '90s is your lifeline," according to entrepreneur Jeri Sedlar, "What people don't realize is it takes time. Some people think of networking only when they have a need, but the smartest person is one who networks when they don't have a need at all. Network is relationship building, it is for the long-term. Get involved, either on the membership committee of an organization or the program committee, because that's the way you meet people and they get to know you. Start first with your community, the Rotary, the Chamber of Commerce. Start volunteering."

❖ Participate in different types of organizations, community, women and business.

❖ Be future-oriented. Get out and about and make the effort to participate in charity and civic events, meet and get to know people in the work force.

❖ Friends are more important than anyone can describe. They are there to hear your troubles, share your achievements and make you laugh. Network first for relationships. It does not matter if they never turn out to be good for business.

❖ Reciprocity is the key to successful networking. Remember to use the network on a regular basis, thus maintaining it and utilize each contact to expand it further.

❖ Don't expect to get, if you're not willing to give.

❖ True networking does not provide platforms for individuals, but extends team spirit to outreach and encompass all races, subjects and actions.

❖ True networking is valuable, but too often it is too superficial to matter. You have to be willing to commit time and resources if you want a return.

❖ Networking has been very important to me. I love meeting people, hearing about their roads to success and helping them in any way I can. The most effective way to network is to just get out there and listen to what people have to say and learn from them.

❖ I think women focus too much on women. Some of my best friends are men and there are more men than women in positions to help us. Women don't think enough about leverage.

❖ Join organizations, business and political.

❖ Networking is really a matter of knowing and being known to a large number of persons, who may have interests or talents that may be called upon to assist oneself or others. There is not just one effective way to network. Some people work better in crowds or professional organizations, others are better able to meet and talk to persons in small groups.

❖ Networking is a numbers thing: the more people you talk to, the better your chances are. Follow up, follow up, follow up.

❖ Networking can validate or change your thinking, create opportunities personally and professionally. You build on one relationship after the other.

❖ Do not limit yourself to business organizations. I meet many people on the tennis courts, golf courses or volunteering for community organizations.

❖ You have to network in many different spheres, among men and women, professionally and personally. If you are networking for information it is important to share information. When you share what you know, others will share with you. Through the exchange of information, you and the group, within which you are working, will be able to succeed. Be willing to give as well as to get.

❖ Circulate, meet people, remember people and be willing to help others. Networking is broadening your base of possible contacts. Building relationships goes beyond knowing whom to call. It requires nurturing, follow through in commitments, staying in touch. Being willing to help and advise others.

❖ Don't operate within a clique. Expand your universe and be generous with one another.

❖ Networking can be a very selfish activity. Relationship building benefits everyone.

❖ It's important to have a small group of alter egos, male and female, whom you can trust for confidence and testing ideas. It is important to remember that networking is not just picking up people and dropping them when your purpose is achieved.

❖ Networking to me is sharing experiences and contacts. This is invaluable for broadening one's own thinking.

❖ Networking gives you the opportunity to explore new territory.

❖ Bring people into your orbit and they will bring you into theirs.

DIRECTOR SURVEY

The National Women's Economic Alliance Foundation surveyed women serving as outside directors on leading U.S. service and industrial corporations about the advice they would give to qualified women candidates for corporate board appointment. With women achieving as business owners, as senior-level managers, as chief executive officers and as political leaders, the number of qualified candidates, who happen to be women, continues to increase. What differentiates candidates with similar qualifications? What steps should qualified candidates take to increase their opportunity of serving on a corporate board? The responses from 500 directors were as follows:

A majority said that the most instrumental factors leading to their corporate board appointment were: credentials, reputation and experience and visibility, which brought them to the attention of the decision-makers.

Over 90 percent said that visibility at the leadership level in one or more nonprofit organizations dedicated to improving the community, or raising money for a health or education cause provided their entry to the decision-makers: "Reputation for community service and involvement coupled with competent and effective business skills." "Make yourself known. If you stay in your office, you'll never be asked out."

Over 60 percent credited visibility through a combination of speaking engagements, articles in business magazines or national/international newspapers, professional journals and trade magazines.

In terms of "strategy," over 95 percent of the respondents agreed:

> It is important to become involved in activities which would provide appropriate visibility. Join pro bono or philanthropic boards. These boards present opportunities to gain experience, as well as provide opportunities for visibility and interaction with corporate chieftains and senior-leaders.

> Identify those who can introduce the candidate to the decision-maker(s).

> Prove you are an expert in your chosen field. Excel at what you do. Earn the respect of people who sit on boards.

The survey respondents identified the following key qualities:

Confidence in one's abilities

Professional competence

Honesty

Integrity

Ability to communicate

Independent thinker

Commitment

Vision/Perspective

Knowledgeable

Authenticity

Judgment

Accountability

The respondents also cited the following steps as important for a qualified candidate to take to make an impact on decision-makers:

Volunteer activities

Writing

Speeches

High profile based on reputation

Spokesperson activities

Excel in your profession

Involvement

Resource to the press

Demonstrate your talents in a variety of arenas

Respect and trust

Utilize established networks

The following pages represent a compilation of survey responses.

NAME/POSITION/COMPANY: Jane Evans, Vice President & General Manager, Home and Personal Services, US WEST Communications, Inc.

CORPORATE BOARD APPOINTMENTS: Philip Morris, Georgia Pacific, Edison Brothers, Inc., Banc One

Most Instrumental Factor

From my own experience, I think two factors significantly increase opportunities for corporation board appointments. First, you need the credentials that come with a proven track record of leadership and professional achievement within your industry or discipline. You also need to be in a job that presents opportunities for visibility within your industry and within corporate America. For example, when I was appointed to the board of directors of Philip Morris in

1981, I had a very strong track record in consumer marketing, and, as an Executive Vice President for General Mills, I was the highest-ranking woman in American industry at the time. As such, my position generated a great deal of visibility and coverage in national newspapers and business publications.

Strategy

Serving on a corporate board is not something you campaign for; you need to be in the right job, at the right time, with the right background that brings the most value to the corporate board. One way to prepare for a corporate board appointment is to join pro bono or philanthropic boards. These boards present opportunities to gain experience, as well as provide opportunities for visibility and interaction with "corporate chieftains" and senior leaders.

Key Qualities

You really need a sense of humor! Never take yourself too seriously. You also need to be confident in your own abilities, and have excellent interpersonal and team skills. Finally, it's important to value the people you work with, and who work with you. Since you won't always be conversant about specific industry or company issues when serving on a corporate board, you need to be able to generalize from your own experiences and extrapolate possible solutions to issues.

Getting in Front of Decision-makers

Serve on pro bono or philanthropic boards. Write articles for widely respected and well-known publications and journals. Establish yourself as a spokesperson for your industry.

NAME/POSITION/COMPANY: Marilou von Ferstel, Executive Vice President/General Manager, Ogilvy Adams & Rinehart

CORPORATE BOARD APPOINTMENTS: Walgreens, Illinois Power

Most Instrumental Factor

Fairly high visibility in the community, first as a newspaper reporter, then as an alderman and public official. My career was open to public scrutiny and I was early-on deemed to be a "leader". I think that gave the business establishment comfort.

Strategy

Make yourself known. If you stay in your office, you'll never be asked out. Our community (the village of Chicago) invest in people in the civic, community affairs arena. It's a good venue to test leadership skills, creativity and initiative. Get on some nonprofit boards. You'll find that your good work, if you do it, will filter up very quickly. That's what men do, too.

Key Qualities

For board service, a woman needs to be intelligent, have good, calm judgment, and be rational. There's no doubt that I have a definite point of view on certain subjects, but I try not to be "causaholic" about it. Then, there is the question of "presence." It's hard to define except you know when it is or is not there. Public speaking seems to help. A comfortable working knowledge of the accounting process is also very helpful, as well as understanding of the earnings performance of the company in question.

Getting in Front of Decision-makers

Again, the best way is to find out what civic and/or community enterprises they are involved in and get yourself on those same committees, boards, etc. Your own boss may be your best friend. As board service demands more time and accountability, there is the believe that we'll have to go farther down in management ranks than CEO. Sit down and talk to her/him, and find out if she/he can be helpful. Board service reflects back well on your own company.

NAME/POSITION/COMPANY: Dr. Gloria S. Hom, Chairman, Economics Department, Mission College

CORPORATE BOARD APPOINTMENTS: Sallie Mae

Most Instrumental Factor

Having a presence in the political party as well as in a presidential campaign was of great assistance.

Strategy

Know other corporate board members who would feed your name into the pipeline.

Key Qualities

She must be articulate, willing to spend hours studying the issues and understand the process and politics of the board.

Getting in Front of Decision-makers

This takes time and cultivation. Spend time understanding the personal sensitivities of the members.

NAME/POSITION/COMPANY: Thekla R. Shackelford, Educational Consultant and Owner of School Selection Consulting

CORPORATE BOARD APPOINTMENTS: Wendy's International, Banc One Corp., and Sundance, Inc., a privately-held radio station in Arizona and Wisconsin

Most Instrumental Factor

My first corporate board appointment was at Wendy's International. Even ten years ago, I began a small entrepreneurial business in Columbus, Ohio, placing boarding school and college students. My personal contacts with the children of top management were what brought me to their attention as a professional person. I had also worked as Development Director at a local treatment center for adolescent boys. In that capacity, I had worked with Wendy's when it sponsored a major tennis tournament. Establishing professional credibility is the single most important factor.

Strategy

The best approach to winning a seat on a corporate board is to prove that you are an expert in your chosen field. Demonstration of good judgment, loyalty, discretion, and vision is vital. Formal and informal interaction with management also positions you well. Head hunter recommendations also seem to yield good results.

Key Qualities

I feel that the important qualities a woman needs to achieve to reach self satisfaction and a high degree of productivity are integrity, ability to communicate, and the ability to sort the wheat from the "chaff." In a recent article in Leader magazine, Jack Welch was quoted as saying that the three things that have made G.E. successful are speed, simplicity, and self-confidence. Those three S's are important. People skills, willingness to work, attention to detail, and follow-through are equally important ingredients to success. It is important to know oneself and one's skills and to learn how to utilize those skills purposefully.

Getting in Front of Decision-makers

Involvement. I would never have gotten in front of opinion/decision-makers had I not been involved in the community and in my professional life. It is an "old person" network, not "old boy" as it used to be. Word-of-mouth means a lot and earning the respect of people who make the decisions will almost always put you in the running. Many folks get nearly to the top but lose it because of one or two mistakes. Willingness to risk but avoidance of irreversible mistakes is critical. Resiliency puts the icing on the cake.

NAME/POSITION/COMPANY: Kitty G. Dickerson, Ph.D., Professor, Department Chairman, University of Missouri, Author, Consultant

CORPORATE BOARD APPOINTMENTS: The Kellwood Co.

Most Instrumental Factor

Having expertise in a subject of value to industry. Having men at the top level in the company who wanted diversity on the board, but who were not willing to choose a token woman.

Strategy

In my opinion, there is no shortcut to development of expertise in areas valued by the business world. To have women or anyone else appointed as tokens to represent a particular group serves no one well, the company, the individual, or women (or other groups) in general. In order for this expertise to be evident to anyone, however, the individual must participate in a number of external groups and activities. One may have tremendous expertise that goes unnoticed unless the individual is involved beyond the office.

Key Qualities

Expertise, good people skills, diplomacy, poise, confidence, and a healthy self-esteem. Without these, one lacks important tools and skills to participate in what may be uncharted waters for a woman.

Getting in Front of Decision-makers

This is not an easy matter. Trying too hard may make one seem manipulative and opportunistic both of which are self-defeating. My board appointment came as a surprise; I did not expect it or probably was not savvy enough to have pursued it, even if I were inclined to do that (which I was not). If I were an upper level male executive, I would be skeptical of individuals who appeared too hard to get attention. In short, my appointment came about because of my expertise in a timely area. My advice is to "work like the dickens, and good things will eventually come your way."

NAME/POSITION/COMPANY: Judith M. Von Seldenech, President/CEO, Diversified Search Companies

CORPORATE BOARD APPOINTMENTS: Meridian Bancorp, Tasty Baking Co., Phillips & Jacobs, Keystone Ins.

Most Instrumental Factor

I sit on four and they were all different. Probably being perceived as a successful businesswoman who had also been active in the community in the business-oriented organizations like the Chamber of Commerce, Economic Development Council, etc. And also for a long time.

Strategy

Impress the CEO or Chair of the nominating committee through some subtle means. Above all, don't be seen as controversial.

Key Qualities

Attractive, smart, articulate, ego in place, clearly successful, sense of humor, confident but not overbearing.

Getting in Front of Decision-makers

Serve on committees which they are involved in, nonprofit, social service organizations.

NAME/POSITION/COMPANY: Judith A. Rogala, President/CEO, The Environmental Quality Co.

CORPORATE BOARD APPOINTMENTS: Butler Manufacturing, Dry Storage Corp.

Most Instrumental Factor

Having the experience the company was searching for.

Strategy

Network. Decision-makers need to know you or trust the person recommending you.

Key Qualities

Integrity in all your dealings, balance in your approach in solving problems and pursuing goals.

Getting in Front of Decision-makers

Participate in business organizations like the Economic Club, Chamber of Commerce.

NAME/POSITION/COMPANY: Margita E. White, President, MSTV, Inc.

CORPORATE BOARD APPOINTMENTS: ITT Corp., ITT Sheraton Corp, Washington Mutual Investors Fund, Growth Fund of Washington

Most Instrumental Factor

Most instrumental in my initial appointments in 1980-81 to the ITT and Taft corporate boards was my governmental experience as an FCC Commissioner, Director of the White House Office of Communications and Assistant Director of USIA. In later board appointments (Armtek, Washington Mutual, Growth Fund of Washington, ITT Sheraton, Rayonier Forest Resources), my corporate board experience and performance likely were the most significant factors.

Strategy

One doesn't exactly "win" a corporate board seat. Luck does figure into being in the right place at the right time and being known by the right people when a board position is to be filled. I never campaigned for a board seat, the recommendation to ITT came from three different individuals without my knowledge. However, having achieved a professional level and expertise where one's credential might be an asset to a board in a particular industry or area, focused research and contacts certainly could be useful.

Key Qualities

To the extent women see or seek power as a goal, I believe they will be disappointed. Power, it seems to me, is a result that is reinforced by a demonstration of leadership that is perceived as effective and meriting of support. Achieving higher levels of power also depends on the ability to motivate and contribute as a member of the group.

Getting in Front of Decision-makers

Professional achievements, if recognized, are their own introduction to the seat at any table, and women have growing choices as to where they want to be seated. I don't know of a "right way" to achieve that recognition but certainly the endorsement, patronage and support of those who best can vouch for your qualifications are far preferable to self-promotion.

NAME/POSITION/COMPANY: Myra Jones, State Representative/Small Business Owner

CORPORATE BOARD APPOINTMENTS: Arkla, Inc. (soon to be renamed NORAM)

Most Instrumental Factor

History of community service and leadership and local elected official with a broad base of support from diverse community groups.

Strategy

Demonstrate leadership through business and community involvement.

Key Qualities

Integrity, loyalty, trust, hard work, good mentors.

Getting in Front of Decision-makers

Become involved in community service. Leadership demonstrated through community, business and charitable organizations.

NAME/POSITION/COMPANY: Laurel Cutler, Vice chairman, FCB/LEBER KATZ partners (advertising)

CORPORATE BOARD APPOINTMENTS: Hannaford Brothers, Quaker State, NY

Stock Exchange Boards (3), Silver Bullets Advisory Board, Advertising Education Foundation

Most Instrumental Factor

Prior working relationships with CEO and/or other board members.

Strategy

Earn the respect of people who sit on boards.

Key Qualities

Be known for doing your homework and speaking your mind.

Getting in Front of Decision-makers

Accept invitations to speak and calls from the press. Become a reliable source.

NAME/POSITION/COMPANY: Jean Patrice Harrington, S.C., Ph.D., President Emerita, College of Mt. St. Joseph

CORPORATE BOARD APPOINTMENTS: Star Bank, N.A.; Carillon Funds, Inc. (Retired from: Star Banc, Inc. and Cincinnati Bell)

Most Instrumental Factor

Reputation for community service and involvement coupled with competent and effective administrative skills.

Strategy

Perform your responsibilities consistently and efficiently and be conscious of the importance of good interpersonal skills. Learn to network well.

Key Qualities

She needs to be intelligent, well-educated, and articulate without being aggressive. She needs to be a woman of principle, but gentle in approach to difficult situations.

Getting in Front of Decision-makers

I have never consciously tried, except to always respond promptly when asked to serve in any capacity.

NAME/POSITION/COMPANY: Dina Merrill, Vice Chairman, RKO Pictures

CORPORATE BOARD APPOINTMENTS: RKO Pictures, Shearson Lehman Brothers Holdings, Inc.

Key Qualities

Clear vision, cool head and a willingness to speak up and stick your neck out for something you believe in.

Getting in Front of Decision-makers

Create the "right" moment for yourself, and then sell your idea and your faith in it.

NAME/POSITION/COMPANY: Joan Roth Herschede, President/CEO, Frank Herschede Co.

CORPORATE BOARD APPOINTMENTS: Fifth Third Bancorp (present)/Central Trust Bank (past)

Most Instrumental Factor

Female, known throughout the business community as a hard worker in the business as well as the civic community. A very capable person.

Strategy

Work hard and be good at what you do. Do not be an activist-do gooder.

Key Qualities

Be very knowledgeable about your job, work hard and be at the right place at the right time.

Getting in Front of Decision-makers

Work very hard behind the scenes, so that the powers that be know you do make a difference; and when it is time to ask for someone to step forward, you have already proven yourself.

NAME/POSITION/COMPANY: Barbara B. Grogan, President/CEO, Western Industrial Contractors, Inc.

CORPORATE BOARD APPOINTMENTS: Deluxe Corp. and Federal Reserve Bank of Kansas-Denver Branch

Most Instrumental Factor

The most instrumental factor without a doubt was "being out there" knowing the players and having them know me. When a board opening came up, I am certain they decided they should be looking for a woman. Two of the directors knew me, one through the U.S. chamber and one through the Federal Reserve.

Strategy

Be the best person you can be. Excel at what you do and give back to your community. Be involved. Follow your passions and lead, lead, lead!

Key Qualities

Honesty and integrity are number one, followed closely by intelligence, guts, determination, perseverance, sense of humor, nerves of steel, compassion, inspiration, decisive, incisive, great communicator, a vision for the future and a passion for life.

Getting in Front of Decision-makers

By being very good at what you do and very involved in your community. By making significant, meaningful, positive contributions while working the "decision-makers and opinion leaders", you eventually become one.

NAME/POSITION/COMPANY: Doug Newsom, Ph.D. (Douglas Ann Newsom), Professor of Journalism, Texas Christian University

CORPORATE BOARD APPOINTMENTS: ONEOK

Most Instrumental Factor

The "good-old girl" network.

Strategy

Get someone to recommend you to the decision-maker.

Key Qualities

Flexibility and the ability to listen. Learn as much as you can about the organization (in addition to being at the highest level of your own profession).

Getting in Front of Decision-makers

Pay attention to what is important to them.

NAME/POSITION/COMPANY: Doris R. Bray, Partner, Schell Bray Aycock Abile & Livingston, L.L.P., Attorneys

CORPORATE BOARD APPOINTMENTS: Cone Mills Corp. Will stand for election to the Vanguard Cellular Systems, Inc. Board at its May, 1994 Annual Meeting.

Most Instrumental Factor

Knowledge of the company, business experience and judgment.

Strategy

Demonstrated competence in one's career.

Key Qualities

Demonstrated professional competence, self-confidence and a lack of self-consciousness about gender, i.e., a woman must think of herself as a professional, not as a female professional, but, at the same time, she should retain her femininity. On the other hand, a woman should not use that fact to attempt to obtain an unfair advantage. She should compete with men on an equal basis.

Getting in Front of Decision-makers

If one is professionally competent, she has no problem getting in front of opinion/decision-makers in the right way. She will be sought out because of the contributions she can make. Of course, one must first establish a professional reputation, but it seems to me that how one does that is dependent upon one's professional, personality and circumstances, which makes generalization difficult.

NAME/POSITION/COMPANY: Ruth Shaw, Senior Vice President, Corporate Resources, Duke Power Co.

CORPORATE BOARD APPOINTMENTS: First Union Corp.

Most Instrumental Factor

Professional and civic leadership. I was president of the state's largest community college when named, had chaired several major charitable campaigns, civic and volunteer boards. High regional, state profile.

Strategy

I was simply doing my best in some important work. Doing that involved building relationships and working in public settings where my abilities were "tested" and I teamed with corporate leaders.

Key Qualities

Important requisites that make one deserving of this responsibility include vision/perspective; professional competence; energy; integrity; authenticity.

Getting in Front of Decision-makers

I believe "the right way" is the way that enables you to use your abilities to their fullest on work you believe is significant and in which you find pleasure. That differs for different people.

NAME/POSITION/COMPANY: Cecily Cannan Selby, retired professor; Trustee/Director

CORPORATE BOARD APPOINTMENTS: Avon Products, Inc. (formerly RCA, NBC, National Education Corp., Loehmanns)

Most Instrumental Factor

My position as COO of the largest nonprofit corporation for girls and women (Girls Scouts, USA); strong academic credentials (Ph.D. from MIT); and a record of management of other enterprises and, being female in 1972 when the cry was out for women on boards!

Strategy

Record of accountability in management in profit and nonprofit enterprise plus visibility (reputation) and leadership.

Key Qualities

Visible evidence of ability and readiness to "take charge", i.e., lead and be accountable; and, thereby, earn respect for judgment. Also, getting along with men!

Getting in Front of Decision-makers

Be up front with good works! i.e., achievement of your organization for which you are credited. Do a great job, be recognized for it, and be liked and respected.

═══════════════════════════════

NAME/POSITION/COMPANY: Jameson A. Baxter, President, Baxter Associates, Inc.

CORPORATE BOARD APPOINTMENTS: Banta Corp., Putnam Mutual Funds, Avondale Federal Savings, Ashta Chemicals, Inc.

Most Instrumental Factor

Demonstrated professional experience and achievement combined with personal knowledge by one of those associated with or recommending to the director search process of my style or comportment in other board or professional settings.

Strategy

Develop a knowledge and insightful understanding of board functioning and the kinds of issues with which boards must deal. Understand that a board membership is not an advocacy platform, but a serious governance responsibility. Gain board experience in not-for-profit settings which are dealing with policy, stewardship, and/or oversight.

Key Qualities

A high level of intelligence, judgment, core integrity and genuine caring. An ability to take risk; articulate and defend views; develop a personal plan for one's future. Keen listening skills and willingness to work with others toward consensus. Strong communication and leadership skills. Solid experience gained in reputable, professional context.

Getting in Front of Decision-makers

Present issues of broad-based concern like expanding representation of women on corporate boards. Use known organizations or associations to help promote issues, presentation should have both substance and grace. Involve politicians, especially growing numbers of women politicians. Take meaningful advantage of developed networks, avoid making opinion/decision-makers seek their help. Use personal abilities or positions to help bring women to the front.

═══════════════════════════════

NAME/POSITION/COMPANY: Dorothy K. Light, Vice President and Corporate Secretary, The Prudential Insurance Co. of America

CORPORATE BOARD APPOINTMENTS: New Jersey Resources Corp. (parent of New Jersey Gas Co., the Paradigm Power Co. and New Jersey Energy Recourse Co.). Trustee for the New Jersey Center for Analysis of Public Issues in Princeton. Member, New Jersey Economic master Plan Commission; member, National Advisory Board of Leadership America

Most Instrumental Factor

My volunteer leadership role in a traditional "old boys" bi-county Chamber of Commerce.

Strategy

Establish beyond question your credentials and expertise in your chosen profession; Network with individuals who influence the power structure, so when they are looking for the right person to do the job, your name will be on top; Extend yourself into the community to broaden your centers of influence.

Key Qualities

Proven accomplishments in your chosen field; Ability to move in circles of power; Incredible commitment and energy; Team player.

Getting in Front of Decision-makers

Find out who the decision-makers are; Public participation in organizations/ activities outside your normal work circle (i.e, committee chair, presenter, publications contributor); Understand that every project or event is a test. Unfortunately, we don't always realize this, even after taking the exam.

NAME/POSITION/COMPANY: Rosemarie Nassif, SSND, President, College of Notre Dame of Maryland

CORPORATE BOARD APPOINTMENTS: Provident Bank

Most Instrumental Factor

They were looking for a woman CEO of a mid-sized company. The "other" woman board member is on the committee that identifies new board members.

Strategy

Making positive connections with present board members and CEO's.

Key Qualities

Being smart. Being dedicated and committed. Being a woman of integrity and spiritual depth.

NAME/POSITION/COMPANY: Luella Gross Goldberg, Board of Trustees, Wellesley College

CORPORATE BOARD APPOINTMENTS: Hormel Foods Corp., The NWNL

Companies, and Northwestern National Life Ins. Co., TCF Financial Corp., and Piper Jaffray Investment Trust, Hercules Funds

Most Instrumental Factor

Personal acquaintance with several members of each board who had worked with me specifically on another corporate or not-for-profit board. In that way, they had seen me "in action" so to speak, and knew what they were getting.

Strategy

Do extremely able, conscientious work wherever you are!

Key Qualities

Exceptional competence, willingness and eagerness to be extremely conscientious, and excellent communication skills, oral and written.

Getting in Front of Decision-makers

By building their confidence, respect, and trust in you over time; by demonstrating in a variety of arenas that you deserve to be respected and trusted.

NAME/POSITION/COMPANY: Marina V. N. Whitman, Professor of Business Administration and Public Policy, University of Michigan

CORPORATE BOARD APPOINTMENTS: Alcoa, Chemical Bank, Browning Ferris Industries, Procter & Gamble, UNOCAL

Most Instrumental Factor

Initially, national visibility (as member of President's Council of Economic Advisers); subsequently, reputation and network.

Strategy

Become widely known for experience and expertise in an area relevant to service on board of the particular company.

Key Qualities

Intelligence, energy, articulateness, good people and political skills and a heck of a lot of luck.

NAME/POSITION/COMPANY: Gail Deegan, Vice President & Chief Financial Officer, New England Telephone

CORPORATE BOARD APPOINTMENTS: Houghton Mifflen, EG&G Inc., New England Telephone

Most Instrumental Factor

Experience with CEO's of these companies who served on Board of company where I was CFO. They got to know me over many years before asking me to serve on their boards.

Strategy

Get to know senior executives through work, possibly on volunteer organizations; distinguish yourself as a competent person in her own right.

Key Qualities

Intelligence. Hard work/commitment. Integrity. Leadership.

Getting in Front of Decision-makers

Do your homework. Be assertive/take leadership role.

NAME/POSITION/COMPANY: Frances Hesselbein, President/CEO, The Peter F. Drucker Foundation for Nonprofit Management

CORPORATE BOARD APPOINTMENTS: Previous: Pennsylvania Power and Light; Crum & Forster. Since 1981 and Presently: Mutual of America Life Insurance Co.

Most Instrumental Factor

Professional search firm used by two corporations.

Strategy

Express yourself in your work and reach a visible level of excellence. Take seriously your leadership role.

Key Qualities

Personal integrity, commitment to mission, ability to communicate vision and values; self-confidence. Seeing oneself as a board member who is a woman, not a woman board member. Focusing on task, not gender.

Getting in Front of Decision-makers

Be generous in sharing ideas, examples, opportunities with others. Believe that leadership is a matter of how to be, not how to do, and "leading from the front."

NAME/POSITION/COMPANY: Zoe Coulson, Consultant

CORPORATE BOARD APPOINTMENTS: Rubbermaid Inc.

Most Instrumental Factor

Because I had worked in two major advertising agencies on consumer product accounts, had held senior responsibilities at two important publishing companies producing profitable, recognized consumer magazines, my background contributed to the needs of Rubbermaid Inc.'s Board of Directors.

As spokesperson for *Good Housekeeping* as a consumer marketing authority, I had interfaced with three board members in business activities, so I was known individually by them also.

Strategy

As a member of a Nominating and Director's Committee, I assist in searching for a board member whose background and experience meet certain needs. For example, a well-grounded board needs members from relevant industries, possibly with international experience, with understanding of financial issues, with business vision and who is dedicated to serving stockholders. Candidates meeting these requirements come from banking, law, manufacturing, service and investment industries. Race, gender, and ethnicity are usually not board criteria, unless other requirements are met.

Key Qualities

Besides a strong academic record relevant to the field of endeavor, any person gaining more responsibilities should exhibit qualities of team work. It is also important to train those employees for whom you are responsible; helping them climb the ladder of success has been important in my progress.

Getting in Front of Decision-makers

Being recognized within a profession as a responsible, creative worker can be achieved by accepting committee work in organizations with a cooperative attitude, by becoming a spokesperson in the industry on specific subjects, and by recognition within your company as important to the company's success.

NAME/POSITION/COMPANY: Judi K. Hofer, President/CEO, Meier & Frank, a division of May Dept. Stores

CORPORATE BOARD APPOINTMENTS: The Dial Corp., Phoenix, AZ; Key Bank of Oregon, Portland, Ore., and Standard Insurance Co.

Most Instrumental Factor

Being a CEO of a major retail company and performing at a top quartile rate. Also, being one of very few women at this level was probably a factor.

Strategy

Achieve CEO status of a major company; have on-line responsibility and accountability, and perform above industry standard.

Key Qualities

Ability, tenacity, strong work ethic, and, most importantly, RESULTS. In addition, the ability to manage people effectively, both male and female, is essential.

NAME/POSITION/COMPANY: Catherine A. Pierce, Executive Vice President, Metropolitan Life Ins. Co.

CORPORATE BOARD APPOINTMENTS: Corning, Inc., General Public Utilities, Bank of New York

Most Instrumental Factor

Other board members' familiarity with my accomplishments.

Strategy

Visibility in your profession!

Key Qualities

Self-confidence, presentation skills, excellence at chosen career, job commitment, social skills, positive attitude, ability to function as a team player.

Getting in Front of Decision-makers

Excel at your profession. Use opportunities such as trade associations, etc., to speak authoritatively on some subject.

NAME/POSITION/COMPANY: Carol Dinkins, Partner & Member of Management Comm, Vinson & Elkins, L.L.P. (law firm)

CORPORATE BOARD APPOINTMENTS: Oryx Energy Co.

Most Instrumental Factor

I doubt it was any single factor. Rather, I believe the invitation resulted from a combination of my reputation as a lawyer, my high level government experience, my professional demeanor, my activities as a member of nonprofit boards in the energy and the environmental area and the fact that the CEO and COO had seen me chair larger meetings, speak before large groups and had visited with me at meal functions associated with trade organization meetings.

Strategy

Participate in trade associations and nonprofit work; develop a grand reputation in your field; become acquainted with many different professionals who might suggest you be considered.

Key Qualities

To be comfortable with herself as a person and to display self-confidence. To be comfortable with and enjoy other people. To be thoughtful and to develop and express ideas clearly and well. to develop a reputation for possessing these characteristics and qualities.

Getting in Front of Decision-makers

Identify such persons. Research and evaluate how to do so effectively, whether as to specific people or for general areas of interest. Thereafter, assure you are introduced by mutual acquaintances who can speak well and knowledgeably of you. Seek opportunities to serve on committees or to speak before groups that include those whom you wish to know.

NAME/POSITION/COMPANY: Sally Gore, Human Resources Associate, W.L. Gore & Associates

CORPORATE BOARD APPOINTMENTS: Delmarva Power and Light, Delaware Trust (bank)

Most Instrumental Factor

Visibility within the community and job responsibilities within my company that are broad and could help with policy development and decision-making for other corporations.

Strategy

I never directly sought one. I think it happens when you know a lot of people from different parts of the community. I've been active on philanthropic boards, have done volunteer work, etc.

Key Qualities

She needs to be: smart, have a vision, have charisma, be a natural leader, have good communication skills , and be willing and able to mentor and guide others. (A good education and a willingness to work hard go without saying).

Getting in Front of Decision-makers

Through working hard on causes, getting to know lots of people within the community.

NAME/POSITION/COMPANY: Ruth Levanthal, Provost and Dean, Penn State, Harrisburg

CORPORATE BOARD APPOINTMENTS: Pennsylvania Power & Light Co. and Mellon Bank

Most Instrumental Factor

Working with members of for-profit boards on volunteer, nonprofit activities.

Strategy

Be educated competent, interested, interesting and a workaholic. Go where the action is — i.e., find out about those activities in which CEO's participate and join in.

Key Qualities

Patience, fortitude, knowledge, skills, curiosity, hobbies, friends, 28-hour days, good people skills, balance, a good therapist.

Getting in Front of Decision-makers

Read *Skills for Success* by Adele Scheele. Risk doing! Success and self-confidence only come from trying new things. Leaders value those who deserve recognition and can publicly toot their own horns appropriately. Volunteer on nonprofit boards and invite CEO's to be advisory to your organization. Speak and write publicly.

NAME/POSITION/COMPANY: Helen Galland, President, Helen Galland Associates (marketing consultants)

CORPORATE BOARD APPOINTMENTS: Whitman Corp., Pet Inc., Woolworth Corp.

Most Instrumental Factor

I was a female and the first board to which I was elected had none (Whitman). They still have only one. Also, my background complimented the strengths of other board members. Woolworth had nobody with retail background on the board. Whitman was loaded with financial people and wanted new input.

Strategy

Straight talk during the interview process. Tell it just like it is. Make a point of wanting to help the company attain the goals it has established and don't seem too anxious — very interested, yes. People react to people — no "airs".

Key Qualities

Tenacity, never give up. Certainly intelligences and street smarts, dedication, knowing your business and being able to communicate that expertise to business associates. A warm and pleasant personality is a major plus.

Getting in Front of Decision-makers

First, it's helpful if your credentials are established. Then, you try to set an appointment by saying that there is something you would like to share with that person or maybe you say that you need some "friendly counsel." Nobody can refuse that.

NAME/POSITION/COMPANY: Lillian Vernon, CEO, Lillian Vernon Corp.

CORPORATE BOARD APPOINTMENTS: Lillian Vernon Corp.

Most Instrumental Factor

Broad background and familiarity with all aspects of the business.

Strategy

You must have a high profile in the corporate world. Make speeches to business groups, be quoted in the business press, etc.

Key Qualities

Determination, persistence and commitment.

Getting in Front of Decision-makers

Determination, persistence and commitment.

NAME/POSITION/COMPANY: Barbara S. Uehling, Chancellor, UCSB

CORPORATE BOARD APPOINTMENTS: Meredith

Most Instrumental Factor

Position and personal knowledge of CEO.

Strategy

It's not the way I did it, but I think talking with representatives of search firms that handle [such things].

Key Qualities

Competence in her chosen field, self-confidence, ability to communicate effectively.

Getting in Front of Decision-makers

Volunteer activities, writing, speeches.

NAME/POSITION/COMPANY: Remedios Diaz Oliver, President, All American Containers, Inc.

CORPORATE BOARD APPOINTMENTS: U.S. West, Inc. (Denver, CO); Avon Products (New York, NY), Barnett Banks of South Florida

Most Instrumental Factor

International expertise.

Strategy

Try to excel in one or two specific areas: finance, international, human resources, acquisitions, etc.

Key Qualities

Educational background, discipline, perseverance.

Getting in Front of Decision-makers

By being truthful and honest.

NAME/POSITION/COMPANY: Ruth Block, Exec. VP and CIO, Equitable Life and Chair/CEO, Evlico

CORPORATE BOARD APPOINTMENTS: Amoco Corp., Ecolab, Inc., Alliance Capital Mutual Fund Finance Corp.

Most Instrumental Factor

Corporate position and responsibilities one level below CEO led to first appointment. Once on one board, other offers of board appointments are made.

Strategy

Same as above, plus contacts made through participation in industry, civic, volunteer groups; expression of interest to contacts; reputation; visible contributions to considerations of issues.

Key Qualities

Aside from hard work and talent. Exceptional accomplishments (track record), people and communications skills, personal integrity, demand for high quality output, commitment, willingness to take risks, self-confidence. (Mostly the same qualities needed by men.)

Getting in Front of Decision-makers

Once reputation for very good work results is in place, ask for what you want if you're not getting it: management job(s), special project assignment, corporate committee or task force assignment. Board presentation(s) and, again, do it exceptionally well each time. These are all high visibility positions. This approach applies in corporate jobs and in industry, etc.

NAME/POSITION/COMPANY: Carol R. Goldberg, President, The AVCAR Group, Ltd.

CORPORATE BOARD APPOINTMENTS: The Gillette Co., America Service Group

Most Instrumental Factor

Joining our company board, The Stop & Shop Companies, Inc., in 1974. It was based on my position at that time as Vice President, General Manager of one of the operating divisions.

Strategy

Building a reputation in the community with those people who make decisions about who is invited onto boards. Those people, almost all male, are usually on boards themselves in other companies and key voluntary organizations.

Key Qualities

A woman needs to build her own professional credentials to even get into the game. But beyond her basic skills and knowledge, she has to develop a broad understanding about rainmaking, personal currency, the power of collaboration, etc.

NAME/POSITION/COMPANY: Katherine E. Smith, Vice President, Consumer Affairs, The Quaker Oats Co.

CORPORATE BOARD APPOINTMENTS: CILCORP, Inc., and Central Illinois Light Co.

Most Instrumental Factor

The CEO had read an article in *The Wall Street Journal* in which I was quoted on "Consumer Service." He followed up with me to determine if I had the qualifications needed for the board opening.

Strategy

A board of directors job requires time, study and dedication. One must have the commitment to make this a priority. Being known and credible in some area of business expertise: consumer expertise, finance, marketing, engineering, executive experience, etc. Ability to build trust and confidence with other directors.

Key Qualities

Qualities for success include leadership, communication skills, decision-making, motivation, flexibility, curiosity or desire to learn, credible business experience, sense of humor.

Getting in Front of Decision-makers

Participate in professional or civic organizations in a leadership capacity that provides visibility and contact. Speaker forums or articles in publications regularly read by decision-makers. Network with people.

═══════════════

NAME/POSITION/COMPANY: Elinor Ferdon

CORPORATE BOARD APPOINTMENTS: UJB Financial Corp., Princeton, NJ; Limited Jersey Bank, Hackensack, NJ

Most Instrumental Factor

Involvement in the community. Well-known as the leader and President of the local Girl Scout Council; was also known personally by Chair and CEO of company, and I chaired a Board of Trustees of a prestigious girls' school in which his brother served.

Strategy

Network among leaders and "shakers" in community; become well known. Volunteer on prestigious, not-for-profit boards. Excel in one's professional field. Understand corporation's business and mission. Meet corporation's senior management and other directors.

Key Qualities

Be well-rounded, know your facts; demonstrate leadership ability either in one's profession or not-for-profit organization; learn to be a good public speaker.

Getting in Front of Decision-makers

Serve on not-for-profit boards whose members are among the prestigious opinion/decision-makers. Use contacts to network, exhibit leadership skills inside your company and recognize unusual assignments focusing on major goals and objectives of company.

═══════════

NAME/POSITION/COMPANY: Jacqueline Grennan Wexler, Retired University President; Agency President

CORPORATE BOARD APPOINTMENTS: United Technologies (since 1978) Interpublic Group of Companies (since 1973)

Most Instrumental Factor

Support of Citicorp President who was chairman of Nominating Committee at UTC. Support of Exec. V.P. of Interpublic. Both knew me as President of Hunter College.

Strategy

Do your job well, both as an executive and on important civic committees, etc. Be yourself, not a studied part player!

Key Qualities

Intelligence; being articulate and at ease with a wide group of people; a strong understanding of finance.

Getting in Front of Decision-makers

Involvement in city, state, and/or national working groups where you work as a peer with the executive group represented on boards.

═══════════

NAME/POSITION/COMPANY: Estelle Ellis, President, Business Image, Inc.

CORPORATE BOARD APPOINTMENTS: Phillips-Van Heusen, Inc.

Most Instrumental Factor

My career in marketing and communication. It singularized me in the CEO's mind as someone who could make a contribution to meetings heavily weighted by "numbers" and finance and legal and real estate dialogue.

Strategy

High visibility as a professional with specific career experience other than routine and stereotypical backgrounds for board candidates.

Key Qualities

Stamina, self-esteem, confidence. Clarity of personal and professional vision. A sense of humor and sense of woman's history in the world of business.

Getting in Front of Decision-makers

By doing what you want to do and not being preoccupied with "strategic" thinking.

RESOURCE LIST

Resource lists are individual. They are made up of the names of organiza-tions that represent areas that are of interest to that individual. But if you're just starting to put yours together, here are some specific suggestions that you might want to include.

Alliance of Minority Women for Business and Political Development
Brassman Research
P.O. Box 13933
Silver Spring, MD 20911-3933
(301) 565-0258
Brenda Alford, President

All Nations Women's League
P.O. Box 428
Jackson Heights, Queens
New York, NY 11372
(718) 672-1243
Madeleine Thibault, President

American Business Women's Association
9100 Ward Parkway
P.O. Box 8728
Kansas City, MO 64114
(816) 361-6621
Carolyn B. Elman, Executive Director

American Council for Career Women
P.O. Box 50825
New Orleans, LA 70150
(504) 525-0375
Joan Savoy, President

American News Women's Club
1607 22nd Street, N.W.
Washington, D.C. 20008
(202) 332-6770
Margo Phillips, President

American Society of Professional and Executive Women
1511 Walnut Street
Philadelphia, PA 19102

American Women's Economic Development Corporation
641 Lexington Avenue
New York, NY 10022
(212) 688-1900
Roslyn Paaswell, CEO

Association of African-American Women Business Owners
Brassman Research
P.O. Box 13933
Silver Spring, MD 20911-3933
(301) 565-0258
Tracy Mason, President

Association of Part-time Professionals
Crescent Plaza
7700 Leesburg Pike, Ste. 216
Falls Church, Va 22043
(703) 734-7975

Black Professional Women's Network
123 W. 44th Street, Ste. 2E
New York, NY 10036
(212) 302-2924
Paulette M. Owens, President

B'Nai B'Rith Women
1828 L Street, N.W., Ste. 250
Washington, D.C. 20036
(202) 857-1300
Elaine K. Binder, Executive Director

**Business and Professional Women's Foundation
and the Marguerite Rewalt Resource Center**
2012 Massachusetts Ave., N.W.
Washington, D.C. 20036
(202) 293-1200
Ms. J. Lyle Martin, Librarian, Resource Center

Capital Rose Perpetual Fund
690 Sugar Town Road
Malvern, PA 19355
(610) 644-4212
Jean Brooks, Director

Catalyst
250 Park Avenue South
New York, New York 10003
(212) 777-8900
Sheila Wellington, Contact

Center for the American Woman and Politics
Eagleton Institute of Politics, Rudgers University
90 Clifton Avenue
New Brunswick, NJ 08901
(908) 838-2210
Ruth B. Mandel, Director

Center for Women's Economic Alternatives
P.O. Box 1033
Ahoskie, NC 27910
(919) 332-4179
Sarah Fields-Davis, Executive Director

Committee of 200
625 North Michigan Avenue, Ste. 500
Chicago, Illinois 60611
(312) 751-3477
Carolee Friedlander, Contact

Cornell University Institute for Women and Work
New York School of Industrial and Labor Relations
15 E. 26th Street, 4th Floor
New York, NY 10010
(212) 340-3800
Francine Moccio, Director

Council of Presidents of United States
Women's Organizations
American Nurses Association
1011 14th Street, N.W., Ste. 200

Washington, D.C. 20003
(202) 789-1800
Chris deVries, Asst. Director

Directors' Resource Council
National Women's Economic Alliance Foundation
1440 New York Avenue, NW
Washington, D.C. 20005
(202) 393-5257
Elise Garfinkel, Executive Director

Executive Women International
515 South 700 East, Ste. 2E
Salt Lake City, UT 84102
(801) 355-2800; fax-(801) 355-2852
Lois Trayner-Alinder, President

Federation of Organizations for Professional Women
20001 S Street, N.W., Ste. 500
Washington, D.C. 20009
(2020) 328-1415
Dr. Viola Young-Horvath, Director

Financial Women's Association of New York
215 Park Avenue South, Ste. 2010
New York, New York 10003
(212) 533-2141
Debra Flanz, Contact

Financial Women International
7910 Woodmont Avenue
Bethesda, MD 20814
(301) 657-8288
Sylvia Straub, Executive Vice President

Foundation for Women's Resources
700 N. Fairfax Street, Ste. 302
Alexandria, Va 22314
(703) 549-1102
Martha P. Farmer, National Executive Director
Arlington, VA 22209

League of Women Voters of the United States
1730 M Street, N.W.
Washington, D.C. 20036
(202) 429-1965
Gracia Hillman, Executive Director

**International Alliance, an Association of
Executive and Professional Women**
8600 LaSalle Road, Ste. 308
Baltimore, MD 21286
(410) 472-4221 (new number)
Marian E. Goetze, Executive Vice President

International Council of African Women
P.O. Box 91812
Washington, D.C. 20090-1812
(2020) 546-8459
Nkenge Toure, Co-Coordinator

International Women's Forum
1146 19th Street, N.W., Ste. 600
Washington, D.C. 20036
(202) 775-8917
Cindy M. Ryan, President

The Leadership Roundtable
1440 New York Avenue
Washington, DC 20005
Mindy Fountain, Executive Director

National Association of Corporate Directors
1707 L Street, N.W.
Washington, D.C. 20036
(202) 775-0509
John Nash, Contact

National Association of Black Women Entrepreneurs
P.O. Box 1375
Detroit, MI 43231
(313) 341-7400
Marilyn French-Hubbard, Founder

National Association for Female Executives
127 W. 24th Street
New York, NY 10011
(212) 645-0770
Wendy Reid-Crisp, Director

National Association of MBA Women
7701 Georgia Avenue, N.W.
Washington, D.C. 20012
(202) 723-1267
Sharon Griffith, President

National Association of Minority Women in Business
906 Grand Avenue, Ste. 200
Kansas City, MO 64106
(816) 421-3335
Inez Kaiser, President

**National Association of Negro Business
and Professional Women's Clubs**
1806 New Hampshire Avenue, N.W.
Washington, D.C. 20009
(202) 483-4206
Ellen A. Graves, Executive Officer

**National Association of Professional
Asian-American Women**
P.O. Box 494
Washington Grove, MD 20880
Vivian Kim, Executive Officer

National Association for Women in Careers
P.O. Box 81525
Chicago, IL 60681-0525
(312) 938-7662
Pat Surbella, CEO & President

National Bar Association, Women Lawyers Division
c/o Brenda Girton
1211 Connecticut Ave., N.W., #702
Washington, D.C. 20036
(202) 291-1979

National Association of Women Business Owners
1377 K Street, N.W.
Washington, D.C. 20005
(202) 737-6501
Patty De Dominic, President

**National Chamber of Commerce for Women
and the Elizabeth Lewin Business Library
& Information Center**
10 Waterside Plaza, Ste. 6H
New York, NY 10010-2610
(212) 685-3454
Maggie Rinaldi, Executive Director

National Commission on Working Women
1325 G Street, N.W., Lower Level
Washington, D.C. 20005
(202) 737-5764
Cynthia Marano, Director

National Council of Career Women
4200 Wisconsin Avenue, N.W., Ste. 106-210
Washington, D.C. 20016
(202) 310-4200
Patricia Whittaker, President

**National Council for Research on Women
and the National Network of Women's Caucuses**
47-49 E. 65th Street
New York, NY 10021
(212) 570-5001
Debra L. Schultz, Assistant Director

**National Federation of Business and
Professional Women**
2021 Massachusetts Ave., N.W.
Washington, D.C. 20036
(202) 293-1100
Dianne Studer, President

National Federation of Press Women
P.O. Box 99
Blue Springs, MO 64013-0099

National Foundation for Women Business Owners
1825 I Street, N.W., Ste. 800
Washington, D.C. 2006
(202) 833-1854
Sharon Hardary, Executive Director

National Network of Hispanic Women
12021 Wilshire Blvd., Ste. 353
Los Angeles, CA 90025
(213) 225-9895
Celia Torres, Chair

National Organization for Women
1000 16th Street, N.W., Ste. 700
Washington, D.C. 20036
(202) 331-0066

Network for Professional Women
216 Main Street
Hartford, CT 06103
(203) 727-1988
JoAnne P. Smith, President

9 to 5, National Association of Working Women
614 Superior Avenue, N.W., rm. 852
Cleveland, OH 44113
(216) 566-9308

Organization of Women in International Trade
1377 K Street N.W.
Washington, DC 20005
Ellen Federman, President

**PanPacific and Southeast Asia Women's Association
of the U.S.A.**
Box 1532, Madison Square Station
New York, NY 10159
(212) 228-5307
Ann Allen, President

United Nations Development Fund for Women
304 E. 45th Street, 6th Floor
New York, NY 10017
(212) 906-6400
Sharon Capeling-Alakja, Director

U.S. Department of Labor Women's Bureau
Frances Perkins Building
200 Constitution Avenue, N.W.
Washington, D.C. 20210
(202) 523-6611

U.S. Small Business Administration
National Women's Business Council
409 3rd Street, N.W.
Washington, D.C. 20416
(202) 205-3850

Office of Women's Business Ownership
1441 L Street, N.W.
Washington, D.C. 10416
(202) 205-6673
Betsy Myers, Director

Women in Communication, Inc.
3717 Columbia Pike
Arlington, VA 22204-4255
Carol Fenstermacher, President

Women in Government Relations
1029 Vermont Avenue N.W.
Washington, DC 20005-3527
Singleton McAllister, President

The Women's Economic Roundtable
866 United Nations Plaza
New York, NY 10017
Dr. Amelia Augustus, Executive Director

Women's Foreign Policy Council
845 3rd Avenue, 15th Floor
New York, NY 10022-6601
(212) 759-7982

Women's International Network
187 Grant Street
Lexington, MA 02173
(617) 862-9431
Fran P. Hosken, Coordinator/Editor

Women's World Banking
8 West 40th Street
New York, NY 10018
Nancy Barry, President

Zonta International
557 West Randolph Street
Chicago, IL 60661
Bonnie Koenig, President

If you don't know where to begin to expand your resource list, consider these resource directories, which should be available at your local library and/or, in most cases, may be ordered.

Business Women's Network Directory
Kate Suryan, Editor
The Business Women's Network
Washington, D.C. (1994)
  This is a new directory. It profiles more than 130 national and 270 local women's business and professional organizations, indexed by organization name and location. The directory was created as an effort to inform the growing cadre of women in business about what their fellow women executives and entrepreneurs are doing. Consequently, the profiles are detailed. A typical entry includes:

> Leadership
>
> Executive Committee
>
> Organization Profile, a brief description of the size, scope
>   and history of the organization.
>
> Focus Areas/Objectives
>
> Membership Criteria
>
> Membership Benefits

Local Chapters

Programs, a listing of what, when, where and who.

Meetings, a notation about who may attend.

Recognition and Awards, those given by the organization

Education, Philanthropic and Community Commitments

Publications, not just a listing, but a description

Opportunities for Corporate Involvement

If you are interested in obtaining a copy of this directory, you may call The Business Women's Network at 1-800-48-WOMEN.

❖ ❖ ❖

Women's Organizations: A National Directory
Martha Merrill Doss, Editor
Garrett Park Press
Garrett Park, MD (1986)

Though this directory is listed alphabetically, it has two cross-reference sections: by State and by Subject. This is particularly nice, if you just want to take a look at those women's organizations that have branches in your state. A typical entry includes:

Name

Address

Phone

A brief explanation of what the organization offers to its membership.

Note: *Women's Organizations: A National Directory* and a special interest publication put out by Garrett Press entitled *The Directory of Special Opportunities for Women*, which includes educational, career, network and peer-counseling information, are out of print, but I was able to find them at the library. Garrett does have in print currently the:

Women's Information Directory: Guide to Organizations, Agencies, Institutions, Programs, Publications, Services and other resources concerned with women in the United States, 1993 Edition
Shawn Brennan, Editor
Garrett Park Press
P.O. Box 190
Garrett Park, MD 20896

The directory contains over 10,800 listings of organizations and services in 26 categories, including the top U.S. women-owned businesses & consulting organizations; national, regional, state, and local women's organizations; and research and government organizations and agencies. A typical entry includes:

Name

Address

Phone

Contact Person

Year Founded

Description

Publications

Membership

❖ ❖ ❖

Encyclopedia of Associations, 1995
Carol A. Schwartz and Rebecca L. Turner, Editors
Gale Research, Inc.
Detroit, MI (1994)

The encyclopedia lists over 22,000 associations in the United States. All entries are listed under topics, so you must first consult the separate index to search for associations in a topic which is applicable and interesting to you and your professional expertise. A typical entry includes:

Name

Address

Contact Person/Top Decision-maker

Phone

Fax

Some historical information, if available

A brief description of why the Association exists and what it does

Awards

Committees

Publications

Conventions/Meetings/Projects

Affiliations

❖ ❖ ❖

National Trade and Professional Associations of the United States,
   29th Edition
John J. Russell, Managing Ed.
Columbia Books, Inc.
Washington, D.C. (1994)

This publication has been completely revised and up-dated yearly since 1966. The best thing about it is that though the listings are all alphabetical, they are cross-referenced in five ways: (1) by Subject; (2) by Budget; (3) by Management firm; (4) by Executive; and (5) by Acronym. Categories (2), (4) and (5) are unique and of particular interest. For instance: If you want to associate yourself with an organization that is budgeted at between $500,000 and $1,000,000 annually, you can turn to that cross-reference section and find only the names of those organization which fulfill your requirement. Or suppose, you've only heard an organization described as NAWBO or NAFE, you can turn to the acronym reference and look them up accordingly. Or, you may have met a network contact at a conference with whom you'd like to touch base. You've lost her card, but you remember her name. You can look her up in the alphabetical Executive reference and find out what trade or professional association she is with! A really excellent resource, a typical entry includes:

> Name
> Address
> Phone
> Fax
> Number of Members
> Number of Staff
> Budget
> History
> Publications
> Annual Meetings

❖ ❖ ❖

Business Organizations, Agencies and Publications Directory
Catherine M. Ehr and Kenneth Estell, Editors
Gale Research
Detroit, MI (1992)

This directory contains over 26,000 entries concerned with United States business, trade and industry. Listed alphabetically under each general area, a typical entry includes:

Name

Address

Phone

Name of top decision-maker

A brief description about the history of the organization, its membership and/or a brief general description of the organizations focus and purpose.

❖ ❖ ❖

For minorities, of special interest are:

Minority Organizations: A National Directory
Garrett Park Press
Garrett Park, MD

Minorities included in the directory are listed as: American Indian, Native Alaskan, Black, Hispanic, and Asian American. A typical entry includes:

Name

Address

Phone

A 3-6 line description of the organizations purpose.

❖ ❖ ❖

Black Americans Information Directory
Darren L. Smith, Editor
Gale Research, Inc.
Detroit, MI

This directory contains listings for "4,500 organizations, Agencies, Institutions, Programs, and Publications concerned with Black American Life and Culture," including:

Associations	Newsletters & Directories
Awards, Honors, Prizes	Newspapers & Periodicals
Colleges & Universities	Publishers
Cultural Organizations	Radio & Television Stations
Government Agencies	Religious Organizations
& Programs	Research Centers
Industrial & Service Co.	Studies Programs
Museums	Videos

❖ ❖ ❖

If none of the above directories suit your needs, you can consult:

Directories in Print, 1995,12th Edition
Terri Kessler Schell, Editor
Gale Research, Inc.
Detroit, MI, 1994

This publication contains 15,400 bibliographical entries of published directories worldwide. Entries are in 26 subject categories, as follows:

1. General Business
2. Manufacturing, Industries & Commercial Services
3. Construction Industries & Real Estate
4. Retail, Wholesale and Consumer Services
5. Banking, Insurance and financial Services
6. Agriculture and Veterinary Sciences
7. Transportation, Utilities and Municipal Services
8. Management, Employment and Labor
9. Advertising, Marketing and Public Relations
10. Library and Information Services
11. Publishing and Broadcast Services
12. Telecommunications and Computer Science
13. Medicine
14. Health Care Services
15. Science and Technology
16. National Resources, Energy and the Environment
17. Social Sciences and Humanities
18. Education
19. Law, Military and Government
20. Community Services and Social Concerns
21. Associations, Philanthropy, Ethnic and Religious
22. Biographical and Genealogy
23. Arts and Entertainment
24. Travel and Restaurants
25. Sports and Outdoor Recreation
26. Hobbies and Leisure

A typical entry includes:

Name

Address

Phone

What the directory includes; what the entries includes; how they are arranged; frequency of publication; editors; advertising accepted; circulation; cost; fax number; and remarks.

❖ ❖ ❖

These directories, resources, and shelves of other reference materials on specific industries and companies can be found at your local library, and offer you a place to begin your research.

❖ ❖ ❖

For information about specific companies and corporations, don't forget references such as:

- ❖ Standard & Poor's Indices
- ❖ Dun & Bradstreet References, such as "The Million Dollar Directory"
- ❖ Moody's Industrial News Reports
- ❖ The Directories of Corporate Affiliations

Thank you to the following leaders for helping women find their Seat at the Table:

Meg Armstrong
Margaret Long Arnold
Jeannie Austin
Paulette M. Balich
Susan Bari
Jameson A. Baxter
Dr. Lillian Beard
Rebecca J. Beverly
Cathleen Black
Gail Blanke
Ruth Block
Elizabeth I. Board
Courtney Spain Boller
Doris Bray
Nancy Brinker
Beth Bronner
Carol Brookins
Karen Caplan
Majorie Bell Chambers
Dinah Lin Cheng
Elaine L. Chao
Sheila T. Cluff
Linda Collier
Zoe Coulson
Carol Cox Wait
Carol Crockett
Laurel Cutler
Carolyn Davis
Susan Davis
Patty DeDominic
Gail Deegan
Kitty Dickerson
Carol Dinkins
Linda Ellerbee
Estelle Ellis
Bonnie Erbe

Jane Evans
Rae Forker Evans
Elinor Ferdon
Barbara Ferris
Richard Ferry
Carolee Friedlander
Helen Galland
Carol Goldberg
Luella Gross Goldberg
Sally Gore
Diane Graham
Barbara Grogan
Claudia Spain Grove
Bonnie Hill Guiton
Judy Haberkorn
Marilyn Hamilton
Jean Patrice Harrington
Jinger L. Heath
Joan Roth Herschede
Frances L. Hesselbein
Patricia Higgins
Judi Hofer
Wilhelmina Cole Holladay
Betty Ruth Hollander
Dr. April C. Hollinshead
Gloria S. Hom
Myra Jones
Andria Jung
Alona Kennedy
Linda Lambert
Paula Lambert
Ruth Levanthal
Dorothy K. Light
Judy McLennan
Lynn Martin
Dina Merrill

William Morin
Georgette Mosbacher
Rosemarie Nassif
Douglas Ann Newson
Remedios Diaz Oliver
Sally A. Painter
Catherine A. Pierce
Barbara Gardner Proctor
Ray C. Robbins
Judith A. Rogala
Marsha Sands
Jeri Sedlar
Cecily Selby
Thekla R. Shackelford
Therese Shaheen
Cathie A. Shattuck
Ruth Shaw

Jean Sisco
Katherine E. Smith
Lorraine Spiess
Diane K. Steed
Nancy Harvey Steorts
Barbara S. Uehling
Lillian Vernon
Jeanne Viner Bell
Marilou Von Ferstel
Judith Von Seldeneck
Jacqueline Greenan Wexler
Margita E. White
Marina V. N. Whitman
Elynor A. Williams
Harriett Woods
Richard Zimmerman

MasterMedia Limited
17 East 89th Street
New York, NY 10128
(212) 260-5600
(800) 334-8232 *please use Mastercard or Visa on 1-800 orders*
(212) 546-7638 (fax)

OTHER MASTERMEDIA BUSINESS BOOKS

POSITIVELY OUTRAGEOUS SERVICE: New and Easy Ways to Win Customers for Life, by T. Scott Gross, identifies what the consumers of the nineties really want and how businesses can develop effective marketing strategies to answer those needs. ($14.95 paper)

POSITIVELY OUTRAGEOUS SERVICE AND SHOWMANSHIP: Industrial Strength Fun Makes Sales Sizzle!!!!, by T. Scott Gross, reveals the secrets of adding personality to any product or service. ($12.95 paper)

HOW TO GET WHAT YOU WANT FROM ALMOST ANYBODY, by T. Scott Gross, shows how to get great service, negotiate better prices, and always get what you pay for. ($9.95 paper)

OUT THE ORGANIZATION: New Career Opportunities for the 1990's, by Robert and Madeleine Swain, is written for the millions of Americans whose jobs are no longer safe, whose companies are not loyal, and who face futures of uncertainty. It gives advice on finding a new job or starting your own business. ($12.95 paper)

CRITICISM IN YOUR LIFE: How to Give It, How to Take It, How to Make It Work for You, by Dr. Deborah Bright, offers practical advice, in an upbeat, readable, and realistic fashion, for turning criticism into control. Charts and diagrams guide the reader into managing criticism from bosses, spouses, children, friends, neighbors, in-laws, and business relations. ($17.95 cloth)

BEYOND SUCCESS: How Volunteer Service Can Help You Begin Making a Life Instead of Just a Living, by John F. Raynolds III and Eleanor Raynolds, C.B.E., is a unique how-to book targeted at business and professional people considering volunteer work, senior citizens who wish to fill leisure time meaningfully, and students trying out various career options. The book is filled with interviews with celebrities, CEOs, and average citizens who talk about the benefits of service work. ($19.95 cloth)

MANAGING IT ALL: Time-Saving Ideas for Career, Family, Relationships, and Self, by Beverly Benz Treuille and Susan Schiffer Stautberg, is written for women who are juggling careers and families. Over two hundred career women (ranging from a TV anchorwoman to an investment banker) were interviewed. The book contains many humorous anecdotes on saving time and improving the quality of life for self and family. ($9.95 paper)

THE CONFIDENCE FACTOR: How Self-Esteem Can Change Your Life, by Dr. Judith Briles, is based on a nationwide survey of six thousand men and women. Briles explores why women so often feel a lack of self-confidence and have a poor opinion of themselves. She offers step-by-step advice on becoming the person you want to be. ($9.95 paper, $18.95 cloth)

TAKING CONTROL OF YOUR LIFE: The Secrets of Successful Enterprising Women, by Gail Blanke and Kathleen Walas, is based on the authors' professional experience with Avon Products' Women of Enterprise Awards, given each year to outstanding women entrepreneurs. The authors offer a specific plan to help you gain control over your life, and include business tips and quizzes as well as beauty and lifestyle information. ($17.95 cloth)

SIDE-BY-SIDE STRATEGIES: How Two-Career Couples Can Thrive in the Nineties, by Jane Hershey Cuozzo and S. Diane Graham, describes how two-career couples can learn the difference between competing with a spouse and becoming a supportive power partner. Published in hardcover as *Power Partners.* ($10.95 paper, $19.95 cloth)

WORK WITH ME! How to Make the Most of Office Support Staff, by Betsy Lazary, shows you how to find, train, and nurture the "perfect" assistant and how to best utilize your support staff professionals. ($9.95 paper)

THE LOYALTY FACTOR: Building Trust in Today's Workplace, by Carol Kinsey Goman, Ph.D., offers techniques for restoring commitment and loyalty in the workplace. ($9.95 paper)

DARE TO CHANGE YOUR JOB—AND YOUR LIFE, by Carole Kanchier, Ph.D., provides a look at career growth and development throughout the life cycle. ($9.95 paper)

BREATHING SPACE: Living and Working at a Comfortable Pace in a Sped-Up Society, by Jeff Davidson, helps readers to handle information and activity overload, and gain greater control over their lives. ($10.95 paper)

TWENTYSOMETHING: Managing and Motivating Today's New Work Force, by Lawrence J. Bradford, Ph.D., and Claire Raines, M.A., examines the work orientation of the younger generation, offering managers in businesses of all kinds a practical guide to better understand and supervise their young employees. ($22.95 cloth)

BALANCING ACTS! Juggling Love, Work, Family, and Recreation, by Susan Schiffer Stautberg and Marcia L. Worthing, provides strategies to achieve a balanced life by reordering priorities and setting realistic goals. ($12.95 paper)

STEP FORWARD: Sexual Harassment in the Workplace, What You Need to Know, by Susan L. Webb, presents the facts for identifying the tell-tale signs of sexual harassment on the job, and how to deal with it. ($9.95 paper)

A TEEN'S GUIDE TO BUSINESS: The Secrets to a Successful Enterprise, by Linda Menzies, Oren S. Jenkins, and Rickell R. Fisher, provides solid information about starting your own business or working for one. ($7.95 paper)

TEAMBUILT: Making Teamwork Work, by Mark Sanborn, teaches business how to improve productivity, without increasing resources or expenses, by building teamwork among employers. ($19.95 cloth)

For further information about Seat at the Table programs, please write to:

Patricia Harrison, President
NWEAF
1440 New York Avenue, NW
Washington, DC 20005.

ABOUT THE AUTHOR

PATRICIA HARRISON is president and founder of the National Women's Economic Alliance, which for the past ten years has worked with leading corporations to identify qualified people who happen to be women for corporate board positions. She is the author of *America's New Women Entrepreneurs*. A veteran businesswoman, she currently heads the Board of Trustees of Guest Services, Inc., and serves as a member of the Services Policy Advisory Council, Office of the U.S. Trade Representative.

Additional copies of *A Seat at the Table* may be ordered by sending a check for $19.95 (please add $2 for the first book, $1 for each extra copy, for postage and handling) to:

MasterMedia Limited
17 East 89th Street
New York, NY 10128
(800) 334-8232
(212) 546-7638

Patricia Harrison is available for speaking engagements. Please contact MasterMedia's Speaker's Bureau for availability and fee arrangements. Call Tony Colao at (800)4-Lectur.